Women and Punishment

Women and Punishment
The Struggle for Justice

Edited by

Pat Carlen

With a Foreword by
Sir David Ramsbotham GCB CBE
HM Chief Inspector of Prisons
1995–2001

WILLAN
PUBLISHING

Published by

Willan Publishing
Culmcott House
Mill Street, Uffculme
Cullompton, Devon
EX15 3AT, UK
Tel: +44(0)1884 840337
Fax: +44(0)1884 840251
e-mail: info@willanpublishing.co.uk
website: www.willanpublishing.co.uk

Published simultaneously in the USA and Canada by

Willan Publishing
c/o ISBS, 920 NE 58th Ave, Suite 300,
Portland, Oregon 97213-3786 USA
Tel: +001(0)503 287 3093
Fax: +001(0)503 280 8832
website: www.isbs.com

First published 2002

Reprinted 2003

ISBN 1-903240-58-1 (cased)
ISBN 1-903240-57-3 (paper)

British Library Cataloguing-in-Publication Data

A catalogue record for this book is available from the British Library

Printed and bound by T.J. International Ltd, Padstow, Cornwall PL28 8RW

Contents

Acknowledgements

The Conference at which several of the papers included in this collection were first presented was sponsored by Economic and Social Research Council Award L216 25 2033: Women's Imprisonment: Models of Change and Cross-National Lessons. The Editor would like to thank: Sir David Ramsbotham for being so supportive of the whole project; Brian Willan for being such an enthusiastic and inspirational publisher; and all the contributors for being such a pleasure to work with.

Pat Carlen, April 2002

Foreword

by Sir David Ramsbotham GCB CBE
H.M. Chief Inspector of Prisons, 1995–2001

Every so often in life, everyone has an experience that will stay with them for ever. I had one of these in December 1995 when, as the newly appointed Chief Inspector of Prisons, I joined my inspectors in an unannounced inspection of Holloway, the largest women's prison in England. It was overcrowded and filthy dirty, its staff overstretched and demoralised and the vast majority of its prisoners locked up in their cells all day, doing nothing. There were wholly inadequate arrangements for caring for the large numbers of mentally disordered women. Rates of self-harm were alarmingly high. In the Mother and Baby Unit new mothers asked me whether it was right that they had been chained to prison officers while they were in labour. There was no induction programme, no sentence planning and no preparation for release. What I found particularly concerning was that there was no one in Prison Service Headquarters responsible for women in prison, merely a civil servant who wrote policy. The Prison Service's attitude was exemplified by the fact that injuries to women were recorded on a diagram of a man's body.

I like to think that the attention the Inspectorate drew to that dreadful situation jolted people into realising that here was an avoidable scandal that did no one any credit. Of course the Prison Service should have managed women in prison better, but Ministers should have insisted that they did. Officials should have taken note of the warning signs made by the Board of Visitors amongst others. But somehow the notion that budgets matter more than people continues to prevail, and doing some-thing about it seems to slip all too easily into the 'too difficult' basket.

Since then a number of things have happened. In the Inspectorate we published a thematic report *Women in Prison* in July 1997, and a follow-up to it in June 2001. The three main penal reform organisations, the Prison Reform Trust, the National Association for the Care and Resettlement of Offenders (Nacro) and the Howard League for Penal Reform, have all produced papers on various aspects of the imprisonment of females. In the Prison Reform Trust report *Justice for Women: the Need for Reform*, its author, Professor Dorothy Wedderburn, recommended the introduction of a Women's Justice Board, with an appointed Chairman, responsible for looking at all aspects of the treatment of women who come into the hands of the criminal justice system. I could not agree with her more.

In addition a number of people keenly interested in aspects of females who come into the hands of the criminal justice system – such as Angela Devlin, Chris Tchaikovsky and Olga Heaven, to name but three – have added their voices and words to the cause of reform and improvement. The Prison Service, in its turn, has formed a Women's Policy Group, without any money, and appointed an operational manager of women's prisons, whose budget is very strictly controlled. However, extraordinarily, the holders of these two posts, currently both men, report to different members of the Prisons Board.

But no one has done more in 'the struggle for justice' for women than Professor Pat Carlen. I first met her during the course of her latest research, and was at once aware that here was someone who not only understood the needs of women in prison, but also had clear ideas of how these might be satisfied. She has promoted at least one most successful conference to explore the issues, including the lack of suitable offending behaviour programmes, the lack of suitable work opportunities, the fragility of health care and particularly the care of the mentally disordered, the need for social skills as well as educational programmes, the importance of maintaining family ties and links, the need to select and train staff working with women and the importance of understanding and making special arrangements for children and young offenders.

Women and Punishment is a very important book, because it brings together not only her expertise and advice, but that of a number of others who are expert in various particulars, both in the community and in prison. Recently the Director General of the Prison Service [for England and Wales] admitted that the Service was in crisis over the rising numbers of women coming into prison. This need not have been so if those responsible had been prepared to listen to all the warnings that many of us have been giving for a number of years. The crisis is not just about lack of available accommodation; it is about lack of understanding or provision to satisfy the needs of women in a way that will help them to lead useful and law-abiding lives in prison and on release – the Statement of Purpose of the Prison Service. This requires not just providing enough prison places, but examining whether prison is the right place for the woman concerned, or whether imprisonment is more likely to cause further problems not only for her but for society as a whole, including her children and those dependent on her.

'Tough on crime and tough on the causes of crime' is an often-quoted phrase used by the Prime Minister. Simply being tough on crimes committed by women, but not being equally tough on the social and economic factors behind the offending or anti-social behaviour that led to them, risks making matters worse not better. Therefore I hope that Professor Carlen's book will be read, marked, learned and inwardly digested particularly by those who, by failing to take remedial action in the past, have precipitated the current crisis. If they exploit all the thought and care that she and her admirable team of contributors have put into its production, the current crisis will be infinitely easier to resolve. But they must make it their business to listen to, and not ignore, such advice in future, so that the damage that imprisonment currently causes to women is eliminated, the public are protected, and no one has to struggle for justice.

Sir David Ramsbotham GCB CBE
March 2002

About the contributors

Pat Carlen is Visiting Professor of Criminology at Keele University and has written on a range of criminological topics. She was a founder member of Women in Prison and in 1998 was awarded the Sellin-Glueck Prize by the American Society of Criminology for international contributions to criminology.

Kate De Cou is Assistant Deputy Superintendent of the women's population at the Hampden County Correctional Centre in Western Massachusetts, and has published several articles on programmes for female prisoners.

Kelly Hannah-Moffat is Assistant Professor in Sociology at the University of Toronto, Mississauga. She has published several articles and books on women's imprisonment, was for ten years President of the Elizabeth Fry Society of Toronto, and has recently been awarded the Radzinowitz Prize by the *British Journal of Criminology* for 'best article' 2000.

Barbara Hudson is Professor in the Lancashire Law School, University of Central Lancashire. She has published several books and many articles in the areas of justice and difference.

Kathleen Kendall is a sociologist in the Medical School at Southampton University. She has published many articles on responses to female offenders, and has worked for the Correctional Service of Canada as a programme evaluator and special advisor.

Jackie Lowthian has worked for the National Association for the Care and Resettlement of Offenders since 1987 and their Women Prisoners' Resource Centre since 1989. Recently she has worked in partnership with the Prison Service on the resettlement difficulties (especially homelessness) facing women leaving prison.

Joanna Phoenix is Lecturer in Sociology at Bath University and has published a book and many articles on female sex work.

Sally Poteat is Executive Director of Repay, a non-profit criminal justice agency in western North Carolina, USA.

General Sir David Ramsbotham GCB CBE MA CIMgt was Her Majesty's Chief Inspector of Prisons for England and Wales from 1995 to 2001.

Jenny Roberts OBE was Chief Probation Officer in Hereford and Worcester from 1983 to 2001 and is currently Editor of *VISTA*, the Journal of Chief Officers of Probation.

Anne Worrall is Reader in Criminology at Keele University and has published widely in the areas of criminal justice in general and female offenders in particular.

Part One
Context

Chapter 1

Introduction: Women and punishment

Pat Carlen[1]

The coupling of 'women' and 'punishment' occurs only infrequently in penological literature[2]. This is not surprising. Theories of punishment are usually expected to be gender-neutral: the state punishes, the citizen submits and the legitimacy of the punishment is debated according to the jurisprudential principles of the time. Of course, punishments are meted out in a range of relationships characterised by imbalances of power and/or legitimated rule-enforcement institutions; but, by and large, even in the literature that has focused on the deliberate imposition of pains or deprivations in return for wrongdoing, there seems to have been a reluctance to conceive of punishments as being gender-specific.

The cause of the general failure to confront the fact that punishment involves gendered bodies most probably inheres in a supermix of political, social and ideological conditions: the recurring modernistic anxiety to move beyond the vengeful and wasteful imposition of pain towards a more economic and productive repair of faulty organisms (Foucault 1977; Kendall chapter 10 this volume); the ideological desirability to repress all knowledge of social inequalities between the punished and the punishers if the legitimacy of the avenger's power to punish might thereby be strengthened; and the postmodern condition of uncertainty and multiple risk awareness wherein the anxious certainty that 'something must be done' about crime is usually balanced by an equally anxious lack of certainty that whatever is done will be either politically warranted or socially efficacious.

When it comes to the 'punishment' of 'women', moreover, there are several additional and more specific difficulties in conceptually linking the punishable wrong with the punishing rite. The first is that women just do not commit so much crime as men and the crimes they do commit are physically less dangerous and socially less injurious. Accordingly, the nightmarish and murderous felon in the shadows has not traditionally lurked in female form. Then, as far as formal criminal sanctions are concerned, women have always been subject more to informal than formal modes of regulation, and that may be another reason why they have appeared in the criminal courts much less frequently than men (Hagan *et al* 1979; Carlen 1995). Thirdly, when they have been brought before the courts for punishment, women have, more often than not, been seen less as criminals and more as either maddened or misguided victims of a variety of malign social circumstances. As a result, therefore, of the different modes of women's social regulation and the sexualised and pathologising popular gender stereotypes of all women (and especially poor or black women) who either break the law and/or deviate from informal social rules, there has been a tendency to talk about the social control of women not so much in terms of 'punishment' – even when that is what is at stake – but more often (and variously) in terms of something else. Sociologists have favoured 'social regulation'; criminologists have analysed very specific aspects of the criminal justice or penal systems; both the lay public and the bureaucratic and professionalised criminal justice and prisons personnel have routinely talked as if women's prisons are really something other than they are (for instance, hospitals or domestic science colleges or, more recently, feminist finishing schools); while prison reformers, many of whom have always been ambivalently 'abolitionist' in their penal politics, have seldom been quite certain as to exactly *what* it is they have been attempting to reform – or why! Finally, the pornographic nuances of 'women and punishment' may also, in some quarters, have been inhibitive of too loose a usage of the phrase. Certainly professional discourses have never fully explicated and confronted the sexual connotations pervasively resonant in the subtext of many personally invasive procedures imposed on female prisoners in the name of security – for instance, strip searches, various forms of physical restraint and a close disciplinary surveillance too often violatory of bodily or emotional privacy (see Carlen 1998:138–143).

Given the extreme plasticity of popular and official conceptions of women's crimes and women's punishments, it is understandable why critiques and assessments of women's treatment in the penal system have themselves been riven with contradictory assumptions, assertions and aspirations (see Hudson, next chapter, for a clear exposition of the changing and contradictory jurisprudential rationales for some recent sentencing policies). Always seen but darkly through the distorting mirror of male criminality, issues relating to women and punishment have been extremely difficult to extricate from the long shadows cast by the much larger male penal estate (see De Cou chapter 5 this volume). Thus, although women have routinely been punished in several different ways to men, it has been a frequent criticism (especially in relation to the design of prisons and custodial regimes) that they have also been punished as if they *are* men. Relatedly, though women's guilt has traditionally been differentially calculated in the courts, it has also been a familiar plaint (especially in relation to women's crimes against violent men) that the logic of the courts has discriminated against women by treating them as if their life experiences (and therefore any reasoning rooted in them) could be assumed to be identical to men's. Furthermore, and at a more material level, though women's prisons in many countries have been organised differently to men's for several decades, a recurring criticism has been that women's custodial facilities have been primarily designed by men and only with men's needs in mind – and that the ensuing disadvantageous differences have tended to stem not so much from any gender-sensitive design, but rather from the repeated losses suffered by women's institutions in the battles with the men's establishments over regime and rehabilitative resources.

More recently there has been disagreement as to the jurisprudential, ideological and practical utility of representing women in prison only – or primarily – as victims of class, race or gender inequities or abuses (Carlen 1994; Bosworth 1999; Denton 2001). And this at the same time as there has been widespread agreement that women who end up in prison are likely to have suffered disproportionately from poverty and racism, a cluster of associated social deprivations (such as inadequate health care, education and employment opportunity) as well as injuries relating to physical, sexual and emotional abuse during childhood! (See Loucks 1997; De Cou chapter 5 of this collection.)

So then, even at the beginning of the twenty-first century, even after several decades of work by campaigning groups and concerned criminal justice personnel for a better deal for women in the criminal justice system, questions of women's punishment are still fraught with confusion and contradiction – many of them having been aggravated, rather than alleviated, by recent twists and turns in the on-going struggle to make the punishment of women less damaging to themselves and their families, and (by reducing the likelihood of recidivism) more effective in diminishing the quantity of social injury suffered (see especially, Hannah-Moffat, chapter 11 of this book).

The following essays address many of the contemporary issues relating to women and their punishment by the criminal justice system.

They are by women who, as criminal justice personnel, campaigners and/or academics, have been closely involved with either the implementation of new approaches to the punishment of female offenders, or in the analysis of why the new forms of punishment[3] have taken the forms they do. The rest of this first chapter will introduce and discuss the book's main themes; and the discussion will be organised around seven questions central to debates about women and punishment:

1. Are women punished differently to men?

2. Should women be sentenced according to different criteria to men?

3. Is a 'gendered justice' viable?

4. Is it desirable or possible for penal institutions to be used for 'treatment'?

5. Is it desirable or possible for the penal system to be used to address non-criminal issues of social justice?

6. What are women's prisons for?

7. What are the possible and desirable relationships between critique and reform?

In the discussion of these questions there is no intention of implying that any of the other contributors to this collection would give the same answers, nor that they are the only questions worthy of address (though it is contended that, apart from the first question, they are questions that are often neglected or conflated with each other). Nor are any of the 'answers' intended as blueprints for reform. Instead, the more modest purpose is to delineate the complexity of the issues involved.

None the less, there is an insistence that these are political questions, the answers to which cannot easily be read-off from either analyses of the social, mental or emotional conditions of female prisoners (see chapter 12), or the ideologies of any one or more of the campaigning groups, institutional interests or contributors to this book. It is hoped, however, that in the future reform bodies and policy writers will address at least some of these questions and work out where they stand on them at the commencement of their reforming endeavours – rather than, by their silence, imply that what is at stake in relation to women and the punishment of the courts is fairly obvious to all people of good heart and sound mind. For, because of the multiple interpretations and contradictions entangled in competing philosophies and practices of punishment (and the human condition) agreement as to what would constitute 'justice for women' (or men) is impossible to achieve. It should be possible, however, for reformers and policy makers – as they struggle to achieve their various objectives – to be more aware of when and where the ideological and policy trade-offs have occurred, and why (see Hannah Moffat chapter 11). Hence these questions.

1. Are women punished differently to men?[4]

There are six main bodies of broadly critical literature which can be mined to provide answers to this question: historical literature which describes the different punishments imposed on women over the centuries and which focuses on both the quantity and quality of women's punishments (e.g. Freedman 1981; Rafter 1985; Knelman 1998; Maybrick 1905; Zedner 1991); sociological literature which locates women's punishments in the broader context of social (and anti-social) controls and argues that as women have become more closely constrained by informal controls of family, factory, fashion, men and medicine so have they appeared less frequently in the criminal courts (Carlen 1995; Hagan *et al* 1979; 1995; Feeley and Little 1991); socio-legal studies which have attempted to establish whether or not women are sentenced more or less harshly than men (Daly 1994); criminological studies which have attempted to gauge and explain the quality of the confinement suffered by women in closed penal institutions (e.g. Carlen 1983; Girshick 1999); a campaigning literature which has argued that, for a variety of reasons, imprisonment for women is a harsher punishment than it is for men (see Owen 1998; Cook and Davies 1999); and an official and administrative literature which, in a number of countries has, for the last decade, been complementing, or responding to, the criticisms of the campaigners (see, for example, Task Force on Federally Sentenced Women 1990 – for Canada; Social Work Services and Prisons Inspectorates for Scotland 1998; Home Office 2000a – for England and Wales; Select Committee on the Increase in the Prisoner Population – Interim Report [on the increases in numbers of women prisoners in New South Wales] 2000).

In sum, the findings of all this research and scholarship suggest that there is no strong statistical evidence to support claims that women are sentenced more harshly than men. Furthermore, such evidence would be extremely difficult to compute because of the difficulties of untangling gender criteria from others such as those relating to racism and class.

During the early 1980s a series of English research studies suggested that in the English criminal justice system women tended to be sentenced more severely than men (e.g. Edwards 1984; Seear and Player 1986). Subsequently, a number of investigators took issue with these claims (see especially Allen 1987a); and the most recent English research concludes that women are *not* sentenced more harshly than men, that they are sentenced less harshly (Hedderman and Gelsthorpe 1997). However, very few commentators have argued that *all* women are sentenced more or less harshly than *all* men. Rather, and on the basis of the demographic characteristics of imprisoned women, this author, for instance, has always argued that although the majority of women are, in comparison with men, treated more leniently by the criminal justice system, certain women – those who have been brought up in the state's institutional care, have transient lifestyles, have their own children already in state guardianship, are living outwith family and male-related domesticity, or are members of ethnic minority groups (see Chiquada 1997) – are more likely to proceed through the criminal justice system and end up in prison (Carlen 1983, 1998). Such an argument does not contradict the findings of those who argue that *overall* women are sentenced more leniently than men. On the contrary, and as the authors of a previous statistical report which concluded that women are not sentenced more harshly than men recognised:

> The likelihood that female offenders may overall receive more lenient treatment than males does not rule out the possibility that individual women receive unusually harsh treatment.
>
> (Hedderman and Hough 1994:4)

Thus it seems that gender considerations do affect sentencing, but that they do so only *obliquely* and *eccentrically:* obliquely rather than transparently primarily because conventional gender typifications are filtered through dominant ideological strictures about the relationships between the formal and informal social control systems, with the dominant assumption being that the formal control system should be used most harshly against those citizens not controlled by informal means: that is, by the family, male-related domesticity and the welfare state in the case of women (see Ehrenrich and English 1979; Eaton 1986; Donzelot 1979; Worrall 1990; Zedner 1991; Smart 1992); and by work in the case of men (see Young 1975; Laffargue and Godefroy 1989; Slack 1990). Yet even that is too simple. For, once gender typifications are read thus, it is very difficult to separate them out from the effects on criminal justice of racism and other socially-structured inequalities. Hence, the effects of gender typifications on sentencing are not only *oblique* – because they are filtered through other ideological forms; but they are also *eccentric* – because they are realised within structural inequities which overdetermine the form of their effectivities in individual cases.

The obscured effectivities of these complex ideological forms both systematically and eccentrically structure all the other criminal justice decisions which (both separately and exponentially) have already occurred prior to the final sentencing decision taken in the court. (As it is these lone sentencing decisions which are used in studies of sentencing – it would not be feasible to unravel all the contributing decisions relating to arrest etc – it is not surprising that gender differences in severity of sentencing are often not apparent in quantitative analyses of this type.)

As a consequence of the systematic but obscure and eccentric embedding of structural inequities and ideological regulatory mechanisms in the final sentencing decision, some of the most significant social characteristics of prisoners are common to both male and female populations (cf Daly 1994). In England, for example, both have disproportionate numbers of people from ethnic minority groups; both have disproportionate numbers who have been brought up in state institutions and both have disproportionate numbers from the most economically deprived social classes (Home Office 1992a). These characteristics of all prison populations of the countries discussed in this book (see, for example, Mauer 1999 for a telling analysis of the effectivity of racism on imprisonment in the United States; Morgan and Carlen 1999 for Europe) suggest that, although gender considerations do indeed affect whether or not a lawbreaker becomes a sentenced prisoner, it is difficult to separate their impact on sentencing from factors such as racism and class.

Once women are in prison, however, there is no doubt that, historically, they have been treated differently to men, and that the difference in treatment continues to the present day (see Carlen 1998; Girshick 1999; Cook and Davies 1999). It is also arguable that because of their previous life experiences, gynaecological needs and the cultural demands made on women outside prison, certain aspects of imprisonment formally imposed on men and women equally are likely to occasion more pain for women than males (for example, separation from children because imprisoned women are more likely to have been the primary carers prior to incarceration; and some of the security arrangements – for the reasons mentioned above).

2. Should women be sentenced according to different criteria to men?

Several penal reformers have argued that whether or not women have been, or currently are, sentenced differently to men, they most certainly should be; and that for a variety of reasons women should not normally be given custodial sentences. Yet most of the reasons given for using imprisonment only exceptionally in the sentencing of women are not gender-specific. Instead, the four main constructs central to the arguments for the differential sentencing of men and women are respectively: *dangerousness; legitimacy of punishment; double regulation;* and *role worth.*

First of all is an argument based on the observation that women's crimes are committed in very different conditions to those in which men tend to break the law, and therefore pose less of a threat to personal safety and public order (cf Messerschmidt 1986; Home Office 1992b). None the less, the central concept here concerns the (low) degree of dangerousness to others which characterises women's typical crimes, and if this should be a major criterion for the imposition (or not) of a custodial penalty, then it is arguable that it is a criterion that should be applied equally to men and women.

Secondly, it is sometimes argued that if the socio-biographies and criminal careers of women in prison are analysed in depth, it will be seen that their criminal careers were precipitated by their responses to being child victims of neglect and physical and sexual abuse; that therefore the sentence of the courts should aim to ameliorate the affects of previous damage done by child abuse, and not aggravate that pain still further.

Arguments like the foregoing, which implicitly question the legitimacy of punishing young persons to whom the state has never fulfilled its duties of nurturance and basic need-fulfilment (Doyal and Gough 1991), draw upon research which indicates that high proportions of homeless or incarcerated young people have had crimes committed against them by adults who will never be brought to trial (Carlen 1996; Loader 1996). Similar research suggests that these adult depredations often occasion their young victims' first steps into criminal trouble (e.g. Carlen 1996). And although this imbalance of punishment between the young and the old does not excuse the crimes of young people who were criminally abused in childhood, it does call into question the moral legitimacy of punishing them as if they were solely to blame for their actions. In chapter 2, Barbara Hudson develops an argument which points to a way out of this dilemma. In the meantime, however, it is difficult to see how arguments about the illegitimacy of punishing lawbreakers to whom the state has never fulfilled its obligations can be sustained in gender-specific mode.

The third argument in support of gender-specific sentencing of women goes like this: that, in any case, women who appear before the courts usually suffer a discriminating double regulation, because they will have already been subjected to innumerable 'anti-social' and informal controls not suffered by their male counterparts, which in turn will have already reduced their opportunities for full citizenship (Carlen 1995). Therefore, the argument continues, in court they suffer a double punishment – as women who have failed the 'gender test' and as women who have broken the law. Maybe so. But this last argument is again based upon the legitimacy of punishment – though this time the focus is upon the legitimacy of punishing people who as a result of *discrimination* have already suffered a punitive exclusion. That being so, however, there is no reason why the argument for lesser punishment on the grounds of previous gender discrimination against women should not be extended to all kinds of systemic discrimination, including any discrimination involving men (e.g. men already unemployed because of racism in employment) in double punishment too.

Finally, the fourth argument, based on assumptions that there are hierarchies of *role worth* is maybe the one put forward most frequently by emotive press articles decrying the imprisonment of mothers on the grounds that young children should not be separated from their primary carers, and that the damage done to babies when mothers go to jail is too high a price to pay in the name of formal equality of sentencing. But this too is an argument difficult to sustain in gender-specific mode. It could be applied just as convincingly to many categories of worker engaged in life-enhancing work or with rare skills.

Thus, on the basis of the usual arguments for sentencing women differently to men it does not seem that gender can be used as a fundamental or sole criterion in sentencing. Then why a book on women and punishment? Is the concept of 'gendered justice' still worth discussing? Is it viable as an organising principle of sentencing policy, non-custodial programmes and custodial regimes?

3. Is 'gendered justice' viable?

The notion of a 'gendered justice' persists because there is ample evidence that at operational levels it is indeed alive and well. Whether or not they should be, women are already punished differently to men because sentencing policies impact differently on different age, ethnic and gender groups (see especially Hudson, chapter 2, Worrall, chapter 3 and Phoenix, chapter 4 of this collection). When women's prisons are organised without benefit of certain (benign) aspects of gender-specificity they rapidly result in regimes that are disadvantageous to women (see De Cou, chapter 5). Moreover, women's in-prison and rehabilitative needs are not only different to those of men but also vary among each other – according to individual mixes of ethnicity, social class, sexual orientation, health and age factors (see Roberts chapter 6 and Poteat chapter 7 this book). So, the question once more becomes a normative one. *Should* the concept of a gendered justice be retained for campaigning or policy purposes in relation to sentencing, non-custodial interventive programmes and prison regimes?

Throughout the following chapters it will be apparent that three main and interrelated concepts inform debates about gender justice: *legitimacy* (of punishment) and *equality* or *parity* (of punishment). Nicole Hahn Rafter has succinctly distinguished between 'equality' and 'parity': 'Whereas the push for 'equality' tends to be translated into the 'same' or 'identical' programs [*sic*], the push for 'parity' leaves room for differences in program [*sic*] content' (Rafter and Stanley 1999: 42)[5] – and most campaigning and policy change for the last decade has focused on achieving parity of treatment for women in the criminal justice and penal systems, though opponents and critics of these campaigns have repeatedly tried to reframe the issues in terms of 'equality' (see also Worrall, chapter 3).

A fourth notion, central to discussions of the operationalisation of gender-specific sentencing or regimes, is that of *feasibility*. In this collection, different authors weight the four concepts differently within differently constituted discourses and, accordingly, come to different conclusions about the viability or importance of gender specificity in the struggle for justice for women. For example, although I have argued here that the usual arguments for greater leniency towards individual women with particular histories or roles are not in fact gender-specific, Barbara Hudson in chapter 2, and taking a different angle, argues that, while not being intentionally or formally 'gender-specific', some penal phil-osophies (for example those giving primacy to the risk of recidivism) demonstrably translate into sentencing policies which disadvantage women, whereas certain defences (for example, a 'hardship' defence) would, if allowed, most probably favour women. Then Anne Worrall (chapter 3) and Jo Phoenix (chapter 4) both demonstrate (from entirely different perspectives again) that changing interpretations of culpability and risk most probably owe much more to wider political, economic and ideological conditions than they do either to changes in offending patterns or to the perennial remixing of old penal discourses in the formation of new sentencing policies.

All of the authors in the second part of the book appear to operate with an assumption that there is a need for parity of provision for female offenders and that gender-sensitive regimes are both desirable and feasible. However, in the last section, contributors examining the histories of recent reforms conclude that the logical and sociological limits to the viability of gender specific or 'women-centred' prison regimes are much more constraining than some optimists have previously supposed. However, as many of these regimes also attempt to address prisoners' perceived medical, psychological or social needs via a range of interventive programmes (see Kendall chapter 10) another question needs to be raised – one much neglected in recent penal discourse. It is not so much a question of the state's rights and powers of punishment, but of its rights and powers to impose therapeutic 'treatment' as a part of punishment.

4. Is it possible or desirable for penal institutions to be used for treatment?

Thirty years ago the American lawyer Nicholas Kittrie (1971: 403) argued that

> the state should be entitled to either criminal or therapeutic controls in a given case. The insistence upon both reveals an incredible disregard for individual liberty and dignity.

The other arguments against the merging of therapy and punishment in custodial settings are: that the desired therapeutic effects are often undermined by the security and other arrangements thought to be necessary to the good order of the prison; that the voluntary element, seen to be a necessary prerequisite to success in many types of treatment, is often absent and, even where seemingly present, difficult to assess in terms of source and strength of motivation; and that knowledge that a certain type of therapy is available in prison and not available to offenders outside may well result in an increase of custodial sentences not warranted by the seriousness of the offence, but emanating from a judicial desire to 'help' the offender. Even some therapists working in non-custodial settings will refuse to take clients referred by the courts because they distrust the coercive element in the referral.

Kittrie was mainly concerned about the involuntary treatment of offenders for various types of mental illness and addictions. But there was also another reason for concern: that in the cause of rehabilitative intervention, offenders selected for 'treatment' might be detained in custody for longer periods than would have been the case had they been awarded straightforwardly punitive sanctions on the basis of desert. In recent years an opposite concern has been voiced – that many mentally ill offenders are going to prisons rather than mental hospitals because psychiatrists are refusing to accept them into hospitals on the grounds that they have untreatable personality disorders (see Carlen 1983, 1985, 1986). Now again, however, and as Barbara Hudson points out in chapter 2, contemporary sentencing trends in England (based on a concept of 'risk' that, having conflated 'risk of committing crime posing a physical danger to the public' with 'risk of recidivism', compounds the confusion with a further conflation – of 'seriousness' with 'persistence') mean that more and more women are likely to be sentenced to imprisonment for the purpose of undertaking 'programmes' of various kinds directed at reducing recidivism. But what happens to prisoners who refuse therapy or fail to make an appropriate response?

In chapter 4 Joanna Phoenix suggests that they may, in effect, be punished for their recalcitrance. Taking the example of contemporary innovations in the responses to young women in prostitution, she argues that new policy directives which are intended to protect them from abuse and 'ensure that they do not end up in custody, create the very conditions for a greater criminal justice punitiveness towards some and, ultimately, the "protective" incarceration of others'.

At the same time as the concept of 'risk' is becoming more and more woolly for sentencing purposes, the boundaries between the various types of 'treatment' and other types of 'intervention' in the name of rehabilitation are also being increasingly blurred (Kendall chapter 10), and given a disarming spin via the employment of populist expressions such as 'empowerment' (Hannah-Moffat and Carlen chapters 11 and 12 respectively) and 'individual choice' (Hannah-Moffat, chapter 11). The question then arises as to how the prison will respond – indeed can respond – if prisoners fail to 'choose' to be 'empowered', or are seen to have an inappropriate response to therapy? These key questions were recently raised by Kelly Hannah-Moffat in her powerful account of ten years of attempted reform of the women's prisons in Canada (Hannah-Moffat 2001) and she considers them further in chapter 11.

But I wish to pause here. And, in fairness to all the prison officials and reformers who, over many years, have achieved a measure of progressive change in the official responses to women in the criminal justice and penal system, consider a justification for therapeutic intervention which is based not so much on a 'reduction of recidivism' argument but more straightforwardly on a social justice plea: that as so many prisoners – especially women – arrive in prison suffering the extreme health and social effects of poverty, addictions and physical and sexual abuse, surely, in the name of social justice (or, less grandly, human compassion) it is desirable that one objective of imprisonment be to ensure that prisoners are released from prison in a better state than when admitted?

5. Is it possible or desirable for the penal system to be used to address non-criminal issues of social justice?

One of the major difficulties of discussing women's imprisonment solely in jurisprudential terms relating to the rights and wrongs of fusing punishment and treatment within therapeutic custodial regimes is that the prime reason for many women (and men too, for that matter) being in prison is not related to the seriousness of the crime for which they were convicted at all, but rather to their social needs, or, once those 'needs' have been translated into a 'risk of recidivism' index, to the likelihood of their committing crime in the future (see Hudson, chapter 2, and De Cou, chapter 5, of this book). Leaving aside the legitimacy (or not) of such 'therapunitive' sentencing objectives, many prison personnel and reforming prison campaigners, when faced with the actuality of women in prison who, on their own admission, are physically, mentally and emotionally in a very bad way indeed, feel that it is better to attempt to 'do something' to help them while they are in custody than to do nothing at all. Others, however, in addition to raising all the same objections that can be made in relation to using custodial institutions for treatment, oppose the 'social justice' argument by insisting that it is morally and economically indefensible for people to be given social benefits in prison which they would not have received had they not committed a crime. Several arguments are marshalled in support of this latter stricture: one involves the old plea of *less eligibility*, the insistence that criminals should not receive preferential treatment over non-criminals; another is based on resistance to any suggestion that it is actually desirable or possible to redress social wrongs in prison.

The last-mentioned objection is itself rooted in at least three other different perspectives. One is the social prevention argument: that if social deprivation is a contributory factor in lawbreaking, it would make more economic sense to address the areas of deprivation in the community than to take resources away from the community in order to address, in prison, problems caused in the first place by lack of community provision; secondly, there is a common-sense viewpoint which observes that if social exclusion is a contributory factor in a person's criminal activity, removing that person to prison will add even more to her exclusion; and a third perspective, perhaps the bleakest of all, is (for a variety of reasons – see chapters 11 and 12) rooted in a well-founded scepticism that prisons can be for anything except punishment. Theorists from this third perspective turn again and again to the question, 'What are prisons *for*?'

6. What are women's prisons for?

Every contributor to this book agrees that the numbers of women given custodial sentences should be reduced. As that is not happening, the question remains as to how best to respond to the increasing numbers of women who are at risk of, or sentenced to, a term of imprisonment. It is a question implicitly or explicitly addressed in this collection by contributors writing from a variety of standpoints (some from more than one) – for example, prison personnel, professionals involved in non-custodial provision, campaigning academics and feminists.

Senior prison managers, like Kate De Cou (chapter 5), do not have the luxury of sitting on the sidelines and talking off the top of their critiques. Many prison personnel who have no choice but to deal with the prisoners sent to their institutions by the courts, are committed to organising regimes and programmes best suited to the characteristics and needs of the specific population they have in prison at any one time. Those who are committed to making women's prison regimes more appropriate to women's needs try to operationalise the parity principle by ensuring that the implications of recognising women's difference inform regime and programme design. However, they also recognise that because a prison necessarily has to keep its prisoners *in*, security constraints place implacable limits on the organisational reach of prison reform … in women's prisons as much as in men's.

Jenny Roberts (chapter 6) and Sally Poteat (chapter 7) have both been involved in the implementation of non-custodial programmes designed to make community provision for women at risk of punishment by imprisonment: in the short term, by ensuring that the programmes are acceptable to the courts; and in the long term by tailoring the programme content to meet the self-defined needs of the populations catered for. The West Mercia (formerly Hereford and Worcester Probation) Community-Based Programme for Women and North Carolina's Women at Risk

Programme have both received favourable publicity (for West Mercia, see Prison Reform Trust 2000; for North Carolina's Women at Risk see Chesney Lind 2000), and have been seen as models of their kind. However, they are unusual in that they have survived for as long as they have (West Mercia eight years and North Carolina's Women at Risk ten years). Indeed, it is because of the short-lived nature of so many non-custodial programmes for women that a whole chapter (8) is devoted to listing the characteristics of gender-specific programmes for women which survive, change according to the requirements of their clients, and yet remain true to their objectives. Yet even in Jenny Roberts' account, when she describes how the acclaimed West Mercia's programme none the less failed to meet the central authority's accreditation criteria, we get intimations of some of the reasons why penal reform (albeit in this case, non-custodial penal reform) has proceeded so slowly.

Finally, in the book's last section, four analytic critiques of the role of the state in prison reform suggest that women's prisons, like all prisons, are primarily for punishment. Analyses of what has happened recently in England and Canada suggest that other proclaimed objectives, however seemingly well-defined, first become muddied by the confused objectives of bureaucracies with opposed interests (see Jackie Lowthian, chapter 9) and then 'disappeared' – either in the ideological maw of the prison (Hannah-Moffat chapter 11) or by its internal security logic (Carlen chapter 12). Prisons are first and foremost for punishment by keeping prisoners securely in prison and any policy changes (such as a meaningful 'empowerment' of prisoners) which would necessarily involve dilution of that primary goal are unlikely to be successful. That being so, you might well ask again, why this book? Why continue to be involved in prison research, prison reform? Why argue for any policy changes at all? Why not merely campaign for the abolition of women's imprisonment altogether, given that at one and the same time, some of us are both campaigning for reforms in women's prisons *and* (wearing our analytic hats) claiming that prisons are organisationally incapable of engendering the very reforms for which we are campaigning? These questions about the relationships between critique and reform constantly gnaw at the resolve of prison campaigners who, though their heads and hearts may be in constant opposition, none the less remain convinced that 'something must be done'.

7. What are the desirable and possible relationships between critique and reform?

A major contradiction was apparent in the Conference which gave birth to this set of essays. On the one hand, a range of very committed practitioners were telling with enthusiasm of the progress they had made in developing gender-specific or women-centred community programmes or prison regimes against great odds; on the other, a series of academics were concomitantly analysing different aspects of prison reform attempts and invariably finding them to be either deeply flawed or impossible to realise; either because progressive innovations are repeatedly being subverted by inappropriate programmes based on a reworking of some old positivistic explanations of crime (Kendall chapter 10 this volume); or because they are repeatedly swallowed up in the logic and culture of state imprisonment and its bureaucratic arrangements (see Hannah-Moffat on *encroachment* and Carlen on *carceral clawback*, chapters 11 and 12 respectively).

Yet, while penal incarceration for women exists there will always be better and worse prisons. For that reason, if for none other, all the contributors to this book are united in the belief that, as Kelly Hannah-Moffat insists in chapter 11, 'It is better to do something than nothing'. And in her ensuing discussion of the lessons to be learned from the Canadian experience of the last ten years, Hannah-Moffat also gives some firm indications of the relationships between critique and reform, seeing continuous and reflexive critique as the necessary prerequisite to an understanding of the limits to penal reform within prisons.

When Chris Tchaikovsky (founder of the Women in Prison campaigning group in England) and I gave our own thoughts on why it is better to 'do something than nothing', in 1996, we argued that:

> Any *intention* to reduce the pains of imprisonment for women is *good in itself*. Secondly, while prisons exist … such a good can only be pursued if campaigners continue to engage in democratic discussion with prisoners, prison staff, prison administrators and opinion leaders. Thirdly, it is essential to keep open to public view the inner workings of the whole carceral machinery, so that its endemic secrecy can be held in check, and its chronic tendency to periodic reversion from progressive to retrogressive practices constantly monitored. The purpose of giving full recognition to the political conditions which may atrophy the radically progressive potential of new penal initiative is not to enable campaigners to take refuge in a 'nothing works' nihilism. Instead the intention in

recognising the contradictions between present realities and utopian desires is to facilitate specification of the conditions in which present realities might be otherwise.

(Carlen and Tchaikovsky 1996: 211)

None the less, critique and policy implementation are separate and distinct activities. The one cannot be conflated with the other, though they can be undertaken by the same people at different times. In order to achieve better rather than worse prison conditions, committed people from a range of perspectives have, over the years, tirelessly worked on the essential contradictions between the defining and exclusionary security demands of 'the prison' and the ideally inclusive (but elusive) 'rights' of the citizen-prisoner. While this imperative to action involves compromises, the contradictory and action-undermining imperative to monitor the reform product of those compromises necessitates continuous and uncompromising critique.

The reworking of policies which have already been much fought over before agreement was reached the first time round is hard for everyone involved – committed practitioners, policy makers and campaigners alike. It is therefore often tempting to espouse a cynical nihilism; or, under governments which do not encourage criticism of government policy, to acquiesce in the incorporation of the most radical and far-reaching reform objectives into mere cosmetic changes which seldom improve, and sometimes worsen, the lot of prisoners.

Incorporation such as that described above has to be resisted; not because (as many practitioners suspect) academics falsely imagine that constant criticism is morally superior to jumping off the fence and doing something; nor because 'critics' or academics know best (in any case, they are always dependent on official and practitioner knowledge and expertise to suggest, implement and monitor policy reforms); but because politicians, civil servants, practitioners, prisoners, campaigners and academics all know *differently* – and the conversation must go on.

The conditions for change constantly change. Consequently, the political struggle to realise a justice for women lawbreakers which would be more effective (than prison ever can be) in addressing their material needs and reducing their recidivism is necessarily never-ending. What would be the alternative? There is no alternative. For, as Thomas Mathiesen (1974:13) (writing against the closing-off of critique from policy-making) quipped long ago: the 'finished alternative' would be finished indeed. It would be 'finished in a double sense of the word'.

Notes

1 The author thanks Joanna Phoenix and Anne Worrall for their critical comments on this chapter.
2 Recent and important exceptions are Howe (1994), Daly (1994), Cook and Davies (1999), Hannah-Moffat 2001.
3 Maybe some practitioners of the new responses to women described in this book would not describe their programmes as 'punishment' but rather as 'welfare intervention'. I have used the term 'punishment' because most participants in the programmes and regimes described would have been serving a sentence for a criminal offence. The only exceptions would be where programmes allowed attendance by women at risk, but not convicted, of committing a crime.
4 Parts of the discussion under questions 1 and 2 were first published in Carlen 2000a.
5 Frances Heidensohn makes a similar distinction when she distinguishes between formal justice and substantive justice (Heidensohn 1986).

Chapter 2

Gender issues in penal policy and penal theory

Barbara Hudson

Introduction

Too often, studies of women offenders and their treatment in the criminal justice system pay little attention to penal policy and penal theory. With, of course, honourable exceptions (who include the editor and many of the other contributors to this volume), work on female offenders lacks a sense of time and of penological context. From student essays through to polished articles in learned journals, there is little reference in writing on female offenders to changes in penal policy or changes in the relative influence of different penal theories. To some extent this contextual neglect is empirically justified: sentencing, especially the sentencing of female offenders, exhibits 'deep structures' that are resistant to nuances of penal policy change and to shifting fashions in penal theory. Nonetheless, the 1990s saw a series of important developments in penal policy, some of which incorporate significant conceptual shifts about the goals of punishment, and it is therefore well worth considering the impact of these developments on the penal response to female lawbreakers.

The new sentencing framework announced in spring 2001 clarifies the aims and priorities which the government intends sentencing to be oriented towards in the 2000s (Home Office 2001a). This framework is based very firmly on the Halliday Report, the report of the review of sentencing announced on 16 May 2000 (Halliday, French and Goodwin 2001, hereafter HR). Legislation from 1993 onwards introduced significant departures from the principles of the 1991 Criminal Justice Act, which was the last Act to contain a very clear enunciation of the principles which it wished sentencers to follow. These legislative departures both reflected and were reflected by changes in sentencing practice. The Halliday Report reviews the trends of the 1990s and makes a case for a new sentencing framework to be implemented through legislation and guidelines. This new framework would clarify the principles and policies that should govern sentencing. To a large extent the suggested framework articulates and clarifies the policy and practice trends emerging between 1993 and 2000; the new legislation and guidelines would, however, introduce an important conceptual departure from key principles of the 1991 Act. On the other hand, however, it would also establish a principled limit to the extent to which the 1991 principles are to be jettisoned. My first theme in this chapter, then, is an examination of key principles of the Halliday Report and their implications for the sentencing of women.

Following on from this, I want to look at some debates in penal theory and reflect on their relevance to the sentencing of females in a post-Halliday climate. Where penal policy is usually analysed and debated in the restricted, untheorised terms of official discourse, penal theory is its mirror image, generally argued in abstract, generalised terms. Whereas penal policy draws on uncontested official statistics, penal theory draws on legal-philosophical discourse, often with no reference to the empirical world of actual crime rates and actual penal outcomes. This grand penal theory is very much a male-dominated preserve; when female theorists have ventured onto this terrain their contribution has been to draw attention to the otherwise neglected issue of the implications of different penal theories on differently situated groups of offenders. The chapter will consider the implications for women offenders of the changes in penological emphasis contained in the Halliday Report.

The final theme of the chapter is to reflect on debates among penal and legal theorists about culpability and responsibility, looking for ways in which women might be constructed as less blameworthy, without thereby being seen as irrational or irresponsible. This will draw on debates in which I have engaged with legal theorists and philosophers about the possibilities of a 'hardship defence' being allowed in English criminal law (Hudson 1999).

From the 1991 Criminal Justice Act to the Halliday Report

To some extent, lack of attention to penal policy in studies of female offending is understandable, since the sentencing of women seems to show a much looser correlation to the supposed aims of sentencing than does that of men. Sentencing of women offenders also shows far less correlation to the offences they commit than does that of men. This is why analysis of sentencing statistics can be used to demonstrate both relative leniency – a smaller proportion of women than men convicted of violent offences receive custodial sentences – *and* relative severity – a higher proportion of female than male prisoners are property offenders (Hedderman and Gelsthorpe 1997). Women's sentencing corresponds more to their social characteristics and their construction as caring or neglectful mothers, faithful partners or promiscuous sluts than to their crimes. For female offenders, 'The "justice" they receive is more to do with **who** they are than **what** they have done' (Cook 1997: 82, emphasis in the original). This is, of course, well-accepted, and sentencing statistics underpin the formulation of models of justice such as 'familial justice' (Daly 1994; Eaton 1986; Worrall 1990) that appear to fit sentencing practice better than official penal objectives such as 'desert' or 'incapacitation'.

Notwithstanding this different logic in the sentencing of female offenders, penal policy does, inevitably, have some influence on decisions made about them in the courts. Many of the observed practices which led to the characterisation of the sentencing of women as 'paternalistic' and 'infantilising' in the 1970s and early 1980s (Edwards 1984), were associated with the influence of a rehabilitative orientation in penal policy. Sentencing studies found that women were likely to receive probation orders for first and/or minor offences, offences for which their male counterparts would receive fines or discharges (Moxon 1988). Women, it was thought, were being accelerated up the sentencing ladder because they were given unnecessarily interventive sentences for first and for minor offences because of assessments of themselves as sick or needy, assessments which had more weight with decision makers than the seriousness of the offence for which they were convicted. Starting half-way up the tariff, women escalated to custodial sentences more quickly than men, who were more likely to start their sentencing 'career' with a fine and therefore had more rungs to climb before receiving a prison sentence.[1] There was, therefore, quite widespread welcome for the 'just deserts' approach which was influential in the late 1980s and which culminated in the 1991 Criminal Justice Act. The main principle of the Act was that punishment should be in proportion to the seriousness of the offence, and this seemed to offer the prospect of more just outcomes for women and for juveniles, whose penal treatment followed a 'disciplinary' mode, of trying to change the offender, rather than a 'juridical' mode of censuring the crime (Hudson 1996, ch.7).

There were, of course, criticisms to be made about the desert approach. It was seen by some as being too rigid, not allowing for differences in the situations of offenders and not allowing for substituting help for punishment when this seemed to be called for by offenders' circumstances, and it was opposed by many penal reformers who advocated parsimony rather than proportionality as the dominant distributive principle in punishment (Braithwaite and Petit 1990; Carlen 1989; Hudson 1987, 1993). Generally, the desert model raised questions about the (im)possibility of 'doing justice' in an unjust society, questions that remain largely unanswered.[2]

Despite these objections, the predominance of desert thinking and its enactment in the 1991 Criminal Justice Act (an Act which can now be seen as the high water mark of the influence of desert theory) did establish some sentencing principles which are worth defending in the present period, when their persistence is in doubt. The first of these important principles is that people should not be punished for things they have not done. As well as securing the prohibition against punishing the innocent more securely than utilitarian punishment theories, desert theory protects against punishment for crimes not committed in the crucial sense of proscribing punishment for crimes that a rightly convicted offender may commit in the future. It is this past orientation that most significantly divides retributivism from future-oriented consequentialist theories (Von Hirsch 1986).

The 1991 Criminal Justice Act established a bifurcated, or twin-track, system of punishment. Most offence types were allocated to the proportionality track, where penalties were to be in proportion to the offence committed, and a small number of offence types were to be on a 'risk' track, where considerations of risk to the public could allow the imposition of a penalty higher than that dictated by proportionality. Violent and sexual offences were allocated to the risk track; property offences were to be sentenced proportionately. As the 1990s proceeded, risk became a more and more dominant theme of law and order politics, and became increasingly influential in penal policy (Bottoms 1995; Ericson and Haggerty 1997; Feeley and Simon 1992; Garland 1996; Stenson and Sullivan 2001; O'Malley 1992, inter alia).

The general cultural influence of 'risk society' thinking and its significance for criminal justice has been written about extensively (Beck 1992; Castel 1991; Garland and Sparks 2000; Garland 2000; Giddens 1990; O'Malley 2000; Rose 2000; Simon 1988), and the story does not need detailed re-telling here. One development that illustrates the extent to which 'proportionality' was displaced by 'risk' as the dominant criminal justice motif – a development which is particularly relevant for female offenders because of their disproportionate involvement with probation, both in terms of pre-sentence reports and of community penalties – is the

24

extent of 'risk thinking' in probation. 'Risk management' became the key objective of probation during the 1990s (Kemshall 1995; Roberts and Domurad 1995; Worrall 1997). An example of this is the way in which the 'gravity of offence' scales, that were devised in the 1980s to guide probation officers in preparing their reports for courts, were replaced by 'risk of reoffending' measures in the late 1990s.[3] One result of this, of course, is that factors which had been seen as bringing about harsher and more interventive sentencing of socially disadvantaged offenders in the days of the rehabilitative ethic have reappeared as 'risk of reoffending' factors. In sentencing, the key development in this respect was the gradual widening of the risk track and correlative narrowing of the proportionality track (Hudson 2001).

For female offenders, what is really significant about this development is not so much the growing preoccupation with risk, but the changing definitions of exactly what order of risk penal policy is targeted against. The 1991 Criminal Justice Act clearly intended the risk track to provide protection from risk of physical (including sexual) harm. Section 31(3) of the Act defines 'serious harm' as 'death or serious injury', and this is the 'risk' that is acknowledged to warrant departing from penalties proportionate to the crime of present conviction. Although the Act allowed for 'psychological injury' to warrant assignment of an offence to the risk rather than the proportionality track and thus blurred the separation of violent and property offences somewhat, it was generally accepted that this provision was to be used where there was demonstrable targeting of special categories of victim who might be expected to be more traumatised by property offences than other victims. Burglaries with repeat targeting of elderly victims was clearly the paradigm case here; but the fact that this was seen as an exceptional category of case signifies that the normal expectation of the 1991 Act was that property offenders would receive community penalties, and only the perpetrators of violent offences would be imprisoned.

Throughout the 1990s, this differentiation of violent and non-violent offences became increasingly blurred. By the time of the 1996 white paper *Protecting the Public: the Government's Strategy on Crime in England and Wales*, the risk of re-offending was seen to be as important as the risk of physical danger. The target of penal policy was, according to this white paper, protection of the public from 'dangerous and persistent criminals' (Home Office 1996). This coupling together of dangerousness and persistence allowed property offences to shift from the proportionality to the risk track, as for example in the Crime (Sentences) Act 1997, which brought the 1996 white paper into legislation, which prescribed mandatory imprisonment for third offences of burglary as well as for

25

third violent and sexual offences. Although the provision of minimum sentences of three years' imprisonment for third-time burglary might not sound unreasonably harsh in comparison with the USA (and although few women are convicted of burglary), the important departure is that a category of property offences was treated in the same way as offences against the person. The incoming Labour Government delayed implementation of the mandatory imprisonment provision for repeat burglary, but did subsequently ratify the clause.

As well as blurring the bifurcation of violent and property offences, sentencing trends in the late 1990s conflated *seriousness* and *persistence*. The Halliday Report pinpointed 'the unclear and unpredictable approach to persistent offenders' as the most compelling reason for a review of sentencing and the introduction of a new framework (HR: ii). At the end of the 1980s, there was almost complete consensus among policy-makers, criminal justice practitioners and penal reformers that petty persistent offenders should not be imprisoned. The so-called 'revolving door' syndrome was frequently invoked, to illustrate the futility of giving short custodial sentences to people who repeatedly commit crime because of the circumstances they face outside the prison. These short sentences offered insufficient scope to achieve any rehabilitative effects on the offender, and in any case made no impact on the situations of poverty, homelessness, addictions and abuse that they might face on the outside. The Prison Reform Trust described the 'identikit' prisoner as someone who was far more likely than non-offenders and non-imprisoned offenders to be homeless, unemployed, with poor educational attainment, drug and/or alcohol dependent, and without supportive partners or other caring relatives. Prison was likely to make their circumstances, and therefore their likelihood of re-offending, worse rather than better:

> the 'Identikit Prisoner' is someone who has suffered a range of social and economic disadvantages. A key argument for reducing the use of prison is that, all too often, a period of imprisonment exacerbates those very disadvantages which have led the person into crime in the first place.
>
> (Prison Reform Trust, 1991: 5)

The Minnesota Sentencing Guidelines, which made clear that some offences were so minor that they should never result in imprisonment no matter how often they were repeated, were widely admired by proponents of proportionate sentencing, and the thrust of policy and practice in the late 1980s was to adopt a similar principle in England and Wales.

Stopping the door revolving with persistent minor offenders on the outside was the reformist tenor of the times. The 1991 Act established the principle through its two *thresholds* of 'serious enough' and 'so serious'. The first threshold prescribed that community penalties should only be used where offences are serious enough to warrant an interventive sentence rather than a fine or discharge; the second threshold prescribed that custodial sentences should only be used when offences are so serious that only such a sentence is a sufficient reflection of their gravity.

This English version of the Minnesota principle was secured by Section 29(1) of the Act which states that an offence is *not* to be regarded as more serious 'by reason of any previous convictions of the offender'. The only way in which previous convictions could affect estimates of seriousness was if they revealed a pattern which aggravated the form of the current offence: for example, revealed a pattern of targeting of elderly or minority ethnic victims. But numbers of previous offences, and the evidence they gave of 'failure to respond to previous sentences', were not in themselves factors which should indicate greater seriousness. Lack of previous convictions could count as mitigating, and the effect of previous convictions would be 'progressive loss of mitigation', which would mean that first offenders could be sentenced at the bottom end of a presumptive band for an offence, but repeat offenders could not be sentenced to more than the 'going rate' for the offence category.

Section 29(1) was one of the main causes of dissatisfaction with the 1991 Act on the part of magistrates, politicians, and the public (at least, the tabloid reading sections of the public). While judges in the higher courts had sufficient powers to incarcerate those they thought of as posing danger-menace to the public because they were mainly dealing with persons convicted of more serious offences who would receive custodial sentences on current offence desert grounds, magistrates felt frustrated by lack of scope to remove offenders from the streets whom they perceived as posing nuisance-menace. At the time, there were moral panics about persistent offenders in general, and about those who re-offended on bail in particular. Whether the intention of the 1993 Criminal Justice Act, which replaced Section 29(1) of the 1991 Act, was to deal with these particular instances and to make clearer the intentions of the original section to consider previous convictions if they had bearing on the nature of the current effect (Wasik and Von Hirsch 1994) or whether the replacement of the section was an example of 'populist punitiveness' (Bottoms 1995) is debatable, but certainly the effect was to signal to sentencers that previous convictions could lead to more serious penalties than indicated by the current offence.

27

The replacement section 29(1), introduced in the 1993 Act, appears to reverse the 1991 Act's clear separation of the ideas of seriousness and persistence:

In considering the seriousness of any offence, the court may take into account any previous convictions of the offender or any failure of his [*sic*] to respond to previous sentences.

Whatever the legislators' intention, the effect has been to reinstate persistence and criminal justice history as important influences on sentencing. The result of this 1991 to 1993 change and subsequent political and policy emphasis on persistent offending, has been, according to the Halliday Report, unpredictable and inconsistent sentencing. While Crown Courts maintain the 'progressive loss of mitigation' approach, reducing sentence for first offenders but maintaining proportionality to current offence for subsequent convictions, magistrates courts have increased their use of short prison sentences for repeat offences. Discussions with magistrates for the report found that they were likely to respond to 'failures' of previous sentences with desperate attempts to 'try something different'. Halliday comments that

As a result, persistent offenders whose offences are not so serious as to land them in the Crown Court, find themselves 'bouncing around' between a variety of custodial and community sentences, without any clear rationale, continuity, or predictability. (HR: 2)

After concluding its review of sentencing to date, the Halliday Report moves to consideration of the principles that should govern sentencing in the future. The concepts of seriousness, persistence, risk and culpability are combined in the three propositions given in section 2.8. This states that:

the severity of the punishment should reflect the seriousness of the offence and the offender's criminal history; the seriousness of the offence should reflect its degree of harmfulness or risked harmfulness, and the offender's culpability in committing the offence; in considering the offender's criminal history, the severity of the sentence should increase to reflect previous convictions, taking account of how recent and relevant they were. (HR: 13)

The report introduces an important conceptual shift in re-defining proportionality as meaning proportionality to 'seriousness of the offence (or offences as a whole) and the offender's criminal history', and re-defining the 'so serious' threshold as meaning that 'Imprisonment should be used when no other sentence would be adequate to meet the seriousness of the offence (or offences) having taken account of the offender's criminal history' (HR: 21).

What is advocated in order to structure sentencing to reflect seriousness of current offence and previous record is a series of 'entry points' that reflect the present offence, which the judge can go above or below according to criminal history. An illustrative example is given:

> Where the 'entry point', for example, was a prison sentence of 18 months, a first offender might receive a non-custodial sentence, but for an offender sentenced on a large number of sufficiently recent occasions for offences of about the same level of seriousness, the sentence might be three years. (HR: 15)

Current offence seriousness is to govern the range of penalty available, but previous record is to govern the point within the range which is chosen, and as the report acknowledges 'the range around the entry point can be quite wide – of the order of, say, plus or minus 100%'! (HR: 16). Previous convictions, then, could influence both whether a custodial sentence is imposed or not, and also the length of sentence.

Risk, as well as persistence, is to be used in deciding sentence in Halliday's proposed framework. Where the seriousness (current offence plus previous record) indicates a prison sentence of over 12 months, risk of re-offending assessments are to determine work to be done with the offender during sentence, rather than length of sentence. Compliance with risk-reducing programmes would, however, influence decisions about early release, and about the degree of continuing control and work to reduce risk of re-offending that would be demanded in the post-release phase of the sentence.

The influence of risk assessments on sentencing, however, is greatest where the sentencer judges that a sentence of 12 months or more is not necessary to reflect seriousness. In such cases, assessment of 'the needs of punishment' (p. 19), which includes both public protection and repara-tion to victims, would determine whether a community penalty would suffice, and risk assessment would be an important factor in the sentencing decision. Programmes to match the assessed needs of the offender would be imposed, which could be supplemented by elements of 'straightforward punishment', such as financial penalties, compulsory work, and/or restrictions on liberty (curfew, electronic monitoring). Rehabilitative programmes would be supplemented by punitive elements if it was felt that the 'punitive weight' of the rehabilitative elements was insufficient.

For offences which are not deemed serious enough for a sentence of 12 months or more, the combination of harm done by the present offence, previous convictions, and risk of re-offending, could result in a 'custody plus' sentence. This means that there would be a determinate period in prison for purposes of punishment, followed by a period of supervision in the community with participation in programmes aimed at reducing the risk of re-offending:

> 'Custody plus' would be the sentence of choice for offenders with high risk of re-offending, whose offences and previous convictions were so serious as to leave no adequate alternative, but not so serious as to require a longer prison sentence. (HR: 20)

To summarise: the key elements of the framework proposed by the Halliday Report are:

> 'seriousness' is re-defined to mean seriousness of current offence *plus* previous record;
> 'risk of reoffending' can influence sentence severity for cases where seriousness does not indicate a custodial sentence of 12 months or more;
> although sentencers are encouraged to substitute community penalties for short prison sentences, there is no clear 'in/out' line.

Implications for women of the proposed new framework

I have examined the Halliday Report in some detail because it provides a useful thematic summary of sentencing trends over the past decade, and because it is likely to provide the basis of penal policy for many years to come. The report is unusual in that it does mention the impact of sentencing trends on women, and the authors claim to have paid attention to evidence about the penal treatment of women, particularly the Wedderburn Report (Prison Reform Trust 2000). What Halliday offers, however, amounts only to a few brief comments on the effects of penal trends on women in the 1990s; there is no discussion of the likely effects of the report's own recommendations.

It is well known that the 1990s saw bigger proportionate increases in the number of women than men receiving prison sentences (87% for women, 33% for men). The largest component in this increase is usually attributed by the Home Office to more women being sentenced, slightly more women being sentenced for violent offences, and in particular, to large increases in the number of women being sentenced for drug offences (Prison Reform Trust 2000: 2-3). However, as the Halliday Report demonstrates, the trend to give short prison sentences for repeat minor offences has disproportionately affected females. Between 1989 and 1999 the biggest rise in prison sentences was in short sentences, imposed by magistrates' courts rather than Crown Courts. Halliday's analysis of sentencing statistics reports that between 1989 and 1999:

- Custodial sentences imposed at magistrates' courts increased from 18,2000 to 53,000 (191%)

- At the Crown Court, the increase was from 42,600 to 44,6000 (5%)

- The number of adults received under sentence increased from 57,270 to 83,100 (45%)

- The increase in the number of women (143%) was over three times greater than the increase for men (40%) (HR: 83).

In that decade the number of sentences up to 3 months increased by 119% and the number of sentences of 3 to 6 months increased by 98%, while the numbers of sentences of 6 to 12 months and 12 to 18 months decreased by 1% and 6 % respectively (HR: 83). In 1999, under the influence of the emphasis on persistence and risk of re-offending, the number of prison sentences for offenders aged 18 and over of under 3 months given for theft and handling was 7,567 more than in proportionality minded 1989, and there were 3,556 more sentences of between 3 and 6 months; for fraud and forgery the increases were 515 and 651 sentences respectively. These increases in short prison sentences were despite a fall in numbers of persons convicted of these crimes between 1989 and 1999 of 6,360 for theft and handling and 2,213 for fraud and forgery. During the 1990s proportionate use of fines for both crime categories declined by 17%; for theft and handling use of both community sentences and immediate custody increased by 10%; and for fraud and forgery community sentences increased by 21% and immediate custody by 7%. Increasing use of community punishments, then, was at the expense of fines rather than at the expense of short custodial sentences.

What is of most significance for the sentencing of women is that the biggest increases in imprisonment were for the offences for which women were already most frequently imprisoned: theft and handling, fraud and forgery. *The new emphasis on persistence and risk of re-offending encouraged and legitimised the imposition of short prison sentences for property offences of no great seriousness.* Magistrates were given the green light to use imprisonment for offences which were not sufficiently serious, and for offenders who were not sufficiently dangerous, to warrant sentences of more than 12 months. The revolving door was not just re-opened, it was given a shove to make it revolve more vigorously. This policy trend is extremely worrying for the prospects for women offenders, because their lower imprisonment rates compared with men's have always been first and foremost due to the fact that women commit less serious offences, and are less dangerous, than men.

The implications for women, and for those who wish to discourage the use of imprisonment for women, are clear. Much of the case for reduction of women's imprisonment, and for its abolition as a normal rather than exceptional response to female crime (Carlen 1990) has been that very few women commit violent offences, and that very few women pose a threat of physical danger to the public. The reductionist case against extensive and routine use of imprisonment for women often rests on the fact that in any year, half the women sent to prison have been convicted of property crimes. Referring to 1998, the Wedderburn report states that

> The most common crimes for which women were being sent to prison that year were still theft and handling stolen goods which, together with offences of fraud and forgery, accounted for almost half (48 per cent) of the 4,778 sentenced women received that year.
>
> (Prison Reform Trust 2000: 6)

The '*still*' here reveals the lack of adequate consideration of general trends in penal policy that I noted at the outset. It would only be surprising that women committing these crimes were 'still' being sentenced to imprisonment if the 1991 principles, with violent and sexual crimes being assigned to the prison track and property crimes (unless aggravated by special factors) assigned to the community penalty track, were still in force.

In fact, with the increasing abandonment of these principles and the new emphasis on risk of re-offending, women have become even more likely to be imprisoned for these offences. What happened as the 1990s progressed was that the disregard for personal situations that was one of the worst possibilities of the just deserts approach meshed with the worst potential of the risk-of-re-offending approach. This meant that more women with children, more women with bleak economic prospects, more women with addictions, were imprisoned for theft and handling, fraud and forgery (Carlen 1998). The conflation of dangerousness and persistence, and the breaking of the consensus that non-violent, less serious property offences should not result in prison sentences, thus has serious implications for female offenders. (It has implications for male offenders, too, of course, especially for men convicted of burglary, which is the crime that results in most male prison sentences.) For women, the real threat is that there is now no sense of a firm lower limit to the offences which are appropriately dealt with by way of imprisonment. According to Halliday, sentencers should be given discretion to impose community penalties instead of short custodial sentences, but they are by no means required to do so. Persistent property offending is the crime pattern typical of the impoverished, addicted, deprived and depressed 'identikit' female offender, and the new sentencing framework makes her more vulnerable to imprisonment than ever before.

Equality and risk

Equality is the other core principle of 1980s desert penal thinking that deserves continuing support. Feminist penologists have rightly been critical of the construction of equality that is inscribed in law and criminal justice, but this does not mean they are opposed to an ideal of equality. The thrust of feminist critique in and beyond criminal justice is that to treat people *equally* has been taken to mean treating them *the same* (Carlen 1990; Eaton 1986; Hudson 1998). In law, as in the other institutions of liberal societies, this means treating women the same as men.

Equality-versus-difference has been the big debate among feminist theorists in so-called 'second wave' feminism. Liberal feminists first of all mounted an internal critique of rights and equality under liberalism, pointing out that these ideals could not be regarded as realised unless they were extended to women as well as to men. This feminist 'first wave' quickly led to a deeper, immanent critique, as the campaigns for existing rights to be accorded to women revealed that the rights that had been delineated by liberal polities were based on the freedoms needed to lead the life of the male citizen – the individualistic, competitive life in the public sphere (Lacey 1996). Rights to vote, to work in the professions, were relatively easy to extend to women, because they were well-established rights and because their extension was clearly a requirement of equality as already understood in such societies, but difficulties arose with demands for rights that were specific to women, for example abortion rights. These difficulties led some to suggest that the emancipatory potential of rights discourse for women is exhausted (Smart 1989, 1995). Any further freedoms from oppression must be argued for on the grounds of the needs to delineate rights that are needed for women to lead their lives *as women* with as much freedom as men have in leading their lives *as men*.

The equality-versus-difference debate takes as its point of departure the realisation that rights and other bedrock concepts of law are constructed from a male view of the world, and furthermore that it is difficult to see how this could be otherwise because the political-legal-cultural structure of modern societies is based on a *masculine imaginary*. That is to say, the cultural complex of which law is part is based on constructions of subjectivity based on masculine philosophies; it is based on masculine desires, masculine imaginings of the life they would lead, and masculine fears about the structures and other subjectivities that are likely to obstruct the fulfilment of their desires and ambitions. Any further gains for women can only be obtained through interposing a feminine imaginary, which can develop its own ideas of the rights, the freedoms, the rules and the protections women need to fulfil their hopes and to permit their development as free, authentic females (Cornell 1995; Irigaray 1994).

In criminal law, as in other fields of law such as employment law and family law, this 'maleness' of law is readily apparent. Examples abound in women's treatment both as victims and as offenders. On the one hand, there is the length of time it has taken for domestic violence to be taken seriously, and for marital rape to be made a criminal offence, whilst on the other hand the standards of culpability and responsibility for crime are based on the idea of the 'reasonable man'. Rape is entirely constructed around the notion of the normality of the promiscuous male sex drive, forever on the alert for sexual opportunity, a sex drive which it is women's responsibility to manage. Hence the centrality of the idea of consent, and the resilience, even in these supposedly gender-conscious times, of the belief that it is the woman's sexual history that is significant in the case, rather than the man's. The 'rape shield', the prohibition on mentioning previous convictions of male defendants, is easy to maintain not only because it is consistent with rules of evidence across all crime categories, but also because it fits with the deep-seated beliefs about sexuality – that men's sexuality is by its nature unconstrained, and therefore coerced sexuality reflects women's failures as sexual managers.

In the cases of women who kill their abusive partners, we see another facet of this maleness of law. Defences and mitigations are constructed on the basis of what the reasonable man would do in the circumstances, which means that self-defence and provocation are generally unavailable to women because they do not kill instantly in the moment of threat, but await an opportunity, usually when the man is asleep or otherwise unawares. Self-defence is still almost unavailable to women in these circumstances, at least in England and Wales, while the idea of 'cumulative provocation' is only gradually and patchily becoming accepted. Women are still getting life sentences for killing after years of abuse and degradation, while men receive non-custodial or short custodial sentences for killing when provoked by revelations of their partners' infidelity, or if they lose their tempers in response to nagging: the 'nagging and shagging' defence fits exactly the male idea of what provocation means and what is a reasonable response (Cooke, in *The Guardian* 30.10.01:8).

Criminal law has been very slow and very resistant to allowing in the feminine imaginary. Some changes have occurred in rape laws, although it remains the case that only a small number of cases result in conviction; cumulative provocation is gradually becoming accepted, and a wider range of expertise, including feminists working with abused women, is being heard in courts. In the Lavallee case, the Canadian Supreme Court recognised the masculinity of definitions of reasonable behaviour, provocation and self-defence (Martin *et al* 1991).[4] The judgement describes the paradigm case for the law of self-defence as a one-off 'bar-room brawl' between two men of equal strength; a brief encounter between strangers, in a public space. Self-defence is not constructed to reflect private contexts; it recognises neither gendered violence nor gendered fear (O'Donovan 1993: 429). Canada's recognition of the restricted construction of defences and mitigations has led to admission of evidence from a wider range of experts (Valverde 1996). What is path-breaking here is that acknowledgement of the fact that courts need special witnesses to interpolate the circumstances under which women act is *de facto* acknowledgement by the Canadian Supreme Court of that maleness of law which is commonplace amongst feminist criminologists and legal scholars. Moreover, the 'reasonable person' of law is not just a male person: it is a white, middle-class male person, constantly repro-duced through legal thinking and legal practice (Lloyd 1984; Naffine 1990).

I have dwelt on these frequently cited examples because this masculinism of legal concepts and legal reasoning is most obvious, perhaps, in relation to rape and abuse killing cases – but it applies to routine crime as much as to these sorts of cases. The 'equality' which law offers is that like cases should be treated alike. This means that equality as sameness is deeply inscribed into law, and sameness in this context means the same as men: being treated the same, certainly, and in significant ways, being the same. Catherine MacKinnon points out in relation to anti-discrimination law that what this amounts to is that only women who are like men in their public social roles and in their economic power will be treated equitably by law (MacKinnon 1989). In the penal realm too, women who are like men can expect to be treated the same as men, for good or ill. This means that middle-class women who commit crimes for reasons that are readily comprehensible to men will receive proportionate penalties, although these penalties will take no account of the circumstances that they face specifically as women.

Equality, difference and penal policy

Disparities in the penal treatment of male and female, black and white, rich and poor, show that law has two ways of coping with difference, whether difference of gender, race, class, religion, mental capacity or anything else. One way is to rule differences irrelevant, by specifying only a narrow range of factors that are relevant to decision making (Hudson 1993, ch.6; Kerruish 1991). An example of this is the way many states in the USA say that age and mental capacity are irrelevant in decisions about capital punishment, with the result that people who committed their crimes as juveniles, or who have well below average mental capacity, are executed. For women, this means that childcare responsibilities, the lack of control that many women have over their supposed incomes, and other gendered circumstances are deemed irrelevant.

Ruling difference out of court was the main strategy for dealing with inequalities in the proportionality era. The deserts maxim of proportionality to culpability – which in theory means seriousness of offences measured both by the harm done and by the degree to which the offender was to blame – was in practice reduced to a simplified proportionality to harm done. Aggravating and mitigating circumstances were restricted, and were linked to the offence not the offender. This meant that an increasing number of women with children were imprisoned; an increasing number of women with addictions, with mental illnesses and with histories of physical and sexual abuse were imprisoned; and it meant that women committing crime out of need were imprisoned as readily as those committing crime out of greed. Of course this insensitivity of a sentencing system which valued formal justice (dealing with like offenders alike) above substantive justice (doing what is appropriate for the individual case) affected men as well as women, but because of the circumstances typically surrounding women's criminality, women were disproportionately affected, and women's imprisonment grew at a faster rate than that of men.

Desert theorists have acknowledged that adverse social circumstances or 'rotten social background' pose a problem for their theories (Bazelon 1976). They generally, however, start from the position that law treats people equally, and conclude that there is no compelling reason to treat impoverished offenders more leniently than others (Morse 2000; Von Hirsch 1992, 1993). To some extent this is because lenient punishments might not, they argue, reflect the harm done by the offence, but even more, it is because notwithstanding their poverty, these theorists maintain, offenders act out of choice. It has been argued by myself and others that this second reason for rejecting a hardship defence conflates the concepts of *agency* and *choice* (Garland 1997; Hudson 1995, 1999, 2000). Offenders may have agency in the sense that they are not acting out of mental or physical compulsion, but they may have a very restricted range of choice compared with the middle-class, white, legal subject.

Apart from the necessity (as they see it) of avoiding 'undue' leniency in order to reflect harm done to victims, desert theorists generally conclude that a mitigation of economic hardship would treat impoverished offenders as less than equal, because it would see them as being of reduced moral agency. This is theoretically inevitable because desert theory, with its essential starting point that offenders are punished because they deserve to be, obviously rests on a notion that they act out of choice. Without freedom of action, there can be no desert. As von Hirsch puts it, proportionality

> concerns the quantum of punishment levied on persons who, in choosing to violate the law, have voluntarily exposed themselves to the consequences of criminal liability.
>
> (von Hirsch 1992:62)

As I have argued elsewhere (Hudson 1999), this assumption may have been defensible in the days of welfare capitalism. If the basic necessities of life were guaranteed by a welfare safety net, then perhaps it was reasonable to assume some degree of choice on the part of offenders. The extent to which the safety net has been removed in the past couple of decades, and the exclusionary, repressive policies that are being pursued in the name of risk reduction, has re-opened this debate between desert theorists and their sociological critics (e.g.: Duff 1996, 1998). At the time of writing, there seems to be some support for widening the idea of a necessity defence or mitigation, which is accepted in Germany and Scandinavia.[5] More often, however, the conclusion is that penalising people who have had few of the benefits supposedly conferred by belonging to a society and obeying its rules – in other words people who suffer extreme social deprivation – must be considered as something other than justified punishment, without offering any guidance as to how such offenders should be dealt with when they do come before the courts (Duff 1998, 1999; Matravers 2000: 265–6).

Desert/proportionality theory and policy leave us unsatisfied with its approach to equality and difference, then, on at least two counts. Firstly, it is unable to come up with a principled accommodation of the idea of reduced culpability because of adverse circumstances due to its Kantian essentialist conception of the moral agent. To treat any offenders as less responsible, desert theorists argue, would be to treat them as less than morally equal. The abstraction of the purely procedural equality of liberal political theory from the material circumstances of real human beings (Sandel 1982) means that desert theory with its liberal philosophical base cannot comprehend the inequalities which offenders bring with them, inequalities which are reconstructed rather than set aside by the categories and reasons of criminal law. Secondly, to the extent that desert theorists and policy advocates are expanding their understandings of culpability and responsibility, these understandings remain essentially male understandings.

However unsatisfactory desert theory and policy might be from the point of view of assessing the range of choices faced by the impoverished women who fill the courts, nonetheless desert theorists do acknowledge the challenge these issues pose. Proportionality theory's commitment to equality means that unfairness and discrimination are serious matters. It is no coincidence that the proportionality era saw greater attention being paid to the work of feminist criminologists and legal theorists than ever before, and that studies of possible race as well as gender bias in criminal justice were taken more seriously than ever before (Hudson 1998). It is only if equality is the goal that discrimination is a problem; indeed, it is only in relation to a norm of equality that 'discrimination' has any meaning at all. If the goal is not to punish equally, but to punish according to risk of re-offending, then not merely is it not a problem if differently situated offenders receive different penalties, but it is desirable. And this of course disadvantages impoverished offenders, especially black impoverished offenders, who are far more likely than others to possess the characteristics actuarially associated with re-offending, such as lack of employment, unconventional family structures, insecure housing etc.

Current policy trends to sentence according to record as well as current offence, and to base important decisions such as early release and levels of interventiveness in community punishments and post-prison supervision on risk of re-offending, run contrary to the ideal of equality in criminal justice. It is important to be aware that just as proportionality's treating people the same is not thereby treating them equally, neither is the present emphasis on 'consistency' the same as equality. Penal policy which looks to re-offending treats differences consistently by defining them as factors in re-offending, so that poverty, minority ethnic origin, mental illness, histories of abuse, consistently correlate with imprisonment. This is the second mode of responding to difference, using it as the basis for enhanced repression and exclusion.

Culpability and rationality

If we look at studies of imprisonment, it would be hard to be convinced that responsibility for childcare; committing crimes to survive or to support one's family rather to satisfy greed, anger or lust; suffering from abuse and/or addictions; lacking supportive family or friends, or other hardships which may be associated with offending, are treated as mitigating circumstances. While studies of sentencing may suggest that childcare is a factor that makes judges reluctant to impose prison sentences on women, and while studies regularly conclude that sentencers deal comparatively leniently with women because of the sort of factors just listed, studies of imprisonment show that women's prisons are full of women suffering these sorts of circumstances (on sentencing, Farrington and Morris 1983; Hedderman and Hough 1994; Hedderman and Gelsthorpe 1997; on imprisonment, Carlen 1983, 1998). How can we explain these apparent discrepancies between sentencing studies and imprisonment studies?

The answer to this conundrum is that penal outcomes depend on constructions of *culpability* – on how much offenders are held to blame for their crimes. What this means is that there is not a hard-and-fast distinction between being a victim and being an offender, but, rather, there is a continuum of blameworthiness which has important criminal justice implications. Black men are at one end of the continuum, constructed as wholly to blame for their crimes. They fit the stereotype of 'suitable enemy' rather than 'ideal victim' (Christie 1986a, 1986b).[6] White women are at the other end of the continuum, with white men and black women in between.

What this means is that for white women, the line between being a victim and being an offender is somewhat blurred, and can be crossed (Daly 1994). Women offenders can be constructed as victims of biology, of poverty, of abuse and addictions, and more than anything else, of men. This construction, however, depends on their congruence with the stereotypes of the 'sinned against rather than sinning', or the 'poor unfortunate', or the sick and inadequate. Women can benefit from leniency through being seen as little to blame for their offences if they are conscientious mothers (the lone mother struggling against the odds, maintaining high standards of cleanliness in the home, going without things herself in order to keep her child decently fed and clothed); if they are faithful, one-man women (dominated by an abusive but long-term partner) rather than promiscuous or independent; if they suffer from depression, inadequacy, helplessness and despair. For women like these, there is a good chance that they will be seen as needing help rather than punishment, and that their identity as victims will mitigate their culpability as offenders.

Black women, independent women, unconventional women, women who are defiant rather than fearful, women whose children are in care, women with a succession of partners, will be held to be more blame-worthy, for similar offences. The same circumstances – having children, needing money, being addicted, being dominated by a man – will be constructed differently by probation officers, magistrates and others with the power to punish, and will appear as mitigating or aggravating according to the woman's race, sexual status, appearance, demeanour and lifestyle. For example, in my own research on probation reports, I found that when officers asked white women who were mothers about the fathers of their children, the point of the questions was to ascertain whether the fathers were supportive, economically and in other ways. When black mothers were asked the same questions, the point was to find out if the children were from different fathers, or whether the women had a record of promiscuity and unstable relationships. In other words, with white women the point at issue was the adequacy of the father's per-formance of his role; with black women the point at issue was the mother's sexual lifestyle (Hudson 1988). These stereotype-led differences in dealing with white and black women meant that for the white women, responsibility for children was likely to be a mitigating factor, whereas for black women it was meant to be proof of her fecklessness, and become an aggravating factor.

Similarly, for foreign nationals, who are accounting for an increasing proportion of the female prison population, the fact that they committed crimes because of extreme poverty – seeing prostitution, carrying drugs or other offences as the only way of providing for their families – is unlikely to be seen as reducing culpability. They are likely to be judged not as women who are going to desperate lengths to support their families, but as women who have left their families, who have neglected their responsibilities to their children and other dependants. From the way the neighbour turns against the wife in the film *Kramer versus Kramer* to the recent press treatment of the journalist detained by the Taliban in Afghanistan, we see constantly how strong the condemnation of women who leave their children, whatever the reason, remains.

Defences and mitigations are differently available, then, to differently situated women. What is common, however, and what feminists critiquing sentencing have objected to, is that if the available repertoire of mitigations is successfully deployed, any leniency comes at a heavy price. For women, being constructed as less culpable does indeed mean being constructed as less responsible, in the sense of being less rational. Being seen as less culpable means being seen as less possessed of agency: women are less culpable if they are sick, dominated, or mentally unstable, in other words if their capacity to act is seen as less than 'normal'. To this extent, desert theorists' objections to mitigation on grounds of economic hardship are correct: leniency comes at the price of being seen as of lesser rationality. What they fail to note, however, is that this is not necessarily the case for (white) men. A good solicitor or probation officer can construct the circumstances which recur in men's accounts of offending – loss of employment, break-up of relationships, problems with alcohol – as mitigatory, as circumstances emanating from outside the individual which make him act out of character, and which do not diminish his essential rationality or indicate lack of morality.

For women, being seen as less culpable is conditional on being seen as unempowered. In the case of black females, stereotypes of strong women, sexual promiscuity, and tolerance of criminality undermine the woman-as-victim perception, and for white women, economic, social or personal difficulties are represented not as situations they face and are trying to deal with as best they can, but as constituting the persons they are.

Circumstances such as poverty and lack of legal opportunities which structure and constrain choice play differently for different offenders because as well as being mediated by stereotypes of criminality attached to different identities, they are played out in a discursive context which has already placed people into categories differentiated by degrees of rationality. As Martha Minow (1990) explains, law's operational categories distinguish the normal from the abnormal, the capable from the incapable, the autonomous from the dependent. Those who are defined as normal, capable, autonomous – as rational, in other words – are dealt with in juridical mode, whereas those who are defined as abnormal, incapable or dependent – irrational or less than rational – are dealt with in disciplinary mode (Hudson 1998). In juridical mode, law and its institutions of control deal with acts, defining acts which transgress the law and acts which are permitted; in disciplinary mode, law and the institutions of control are directed at individuals *qua* individuals (Tadros 1998). In juridical mode, what is of interest is the act, and therefore any circumstances surrounding the act will be seen as bearing upon, and illuminating, the act itself; on the other hand, in disciplinary mode, what is under scrutiny is the self, so judgements will be in terms of whether the self is more or less rational, more or less damaged, more or less wicked, rather than whether the act is more or less culpable. While law in juridical mode is interested in intentionality (the *mens rea*) and motive, this is in order to name the act; in disciplinary mode law is interested in the act, but in order to label the person.

Women, along with children, are dealt with in disciplinary mode. Although the extent to which this is the case varies with time and place, because the white male abstract legal subject is the exemplar of rationality, any transfer to the rational-juridical mode of legal processing comes at the price of being assimilated to the ungendered, unracialised, white male penal norm.

Juridical processing applies standards of formal procedural equality, and the cost to defendants is the denial of difference. This is what happened to some extent in the desert/proportionality era of the 1980s, and meant that many men who needed help with addictions, psychiatric illnesses, poverty and marginalisation were consigned to warehouse prisons, with little help or treatment. Where this ethos penetrated furthest into the penal treatment of women, for example in the USA, female offenders experienced 'equality with a vengeance' (Daly 1994). Like men, they were imprisoned without regard to their needs, or given community penalties which emphasised punishment rather than help. The cold hard logic of identity in times of over-emphasised and decontextualised due process makes criminal justice turn a blind eye to differences between offenders. In times when preoccupation with risk of reoffending re-centres difference, the categories of difference re-emerge as indicators of control and repression: the deranged, the poor, the marginalised are subject to ever-increasing imprisonment, curfew, surveillance and exclusion.

Minow (1990: 20) poses a question which she describes as 'the dilemma of difference':

When does treating people differently emphasize their differences and stigmatize or hinder them on that basis? And when does treating people the same become insensitive to their difference and likely to stigmatize them on *that* basis?

The key to resolving this dilemma of difference is to widen law's understanding of choice, and to appreciate that people can act rationally, but within different ranges of choice. What women who become entangled with criminal justice need (and indeed what men who do not conform to what has become known as 'hegemonic', or dominant, masculinity need too) is for law to accommodate the fact that although persons may be equally and fully rational, they may be acting within a constrained range of choices. For women, appreciation of their limited range of actual or perceived choices leads to typification of themselves as less rational rather than of their acts as less culpable. We can see this in the fact that diminished responsibility is a more accessible defence than self-defence or provocation for battered women who kill (McColgan 1993), and self-presentation as a victim is more likely to be successful than self-presentation as a rational and moral chooser from among a limited set of alternatives for economic crimes.

What steps are needed for law to develop much fuller understandings of the idea of choice and the importance of appreciating the range of choices available to individual, flesh-and-blood, differently situated offenders? First of all, the distinction between agency and choice as the two components of responsibility needs to be strengthened. Agency is the capacity to do a certain act, and necessitates both mental capacity and physical capacity. Agency means both being able to decide to act rather than following some compulsion, and having neither physical coercion nor constraint to compel or prevent the act. Choice, on the other hand, is a range of possible actions, from which the rational agent selects the best, or more often for the women who come before the courts, the least worst. When conflated with agency, choice becomes a synonym for will, and assumes an either/or character, such that persons have (freedom of) choice or they do not. When uncoupled from agency, it is revealed as being a matter of degree: some people have far more choices than others. For assigning culpability, what matters is the degree of opportunities people have to obtain the 'primary goods' of our society - food, shelter, family life, pleasure and social esteem - legitimately. Only if people have such opportunities and nevertheless seek to achieve them through illegitimate means can they be said to have made positive criminal choices.

Much of the legal theoretical debate about allowing economic hardship as defence or mitigation is concerned with an absolute lack of choice. For those who are attracted by the idea of a defence of economic necessity, the demand is that such a defence should be able to be operated consistently, so that it is not a matter of a skilled lawyer producing leniency for a particularly well-favoured offender. Various criteria have been suggested for such a defence, usually involving a combination of low income, low educational attainment, and other personal-social problems which would make gaining a livelihood more than ordinarily difficult (Groves and Frank 2001). In my own work on this topic I have also suggested some situations which would bring a hardship defence into consideration: for women these would include such circumstances as being controlled by men who only give them money if they engage in prostitution or theft; having a 'benefit gap' after leaving care or custody; being homeless and having chaotic lifestyles which prevent them claiming benefits, for example (Hudson 1995, 1998). It is a criticism of our present society that such categories are not only thinkable but that people who belong to them actually exist in considerable numbers, and it is arguable that they should never be punished at all because the conditions of criminal liability do not exist in such cases (Duff 1998).

Aside from these extreme (but by no means unusual) cases where the idea of punishment should have no purchase, in more run-of-the-mill circumstances women's offending is often rational action, within a constrained range of choices. Mothers living in tower blocks who fail to purchase television licences are not acting irrationally, but following a reasonable set of priorities; mothers who turn a blind eye to the provenance of desirable consumer goods we are all induced to want through relentless advertising, or about which their children inflict endless pressure of the 'everyone has one', 'I'll get dissed if I don't have the right brand of trainers', variety are acting rationally and caringly.

Those of us who are affluent can provision our families without such endless prioritisation; those of us who may not in fact be so affluent but have good credit ratings can provision by overspending on our cards: we have a wider choice of available strategies than the impoverished. Furthermore, the affluent can indulge addictions to alcohol or drugs in private, without resort to robbery, theft or prostitution.

Without knowledge of the circumstances obtaining and the degree of available choice, it is impossible to assess culpability. Such knowledge can contribute to justice for all offenders, not merely the 'normal' white male who is the beneficiary of present constructions of mitigating circumstances and reasonable choices, only if it is gendered understanding, understanding which is also open to the standpoints of the poor, the minority, and the otherwise 'different'.

Conclusion

These reflections on penal policy developments in the 1990s and into the 2000s, and on penal theory as it concerns equality and responsibility, come together if we think about the vulnerability to imprisonment of the most disadvantaged female offenders. Although I have concentrated on an example of penal policy drawn from the UK, similar tendencies are apparent in many other countries. The USA, Canada, Australia, and other jurisdictions which embraced just deserts thinking in the 1980s, have placed increased penal emphasis on persistence (for example, the notorious three-strikes laws in California and elsewhere), and introducing actuarially-based risk assessments.

If sentencing is concerned with previous record and with risk of re-offending, then the number of women prisoners can be expected to rise still further, as dangerousness and seriousness become even less significant as the thresholds for imprisonment. If women are no longer to be judged as not warranting imprisonment because they do not pose a threat of physical harm to the public, then the only thing that can keep them out of prison for repeated but less serious offences is their construction as less blameworthy than the standard case.

If law continues to be built around masculine notions of responsibility and culpability, then women will continue to face the alternatives of being treated like men, or being treated as of diminished rationality. It may be that we need to expand conceptions of rationality, including ideas that are being put forward by some feminists working on women and economic activity, notions such as *provisioning*.[7] We may also need to develop more relational understandings of both rationality and morality.

Current penal policy is bringing the circumstances and choices involved in women's offending back into the sentencing reckoning, but it is bringing them in as risk of re-offending factors, factors which, if present, will legitimate further intrusions into and control over the women's lives. These factors should not be irrelevant, as they may be in simplistic proportionality policies and practices, but nor should they have the potential to make the punishment of already disadvantaged women more severe. They should be seen as mitigatory factors which reduce culpability without diminishing rationality.

Notes

1 This 'up-tariffing' also affected the sentencing of black offenders, who often missed out on probation orders, which were associated with help or treatment, and fines, because so many black offenders were unemployed, thus starting their sentencing 'careers' with community service or suspended imprisonment (Hudson 1988).

2 See Ashworth and Wasik (1998) for reflections by desert theorists and sympathetic critics on these and related questions.

3 At the time of writing (October 2001), the OASYS system of calculating and recording risk of re-offending is being implemented nationwide, and while probation officers may often fail to complete the forms fully or rigorously, its introduction clearly indicates that 'risk' is firmly established as the main preoccupation of the National Probation Service.

4 R. v. Lavallee [1990] 1 S.C.R.852.

5 Von Hirsch, private communication.

6 So strong is this stereotyping of the black (Afro-Caribbean) man as criminal rather than victim that in the Stephen Lawrence and other prominent recent cases, someone who was in fact a victim was initially presumed to be part of the trouble.

7 I am grateful to Pamela Davies for bringing this to my attention.

Chapter 3

Rendering women punishable: the making of a penal crisis

Anne Worrall

> Now what is striking is that when each discovery [of abuse] is made, and somehow made real in the world, the response has been: it happens to men too. If women are hurt, men are hurt. If women are raped, men are raped. If women are sexually harassed, men are sexually harassed. If women are battered, men are battered. Symmetry must be reasserted. Neutrality must be reclaimed. Equality must be re-established.
>
> (MacKinnon 1987:170)

Catharine MacKinnon wrote these words in an article about pornography, which she defined as 'the graphic sexually explicit subordination of women through pictures or words' (1987:176). Her argument was that pornography, which reinforces the objectification and dehumanising of women and the dominance of men, is often portrayed by men (and women) as being no more than *erotica* – something which is based on sexual equality and which is equally pleasurable for men and women. In this symmetrical world, men suffer *from the same things* as women and, conversely, women find pleasure in *the same deviant behaviour* as men.

Building on this assertion, it would thus be only a small step from claiming that women enjoy pornography to claiming that women are as likely as men to commit acts of sexual deviance. It is this 'search for equivalence' which Joan Forbes (1992) explores in a professional journal, in a modest article about the 'discovery' of female sexual abusers. Following the first national conference organised by Kidscape in 1992, this new problem was identified and named. A new category of female offender was constructed. Prior to this, isolated women had been convicted of the sexual abuse of children but almost always as passive or coerced accomplices of men. The difference now was the issue of agency – the extent to which women were to be seen as both willing accomplices and as initiators of such abuse (Matravers 1997, 2001). The emergence of female sexual abusers had an underlying political message which challenged feminist claims that violence and abuse were predominantly perpetrated by powerful men against powerless women and children. The apparent realisation that women might deliberately sexually harm children, rather than protect them from sexual harm, justified an ideological and moral retreat by professionals and policy makers. Violence and abuse could again be analysed legitimately in terms other than those of gender inequality. This is not to argue that anyone believed that women committed *as much* sexual abuse as men. However, the very recognition of a category of 'female sex offender' was sufficient to loosen the conceptual inhibitions against believing women to be capable of such abuse that liberal and radical feminism had instilled in most social work and criminal justice professionals trained in the 1980s.

This chapter aims to explore the 'contemporary search for equivalence' (Forbes 1992) in offending. It will trace the emergence, in England and Wales (but drawing on examples from the US and Australia), of categories of female offender that disguise the interplay of gender, age, class and race, and serve instead to produce and reproduce a spurious categorical equality that renders women punishable and makes it not only possible, but necessary, for increasing numbers of them to be punished. The political and moral justification for such punishment is that either more women are committing punishable acts or more women are being *discovered* committing punishable acts. This chapter aims to argue that, while both these claims may be true, crime, as Nils Christie (2001) has asserted, 'is a limitless natural resource' which we can mine as much or as little as we wish. The desire to 'mine' women's crime in the 1990s has been driven by a creative political will, not a reactive one.

The search for equivalence involves more than the social construction of women as 'real criminals'. The battle to have women's crime taken seriously and not medicalised or sexualised away was won in the 1980s (for a review of the international literature, see Naffine 1997). In contrast, the search for equivalence is the product of the 'backlash' of the 1990s that has been founded on a denial of the context of victimisation in which women offend. As MacKinnon (1987:171) says 'all of this "men too" stuff means that people don't really believe' that women are victims of anything any more, though there is little question about the empirical evidence for such victimisation[1]. And if women are no longer victims of gender-specific oppressions, such as domestic violence, rape and sexual abuse, because men are also victims of these things, then there is no need for gender-specific approaches to these offences after all and certainly no need for gender-specific ways of dealing with offenders. Furthermore, the denial of *sex* (biological) differences in offending has been used to justify the utilisation of supposedly *gender*-neutral tools of risk assessment and categorisation. But a truly gender-neutral (and sex-neutral) tool of risk assessment would show women, as a category of offender, consistently to be at low risk – both of re-offending and of causing serious harm. But because it is no longer acceptable to have a sex-specific category of offender, each category of offence now has its sex-specific sub-category, with the result that risk assessment for *sex* becomes subordinate to risk assessment for the *offence*. Since domestic violence can be committed by both men and women, women who kill their abusive male partners are *murderers who happen to be women*. Since rape and sexual abuse can be committed by both men and women, women who sexually abuse children are *paedophiles who happen to be women*. Since public order offences are committed by gangs of both boys and girls, girls who are drunk and disorderly are 'ladettes' – *lads who happen to be girls*. And since both men and women take illegal drugs, women who carry and supply drugs are *drug-dealers who happen to be women* – and also *happen* to be black and/or foreign nationals. But the very effort of creating this kind of gender-neutrality contains within it an asymmetrical moral judgement (or double-standard). '*Women* who kill', '*female* sex offenders', 'violent *girls*' and '*women* drug-dealers' are implicitly *worse* than their male counterparts because (and here we return full circle to a very old argument) they are 'doubly deviant' – violating both the law and gender-role expectations.

The search for equivalence rests on the premise that sexual categories are factual and symmetrical and that gender is a matter of socialisation. Changes in socialisation, it is argued, introduce agency or volition into women's behaviour and crime becomes as much an expression of disaffected femininity as of rebellious masculinity. Thus, it is no longer sufficient to analyse crime as 'a resource for doing masculinity' (Messerschmidt 1993, cited in Daly 1997:37), as a means of distinguishing between men and women. Crime is now a resource for both men and women to 'do gender'. But, as Daly (1997: 37) asks:

Would the claim that crime is a 'resource for doing femininity' – for women and girls to 'create differences from men and boys or to separate from all that is masculine' – have any cultural resonance? Probably not.

Yet it is this very assumption that, now more than ever, sex differences are irrelevant because crime and punishment should – and can – be gender-neutral, that masks ways in which penal policy continues to produce and reproduce punishable 'sexed bodies' which are also 'racialised' and 'aged' bodies.[2]

Using the four examples already cited, this chapter will explore the ways in which the actuarial justice of the new penology (Feeley and Simon 1992) has served to justify – in the name of anti-discrimination – a moral retreat from the traditional sexualisation, medicalisation, welfarisation and domestication of women's offending. The implications of this moral retreat for the management of women offenders both in the community and in prison will be analysed by considering the responses of the Probation Service and the Prison Service. The debate about 'adapting' drugs treatment, risk assessment and cognitive behavioural programmes to meet the 'criminogenic needs' of women offenders will be introduced as a background to more detailed discussion of women's imprisonment in the following chapters.

Female sex offenders – the retreat from sexualisation

In 1988, a consultant psychotherapist named Estela Welldon 'discovered' the female sex offender in the UK with this stunning statement:

> Odd though it may sound, motherhood provides an excellent vehicle for some women to exercise perverse and perverting attitudes towards their offspring, and to retaliate against their own mothers.
>
> (Welldon 1988:63)

This is not to suggest that no-one had previously recognised that women might commit sexual abuse. A number of studies had indicated that women might be responsible for somewhere between 5 and 20% of the abuse of girls and boys respectively (Hetherton 1999) and a pioneering sex offender treatment programme for women was run at Styal Prison in the late 1980s (Barnett *et al* 1989). But such women were considered pathological exceptions, most of whom were accomplices of male abusers. Welldon's thesis, however, was that motherhood itself was dangerous and contained within its ideological and material conditions of existence the potential for abuse – or 'perversion'. Welldon's concept of 'female perversion'[3] and the 'intergenerational transmission of perverse and abusive mothering' (Motz 2001:4) allowed the phenomenon of child sexual abuse to be reconstructed from something which women 'don't do' (because of their sexual passivity and maternal instincts) to something which all women are capable of and which a substantial number choose 'to do'. The traditional sexualisation of women's offending as being a reflection of sexual and emotional neediness has been replaced by the exposure of sexual predacity. Studies began to emerge that put the proportion of sexual abuse committed by women at nearer 50% and, in one study, 75% (Hetherton 1999). The Kidscape Conference, mentioned above, met with a great deal of hostility from women's organisations but was praised by Kirsta (1994) for challenging a feminist perspective which perpetuated the suffering of children by refusing to acknowledge female abuse.

Hetherton (1999) argues that professionals are vulnerable to popular myths about female child sexual abuse. Even when faced with incontrovertible evidence of its existence, they are inclined to minimise its damage, believing that it is 'gentle' and 'harmless'. When it is patently neither, it is then assumed to be the behaviour of a 'mad' or a 'coerced' woman. Instead, Hetherton urges professionals to suspend their disbelief and cease trivialising this under-reported abuse.

But exactly where this evidence comes from, apart from victim disclosure, is difficult to identify – which is, of course, the point. In 1999, it would appear that only 16 women over 18 years of age were imprisoned for sexual offences, compared with 2,492 men (Home Office 2000b). The gap between the official statistics and the research studies on which the recent 'discoveries' of female sex offenders are based is not, of itself, evidence one way or the other of the extent of the phenomenon. Nevertheless, the disproportionate interest in the subject by sections of the media, especially following the conviction of Rosemary West (Birch 1995; Welldon 1985), raise the question of whether female sexual abuse is really anything more than an example of old-fashioned deviancy amplification. The same cannot be said, however, of women's involvement with illicit drugs.

Women and drugs – the retreat from medicalisation

The history of women's imprisonment has been a history of the medicalisation of women's problems (Carlen 1983, 1998; Sim 1990) or, as Hannah-Moffat puts it, the power of *pastoralism* – the secular version of concern for the soul of the individual (2000:8). The rebuilding of Holloway Prison in the 1970s was based on the assumption that women in prison needed medical and psychiatric facilities rather than punishment. Women's prisons were at the top of the prison 'league table' for the prescription of drugs that affected the central nervous system and the psychiatric control of difficult women through medication became one of the main concerns of the campaigning group Women in Prison in the 1980s. But, even at the height of this concern, it was acknowledged that prisons were doing no more than reflecting women's widespread dependency on prescribed drugs and that prison doctors were in a 'no win' situation:

> If the prison doctor then stops prescribing drugs which the women have been legitimately prescribed outside s/he is likely to be accused of being punitive. If, on the other hand, s/he continues to prescribe large doses of drugs then s/he is likely to be accused of drugging women solely for penal control purposes.
>
> (O'Dwyer and Carlen 1985:165)

Increasingly, the view was formed among both those working in prisons and in campaigning groups that women turned to drugs – both prescribed and illegitimately obtained – in order to survive the pains of imprisonment. What was not conceded at that time was that women were themselves *drug offenders*.

The recognition, or over-recognition, of women as drug offenders came with the emergence into professional discourse of anti-discriminatory practice and anti-racism training in the late 1980s and early 1990s. In an attempt to counter accusations of discrimination, the first Section 95 publications[4] on Gender and Race in the Criminal Justice System (Home Office 1992b, 1992c) acknowledged:

1. that women committing drug offences were likely to be cautioned at a similar rate to men (and not at the much higher rate of cautioning that women experienced for other offences);

2. that women sent to prison for drug offences actually received, on average, longer sentences than men; and

3. the 'apparently dramatic rise' of female prisoners from ethnic minorities 'may be accounted for by an increase in those convicted of drug smuggling, many of whom are foreign nationals'

(1992c:16)

The received wisdom that black and foreign national drug-offending women were inflating the otherwise insignificant numbers of women in prison (and undermining an otherwise benign approach to the sentencing of women) became embedded in official discourse. By 2001, the Section 95 publication (Home Office 2001c) on women was confident that:

> the proportion of black sentenced women in prison for drug offences (69%) was almost double the proportion of all sentenced female prisoners in prison for drug offences (36%). Excluding foreign nationals, the proportion of black women serving sentences for drug offences (52%) was still considerably higher than that of white women (24%) and black men (19%).
>
> (2001c:29)

By the mid 1990s, concern about drugs in women's prisons reached the point where the Chief Inspector of Prisons expressed the view, after visiting one women's prison, that it was possible for a woman 'to enter a shoplifter and leave an addict' (cited in Malloch 2000:7). This level of illicit drug use in women's prisons was leading to bullying, trading and violent sexual assault among women (conducting internal searches on other women) (Malloch 2000). Officers began to view drug-users as the most aggressive and disruptive women in the prison: 'The biggest problem in here isn't the murderers, it's the addicts – they're far more devious' (Malloch 2000:113).

Hedderman and Gelsthorpe (1997) discovered that, although many women offenders were, statistically, still being dealt with more leniently than men offenders by magistrates, the two groups for whom this was no longer true were women who were first-time violent offenders and women who were recidivist drug offenders. The increase in the number of women charged with drug and drug-related offences is undeniable, though this is also true for men, and women still constitute only 21% of drug offenders (Home Office 2001c). Nevertheless, levels of substance misuse among prisoners are roughly comparable for men and women (ONS 1999 cited in Howard League 2000:5), though women are pro-portionately more likely than men to be users of opiates and crack cocaine – the drugs most strongly associated with offending. For this reason, the Prison Service Women's Policy Group regards the misuse of drugs as a 'major issue for women in prison' (Stewart 2000:42) and increasing resources are being made available for drugs treatment in women's prisons (e.g. at Holloway and Drake Hall). But there is now a danger that courts will send more women to prison precisely because this is the one place in the criminal justice system where such treatment may be available.

A recent briefing paper from the Howard League (2000) argues that the introduction of Drug Treatment and Testing Orders[5] could provide a promising diversion from custody for women, if probation officers are willing to give special attention to the needs of women who misuse drugs. But if from the outset no attention is given to women's practical difficulties (suitable accommodation, pregnancy issues and child care) the DTTO will become yet one more male-centred provision that will be only half-heartedly 'adapted' for women.

The extent to which women participate in the illicit drug economy has been the subject of a number of studies (see, for example, Green 1991, 1996 in England and Wales; Maher 1997 in the US; Denton 2001 in Australia). Green notes that, although 80% of couriers are men, 'virtually all journalistic and pressure group interest in couriers has been on women' (1996:13). Couriers – 'poor, foreign, visible and vulnerable' – have been reconstructed as traffickers – 'wealthy, powerful, manipulative and dangerous' (1996:3). In recent studies, women's active participation as drug users and drug dealers has been used as an example of women's *agency* or *volition* in offending. As Maher argues, there are two readings of women's agency – 'the first practically denies women any agency and the second over-endows them with it' (Maher 1997:1). In contrast, Maher maps out the 'intersectionalities' of race, gender and class in the drug economy, demonstrating the intricacies of the structural relationships between European American, African American and Latinas women on the streets of Brooklyn, where sexwork is the only way that women can generate income to sustain their drug involvement. Within such constraints, choices are made and there is a degree of volition, but it should not be over-stated. Challenging traditional stereotypes in Australia of drug-involved women as 'dope chicks' or 'prestigious escorts', however, leads Denton (2001:58) to view women drug dealers as feisty business women, using their inter-personal skills to further their careers and not being averse to the occasional act of intimidation or violence. Sexwork plays a less significant part in income generation than burglary, bank fraud and handling stolen goods. Arrest and imprisonment are occupational hazards, time to renew acquaintances, reinforce networks and carry on business (nearly) as usual. Denton's sophisticated ethnographic study offers great insight into the gendered nature of the illicit drug economy but, by focusing on a small number of more or less 'successful' women, it tends to fuel the growing view that women involved in drugs are no different from men involved in drugs and should be dealt with in the same way. Maher's North American study suggests that there is still little evidence to support the view that women drug users are 'hypersexual' (willing to do anything for a 'hit'), 'emancipated' or part of a 'new' breed of violent female criminal (1997: 195–197). On the contrary, the war on drugs in North America seems to have become a war on minority and poor women, where punishment comes before treatment (Van Wormer and Bartollas 2000). Women's violence within the home, however, is subject to a different kind of moral retreat.

Women who batter and kill – the retreat from domestication[6]

Although twice as many men as women are victims of homicide in England and Wales every year, the pattern of victimisation is highly gendered. A third of female victims of murder or manslaughter have been killed by current or former spouses or lovers, compared with fewer than 10% of male victims (Home Office 2001c). There is, however, another way of viewing these statistics. As P.W. Cook (1997) points out, women convicted of a homicide offence in the US are much more likely than men to have killed their partner or child, as opposed to someone less intimate. At the same time, evidence from the British Crime Survey self-completion (CASI) questionnaire (Mirrlees-Black 1999) has suggested that the proportions of men and women experiencing physical assault by a current or former spouse or lover in the previous year were identical at 4.2%. When 'frightening threats', 'injury' and repeat assault are added in, the gap begins to widen. Stanko's (2001) innovative audit of domestic violence suggests that 81% of incidents reported to the police in England on 28 September 2000 were male on female, 8% were female on male, 7% were male on male and 4% were female on female. Nevertheless, the message that 'women do domestic violence too' now has official confirmation.

The literature on the extent and causation of women's violence within the home is much more established than that on women's perpetration of other criminal activity. Otto Pollak's (1950) strange contribution to the theorising of female criminality asserted that women's domestic role and men's sense of chivalry resulted in the masking of much criminally aggressive behaviour by women. Additionally, recognition of mothers' propensity to kill their own children, especially within the first year of their lives, led to the passing of The Infanticide Act in 1922, when the public became increasingly alarmed at the number of women being sentenced to death for such offences (Ballinger 2000). More recently, Wilczynski (1997) has argued that women who kill their own children (provided there is no prior abuse) are still likely to receive more lenient treatment than fathers who commit the same offences.

The more controversial area of debate, however, is that of 'domestic violence' or 'spouse/ partner abuse'. Here, too, there has existed a body of (American) 'family violence' research literature since the 1970s, which has persistently refuted the feminist view that women are always the only victims of domestic violence. Straus (1993) summarises this literature and expresses exasperation at those who accuse him and his colleagues of 'letting men off the hook'. He puts forward three reasons for recognising women's part in domestic violence: first, despite the lower probability of injury, assaults by women should be taken seriously in the same way that men who 'only slap' women are also censured; second, 'minor' assaults by women put them in danger of more serious retaliation by men; and, third, ignoring minor assaults by women reinforces the 'implicit cultural norms that make the marriage licence a hitting licence' (Straus 1993:67). The family violence literature and its use of the gender-neutral Conflict Tactics Scale has been strongly criticised for ignoring gender and power dynamics within the family (e.g. Kurz 1993). Whether or not such criticism is fair, there is little doubt that this literature has been appropriated to support the 'discovery' of 'battered husbands' in England and Wales in the 1990s. Although there are still very few British studies (George 1994; Stitt and Macklin 1995; Brogden and Harkin 2000) those that exist do *not* appear to set male victimisation within the context of marital dynamics (as do family violence theorists). Instead, they present male victims as 'invariably the nice sensitive ones' (quoted in Kirsta 1994:229). The men interviewed in these studies saw themselves as being socialised into not using violence against women and believing themselves to be bullied and controlled by their female partners. Such 'role reversal' is reinforced by the ironic treatment of traditional masculinity in the media, especially in advertising, where men are increasingly portrayed as 'incapable, stupid wimps' (Stitt and Macklin 1995:10). In the BCS study (Mirrlees-Black 1999), more male than female victims denied contributing physically to the assault (though more men than women blamed themselves for allowing it to happen – for what reason is not explored). In other words, 'battered husbands' saw themselves as mirroring 'battered wives' in being victims of irrational and unprovoked violence – a search for equivalence rather than any acknowledgement of the complexities of interpersonal relationships. Although family violence theorists cannot be held responsible for the misappropriation of their research, it is understandable that women's organisations feel frustrated that Straus and his colleagues cannot see their contribution to the 'deadlier than the male' claim.

The 'discovery' of the 'battered husband' has also served to undermine the emphasis on the self-defence aspect of female homicide offences. The belief that women who kill their partners invariably do so in retaliation for years of abuse was institutionalised in legal proceedings by Leonore Walker's (1984) naming of 'battered woman syndrome':

> The syndrome is based on a body of research which suggests that domestic violence is of a cyclical and escalating nature and that the cumulative effect of surviving such violence for the women concerned may be a particular state of mind characterised by features such as 'learned helplessness' and 'chronic fear'. These features mean that a woman is psychologically unable to escape a violent relationship, or particular incidents of violence, even when the opportunity is ostensibly open to her to do so.
>
> (Stubbs and Tolmie 1994: 197)

'Battered woman syndrome' is not a defence to murder but it answers the question 'why didn't she leave?' and was introduced to assist women's claims that their perceptions and actions were reasonable, given the circumstances. However, it is most frequently used to support the partial defence of diminished responsibility, reducing a charge of murder to one of manslaughter. The controversy surrounding its use centres on feminist concerns that the concept of a 'syndrome' reduces multi-layered *social* problems to a matter of individual personality and *psychology* (Bowker 1993). To the extent that BWS evidence is accepted by courts, it lends medical and professional credibility to the very stereotypes of female passivity and masochism that it was meant to challenge (Stubbs and Tolmie 1994). It is also based on the experiences of white, middle class women and may thus misrepresent the experiences of other women. As Stubbs and Tolmie argue, such representations may prove damaging for ethnic minority women, such as Aboriginal women in Australia, who are 'assertive, economically independent and who fight back against the violence that they experience' (1994:212).

Expressing concern about the construction and use of 'battered woman syndrome', however, has allowed attention to continue to be focused on the 'search for equivalence' in domestic violence. Mann (1988, cited in P.W. Cook 1997) claimed that 30% of the women convicted of killing their partners in her US study had previous arrests for violence, 60% had preplanned their killings and 70% had killed their partner when the latter was asleep or drunk. Similarly, Pearson (1998:239) claims that women who kill commit an 'antinurturant act' and that, at the moment of their crime, their world does not revolve around their families but around themselves. 'Battered husband syndrome' has a long history – the term having been first coined by Susan Steinmetz in 1975 (Kirsta 1994:232).

Although the term is never used explicitly in court cases, Lloyd (1995) is one of several writers who give examples of men who have been treated leniently by the courts after killing their 'abusive' wives:

> Joseph McGrail killed his drunken, abusive common law wife … after ten years of torment … and walked free … with a two-year suspended prison sentence. The judge … said the woman … 'would have tried the patience of a saint'.
>
> (1995:72)

A glimmer of hope that the search for equivalence is being challenged can be found in the work of Keller *et al* (1999) in California. Alarmed by the ascendancy of a 'mutual combat' discourse, leading to a 'dual arrest' policy, the inappropriate re-definition of female victims as perpetrators and their direction into 'court ordered domestic violence interventions', Keller and her colleagues have sought to establish clinical criteria which distinguish between women who use violence as aggression and those who use it in self-defence or self-preservation. Acknowledging that such distinctions are not always clear, Keller *et al* are, nevertheless, able to report that recent legislation in California now requires police officers to 'make a good faith effort' to identify the primary aggressor, rather than take the easy option of dual arrest (1999:364).

Violent girls – the retreat from welfarism

By the early 1990s feminist analyses of violence by women had revealed that the overwhelming majority of 'violent' women were themselves victims of violence. 'Battered woman syndrome' – though a highly contentious concept – was slowly being accepted by courts as, at the least, a mitigating factor in domestic violence committed by women (Stanko and Scully 1996). Campaigning groups such as 'Women in Prison' demonstrated that violent young women (such as Josie O'Dwyer – see Carlen *et al* 1985) had been abused by individual men and by the prison system from an early age. Despite this, a moral panic developed in the early 1990s in England and Wales when, alongside concerns about persistent juvenile delinquents and children who killed (Worrall 1997), journalists 'discovered' girls behaving badly. In a much-quoted article, Brinkworth (1994) claimed to have discovered 'all-girl gangs menacing the streets' and 'cocky, feminist, aggressive' superheroines targeting vulnerable women and other girls (Worrall 2000a; Muncer *et al* 2001). This was not the kind of violence born of victimisation. Brinkworth was clearly on a different mission – the 'search for equivalence'. Her concern was to demonstrate that 'girls do it too'. And in so doing, she set in train a particular media 'hunt' characterised by the oft-repeated themes – younger and younger girls becoming increasingly aggressive, mush-rooming girl gangs, increased use of drugs and, especially, alcohol, and the wilful abandonment of gender role expectations.

In 1996, Jo Knowsley in *The Sunday Telegraph* used the manslaughter of 13 year old Louise Allen by two girls of a similar age to claim the mushrooming of 'girl gangs, apeing American gangs. … fuelled by cheap, strong wine … [who] travel in pairs or packs, carry baseball bats, mug for money and jewellery, and stage shoplifting raids on designer shops'. No, that was *not* what happened with Louise Allen (where an argument between a group of schoolgirls got disastrously out-of-hand), but who cares? It makes for a good, coherent news story which offers some, albeit distorted, explanation for a horrible but rare incident.

Such distorted reporting was not confined to the UK. The following year, in Canada, a 14-year-old south Asian woman called Reena Virk was attacked and killed by a group of young women and one young man. According to Sheila Batacharya's account (2000) the media coverage appears to have been very similar to that surrounding the death of Louise Allen in England. The difference was that Virk was a young woman of colour and 'the narrative of girl violence obscures race' in the analysis of her death. By constructing a category of 'girl violence' the media was able to proffer explanations devoid of dimensions of racism, classism, ableism and heterosexism (Batacharya 2000). The sole relevant risk factor to be considered was that of gender.

Journalists are now warning us that 'psychologists have projected that by the year 2008, the number of girls reverting (*sic*) to violence will outnumber boys if they carry on lashing out at this rate' (Fowler 1999). This prediction is, it seems, based on a claim that the number of women sentenced for violence against the person 'has quadrupled from just a handful of cases in the 70s'. The fact that the numbers (according to Fowler's own, inaccurate, statistics)[8] are now 460, compared with over 11,000 crimes of violence committed by men, does not cause her to reflect on her hypothesis. In fact, although there has been an increase in violent crime committed by young people (Home Office 2000b), the gender ratio of such offences has remained that of around one female to five males throughout the 1990s.

In August 2000, *The Guardian* reported on an 18 year old girl charged with rape (Chaudhuri 2000) and asked 'A shocking lone incident or a sign of rising woman-on-woman violence?' Again, we hear the garbled statistics about the apparent increase in violence by women; again, the attribution of bad behaviour to girl gangs and alcohol misuse; again, the role of feminism in making women more aggressive yet, because of their continued powerlessness in relation to men, causing that aggression to be displaced on to other women. These are no longer fantasy Tank Girl figures (Brinkworth 1994); these are the girls 'next door'. In their more benign form, these are 'ladettes'; in their more sinister form, the sisters have become 'twisted'.

The extent to which girls participate in gangs has been a question that has intrigued both researchers and the media for many years. But the evidence for 'all-girl' street gangs is virtually non-existent in the UK and, according to Miller (2001), consistently sparse in the USA. Girls who participate in street gangs still belong overwhelmingly to mixed-gender gangs with male leaders and male-dominated hierarchies of member-ship. They are also lower working class girls – middle class girls form 'cliques' or 'groups', but not 'gangs' (Laidler and Hunt 2001).

That is not to imply, however, that the role of girls in gangs is one of traditional or passive femininity. Miller's detailed ethnographic study of gang girls in two American cities demonstrates that the interplay between victimization and agency in the daily lives of such girls is complex and often contradictory. Belonging to a gang both empowers girls to resist traditional gender role expectations and provides protection and escape from violence and oppression within the family. Yet, as Miller demonstrates, belonging to a gang carries its own risks of victimisation and criminal involvement. 'These young women in gangs had traded unknown risks for known ones' (2001:177). Despite gender inequalities and mistreatment, gang membership was one of the ways in which young women 'bargain with patriarchy' (2001:192).

The history of juvenile justice has been a history of the conflict between 'justice' and 'welfare' concerns and girls have tended to experience both the advantages and disadvantages of 'welfarism' to a greater extent than boys, on the grounds that they are 'at risk', 'in moral danger' and 'in need of protection'. Feminist critiques of 'welfarism' in the 1980s resulted in moves towards 'just deserts' for girls which promised much but delivered greater criminalisation and incarceration in the 1990s. But, as Muncie points out (2000:29) the political agenda for the New Youth Justice is no longer based on matters of just deserts, deterrence and rehabilitation, but on the actuarial principle of risk assessment and techniques of 'identifying, classifying and managing groups sorted by levels of dangerousness'. So while common sense (and official statistics) may tell us that girls – even violent ones – are neither high-risk (in terms of the predictability of their violence) or dangerous (in terms of the harm they cause), they must nevertheless be made 'auditable'. They have to be given a risk classification and be subjected to objectives and techniques of management.

Kemshall (1998:39) has suggested that 'there is the possibility that the pursuit of risk reduction may eventually outweigh the pursuit of justice'. She warns that concerns for public protection and victims' rights may eventually lead to an unacceptable (though to whom?) erosion of the rights of the offender. In the case of girls it could be argued that, rather than the pursuit of risk *reduction*, it is the pursuit of risk *amplification* that is outweighing justice. No-one would deny that troublesome and sometimes violent young women exist but categorising them as 'nasty little madams' (Worrall 2001) and managing them in the same way as boys serves only as a mechanism 'for the colonisation of the future and for managing the uncertainty of contingency' (Kemshall 1998:38). It is no more than a way of managing the anxiety, fear and suspicion which troubled and troublesome girls and young women provoke in respectable citizens.

The new psychology of female violence

Media constructions of 'twisted sisters' have claimed to be based on pseudo-scientific psychology, such as that reported in *Psychology Today* by journalist Barry Yeoman (1999), who quotes randomly from seemingly respectable studies to move from factual statements about the few women *who commit violent acts* to the generalisation that:

> Violence by women has skyrocketed in the latter part of this century. Have they taken 'women's liberation' one step too far, or are they just showing their natural killer instinct?
>
> (1999:54)

Similarly, James (1995) reproduces the cliché that men are socialised to be violent and women to be depressed (and that depressed mothers produce violent sons) but predicts that:

> If women are not genetically prone to depression, then, as the restraints on their expression of aggression are lifted, so their rates of depression should drop to those currently found in men. Like-wise, if men are not genetically prone to violent externalizations of frustration, as their role changes and if the much-heralded 'New Man' ceases to be a myth, their rates of violence should drop, and of depression rise proportionately.
>
> (1995:90)

While it may be relatively easy to dismiss popularised psychologising, it is perhaps more important to confront a new discourse of causation that has emerged from the tradition of feminist psychotherapy and, in particular, the work of Estela Welldon (1988), which has been further developed by Anna Motz to challenge the denial of women's capacity to commit acts of violence. 'It is essential', Motz argues, 'to recognise the violence which is done to [women] through the denial of their capacity for aggression, and the refusal to acknowledge their moral agency' (2001:3–4). The idealisation of motherhood and subsequent denigration of women who do not fulfil gender role expectations contribute to this denial, as does the private nature of much female violence. Female violence is more likely to be against children (physical and sexual abuse, infanticide and Munchausen's syndrome by proxy), against abusive partners or against themselves (self-harm and eating disorders). In all these situations, Motz argues, women use their bodies to communicate distress and anger (2001:7).

The women about whom Motz and others with similar views (Bailey 2000) talk are undoubtedly 'extreme cases' and the development of a feminist psychotherapeutic approach to understand and help such women is arguably extremely valuable. The emphasis on exploring the 'meaning' of the violent act for the woman who engages in it, rather than imposing pre-conceived categories and explanations on it, is an important contribution to the discourse of prevention. It is also true that theorising about women's uses of their bodies to convey negative rather than positive emotions offers an insight into the 'physicality' of girls' public behaviour which so alarms the socially-constructed 'decent citizen'.

What is more concerning, however, is Motz's view that psychological explanations of this kind can be given for *all* manifestations of violence by women, including, for example, gang violence. By including this term, Motz invites the reader to view all violence by women as being 'linked to a developmental failure to conceptualise one's own and other people's states of mind' (2001:2). Despite Motz's concern not to classify and manage all acts of female violence, the effect of her work is to hold out the positivistic possibility of precisely this – a new taxonomy of female violence. By constructing an implied continuum of female violence ranging from public incivility to homicide, Motz reinforces, however unwittingly, journalistic stereotypes of 'ladettes' and 'twisted sisters'. While Motz is arguing for a 'thoughtful and sensitive understanding of female violence' (2001:260) which avoids the sentimental (but violent) objectification and dehumanisation of women, Pearson cries 'let the gun smoke!':

Women have virtually no access to anger management counselling, sex offender therapy, child abuse prevention, and prison security – all because we won't concede their fundamental agency.

(1998:238)

Both call for women to be held more accountable for their actions and both argue that this can only be in the interests of women themselves. This is *empowerment*.

But, as Shaw and Hannah-Moffat (2000) have argued, the concept of *empowering* women has now been appropriated by the *What Works* agenda as a means of *responsibilising* women – making them responsible for engaging with programmes of change and managing their own *risk assessment*. Kendall's warning that anger management programmes for women in 'coercive environments' may be helping them to 'tolerate oppression' (2000:39) should not be ignored and Hannah-Moffat (1999) warns us about the danger of redefining women offenders' 'needs' as 'predictive risk factors'. When policy-makers start talking about 'adapting' programmes and risk assessment tools for use by women, they rightly adopt the language of 'need'. However, rather than analysing and seeking to meet those needs through better access to community resources, 'needs talk' may merely replace 'risk talk' and 'high need' women become 'high risk' women who can then be subjected to the same programming as 'high risk' men.

The Chief Inspector of Prisons' thematic report (HM Inspectorate of Prisons 1997) on women's prisons recommended that 'every women's prison should have a psychology team to inform and take part in offending behaviour programmes' (1997:159) Although his follow-up report (HM Inspectorate of Prisons and Probation 2001) noted that this had not been achieved, almost all women's prisons now run cognitive skills programmes, having adapted Reasoning and Rehabilitation, Enhanced Thinking and Problem Solving Programmes for use by women (Stewart 2000). Probation officers are involved in the delivery and management of these programmes but psychologists play increasingly significant and leading roles. The ascendancy of psychology in both male and female prisons has been at the expense of the traditional role of the prison probation officer. In one women's prison, psychologists have moved into brand new, centrally located premises, while probation officers have been relegated, literally and symbolically, to a temporary building on the periphery of the estate (Worrall 2000b). Cognitive behavioural programmes are now viewed as the domain of psychology within the prison and increasingly in the community as well. Despite the fact that we still know very little about the differences in risk factors for men and women there continues to be an assumption that their thinking skills are similar and that programmes need only minor modifications of delivery to diverse offenders (Gelsthorpe 2001).

Conclusion

In this chapter I have attempted to argue that in the past decade in the UK, US and Australia, penal policy-makers have shied away from the obvious implication of both 'just deserts' and actuarial justice – that women still commit very little crime and are not at high risk of either re-offending or causing serious harm. Instead, the 'search for equivalence', driven by a misunderstood feminist hegemony calling for the em-powerment of women by making them accountable for their deeds, has resulted in an inevitable increase in the numbers of women rendered punishable. A combination of a spurious gender-neutrality (which denounces the traditional sexualisation, medicalisation, welfarisation and domestication of female offending) and a 'new psychology' of female aggression (which views motherhood as a dangerous risk-laden site) has masked the interplay of gender, race, class and age in the production of 'sexed bodies' and has reinforced the perceived appropriateness of ('adapted') cognitive-behavioural programmes for the treatment of women's 'gender-neutral' problems of anger, drugs, sex offending and general loutishness. In the effort to retreat from traditional paternalism and maternalism, the making of the penal crisis in relation to women has been instead the *unmaking* of 'women' as a category of offender requiring any special attention at all.

All of which begs two questions: 'why?' and 'so what?'. The latter question invites debate about what, if any, gender considerations should influence sentencing (see Carlen 2000a). The former can only be answered by revisiting classical debates about the relationship between economy, culture, politics and punishment (Melossi 1998). [See also Hudson, chapter 2 this collection. Ed.]. As I have attempted to show, there is no mono-causal explanation for the increase in female imprisonment. Rather, the increasing visibility of women in the public arena, for both legal and illegal purposes, has had a complex influence on the 'culture' of punishment in England and Wales.[8] Even when women enter the public arena, there remains the belief that 'our' women do not require control beyond that of the family and domesticity. But 'other' women do:

> Prisons have been reserved in the past for the working class and today, more and more, for an 'underclass' … conceived as tied to

male images (conceptions of hardness, lack of 'civilised' manners, and so on) … only 'other' women – women of others, that is – may be conceived as belonging in that framework and therefore admitted to prisons.

(Melossi 1998:xvi–xvii)

And 'that framework' increasingly denies differences of sex and gender, focusing rather on differences of race, class and age.

Notes

1 It is not insignificant that the one area where empirical evidence of victimization remains beyond dispute (Phoenix 1999) – female prostitution – is increasingly regarded as a non-criminal career choice.

2 I use the term 'sexed bodies' here to indicate the work of those theorists who challenge the existence of a clear distinction between 'sex' (as biological fact) and 'gender' (as socialised construct). My argument throughout is that penal policy-makers, by focusing on gender differences, which are (arguably) being eroded, justify so-called 'gender-neutral' measures which serve to hide the continued inscription of sex, race and age differences on punishable men and women.

3 Welldon defines the 'perverse' woman as one who 'feels that she has not been allowed to enjoy a sense of her own development as a separate individual, with her own identity; in other words she has not experienced the freedom to be herself. This creates in her the deep belief that she is not a whole being, but her mother's part-object, just as she experienced her mother when she was a very young infant' (1988:8–9).

4 Section 95 publications are the result of the clause in the 1991 Criminal Justice Act which requires the Secretary of State to publish information each year 'as he considers expedient for the purposes of facilitating the performance by [persons engaged in the administration of criminal justice] of their duty to avoid discriminating against any person on the ground of race or sex or any other improper ground.'

5 Introduced by the Crime and Disorder Act 1998, piloted in Croydon, Gloucestershire and Liverpool and operating nationwide from December 2000.

6 I am grateful to David Gadd for directing me to some studies on men as victims of domestic violence.

7 I am not sure where Fowler's statistics come from. Official criminal statistics indicate that young women of 14-17 years accounted for about 1,800 offences of violence and robbery in 1996, compared with 11,000 young men. The figure of 460 seems to refer only to robbery committed by young women (HM Inspectorate of Prisons 1997).

8   As Melossi (1998) argues, great care should be taken in making cross-national comparisons of rates of punishment, because of the culturally-embedded nature of punishment.

Chapter 4

Youth prostitution policy reform: new discourse, same old story

Joanna Phoenix

We think that much useful work could be done if every young prostitute brought before the courts … were remanded for a few weeks, in custody if necessary. Short remands such as we have in mind have enabled probation officers and other social workers to smooth out difficulties which have prevented young offenders from obtaining employment and so compelled or encouraged their continuance in crime.

(Home Office 1957:93–4)

It is a tragedy for any child to become involved in prostitution: it exposes them to abuse and assault and may even threaten their lives … Children involved in prostitution should be treated primarily as the victims of abuse and their needs require careful assessment. They are likely to require the provision of welfare services and, in many cases, protection under the Children Act 1989.

(Department of Health and Home Office 2000:3
hereafter DOH/HO)

Offenders or victims of abuse? Two fundamentally different ways of seeing girls who sell sex.[1] In the space of only 40 years, these two approaches have been advocated and adopted by differing British governments. The Home Office's Wolfenden Report (1957) recommended that girls in prostitution should be treated as offenders. It made no distinction between them and their older prostitute sisters. Any woman convicted of soliciting, loitering, or any other prostitution-related offence, could be fined, given a probation order or imprisoned as long as she had reached the age of criminal responsibility. In contrast, the Department of Health and Home Office (DOH/HO 2000) guidance describes them as victims and directs local authorities and the police to treat girls in prostitution as very different from adult women. Young prostitutes are to be cared for, rather than punished. Two more widely differing approaches could not be envisaged. Or so it would seem.

This chapter examines one moment in the history of prostitution policy reforms: the current attempts to ensure that young prostitutes are not criminalised or punished for their involvement in prostitution.

'Liberal' innovations involving reforms to ease the burden of punishment in relation to prostitution issues have often had ironic results. For example, in the early 1980s, sentencing orthodoxy was changed following the success of various campaigns making two main claims: that most women in prostitution are motivated by poverty; that the punishment of imprisonment for soliciting is out of all proportion to the crime.

Following the implementation of the Criminal Justice Act 1982, magistrates could no longer imprison women convicted of soliciting or loitering for the purposes of prostitution. The unintended consequence was an increase in the numbers of women going to prison for defaulting on the fines that magistrates meted out (see Matthews 1986 for a fuller discussion of the failure of this reform). The policy innovation (DOH/HO 2000) examined in this chapter is of a very different order. Rather than merely changing one dimension in the regulatory response to prostitution i.e. sentencing, it is altering how the entire criminal justice system responds to a particular group of people. But this seemingly benign innovation has resulted in an equally ironic outcome. The strategies adopted in a reforming process intended to protect young girls in prostitution from abuse and ensure that they do not end up in custody also create the very conditions for a greater criminal justice punitiveness towards some and, ultimately, the 'protective' incarceration of others. For, when youth prostitution is symbolically divorced from its social and material context, and especially when it is divorced from the anti-youth social policies of two decades, there exists only the thinnest of lines between the official recognition of victimisation, the emergence of an official ideology of young prostitute victimhood and increased levels of state disciplinary regulation in the name of protection. The argument of this chapter is that:

1. *The reforming process vis-à-vis youth prostitution is limited by the very techniques and strategies that were used to introduce the process and implement changes in practice. Specifically, a 'renaming game' took place*

which whilst privileging a newly emerging ideology of young prostitute victimhood simultaneously sidelined the material and social conditions and realities of young people's involvement in prostitution. From the outset, the reforming process was a process geared towards changing the symbolic framework previously shaping the practice of the statutory and voluntary agencies that come into contact with young people in prostitution. Guidance was given (DOH/HO 2000) on how such agencies and individuals were to *understand* and *make sense of* youth prostitution. This strategy had two unfortunate results:

i) *it left two dominant perceptions – 'prostitution is a crime problem' and 'prostitutes are offenders' – untouched and unchallenged.* By arguing that young prostitutes are different to older prostitutes, DOH/HO guidance made it easier for agencies to construct these under 18 year olds as vulnerable victims and girls 'in need'. However, in leaving unchallenged the dominant criminal justice construction of prostitutes and prostitution as a public nuisance and law-breaking problem, the guidance has created a policy in which young prostitutes are known oppositionally as either victims *or* as offenders and *not* both. Young prostitutes are victims *except* when they are offenders.

ii) *it rendered youth prostitution epiphenomenal to sexual abuse and, in so doing, has created the conditions in which the social and material circumstances that structure young people's involvement in prostitution are perceived as less relevant than their lifestyles and their relationships with men.* In other words, the guidance elevates a 'moment' in time (the 'moment' of prostitution), and in so doing, wipes out the young women's previous history.

2. *The techniques and strategies used to facilitate change have created the conditions in which young prostitutes are brought into greater contact with statutory agencies and criminal justice bodies.* It is not just that the intensity of contact between young prostitutes and statutory and criminal justice agencies has changed; the nature of the contact is different. Prior to these innovations, the type and intensity of contact between young girls in prostitution and official agencies might best be described as 'marginal' (consisting of sexual health outreach input and police arrest, caution and occasionally conviction resulting in conditional discharges and fines). Now, as a result of the discursive strategy of constituting 'young prostitutes' as victims of child abuse and, by extension 'youth prostitution' as a child protection issue, statutory and voluntary welfare and criminal justice agencies are *obliged* to investigate and act upon every aspect of the young girls' lives, both in relation to their involvement in prostitution and, more

importantly, beyond it. Thus, such agencies have more (obligatory) regulatory and disciplinary powers over young prostitutes than they did before.

3. *At the same time, the techniques and strategies adopted have created the conditions in which official responses are organised around 'risk assessment' which in turn has created the conditions for both a greater official punitiveness towards some young prostitutes and a blurring of the boundaries between protection and punishment for others.* For, by constituting young prostitutes oppositionally as either victims of child abuse or offenders, a model of intervention has been established that is concerned almost exclusively with differentiation and categorisation. Official attention is turned towards adjudicating motivation (of the young person) and risk (to the agency). For those young girls whose perceived 'voluntarism' leaves them outwith the ideology of victimhood, new and different punishments to those meted out to older prostitutes have been instituted. The result is that there now exists the possibility of using higher and higher tariffs of punishment than were possible before. Additionally, for young girls seen to be 'risky', 'protection' and 'punishment' blur as deeper levels of personal intrusion and more punishing care regimes become possible and indeed justified.

4. *In short, the discursive strategy of constituting young prostitutes as victims of child abuse has created the conditions in which some young people will be treated more punitively than prior to the reform process with the result that even more young women (rather than fewer) will end up locked up for indeterminate periods in secure accommodation.* As agencies come to define more and more aspects of young prostitutes' lives as toxic and harmful, as they struggle with having only individualised solutions to decontextualised social problems, the provision of safety for these young people through the mechanism of secure containment becomes more and more plausible, possible and warranted.

The chapter is divided into seven sections. The first section briefly outlines some of the material and social conditions that structure young people's involvement in prostitution. In the second and third sections, the DOH/HO guidance is deconstructed and the oppositional construction of young people in prostitution as either victims of child abuse or offenders is detailed. Following this are four sections in which the strategies and rationales employed by official agencies as they focus on young people are demonstrated.[2] Collectively, the chapter concentrates on the ways in which youth prostitution as crime and/or victimhood is understood and recognised.

The realities of youth prostitution

Poverty and anti-youth social policies[3] not only constrain the choices of, and limit the opportunities for, young people in Britain, they also structure their involvement in prostitution. Study after study indicates that many young people engage in prostitution as a matter of survival and that the survivalism of many of Britain's impoverished youths has been increasingly criminalised (Carlen 1996; Pitts 1997; Melrose *et al* 1999; Lee and O'Brien 1995; Barnardos 1998). Other studies reveal the utter desolation that poverty creates in the lives of young people and how that poverty is structured by the specific anti-youth social policies adopted in the last two decades (MacDonald 1997; Coles 1995). So, for example, only 12 years ago the right of 16 and 17 year olds to claim social security benefits was removed, at the same time as the then Conservative government introduced a lower rate of benefits for under 25 year olds. Moreover, the last two decades have seen a decrease in the number of agencies that specifically work with and for some of Britain's most vulnerable young people. Other anti-youth policies have resulted in: reduced youth training schemes for those who have left education; the exclusion of the under 18s from minimum wage protection; the institution of a lower minimum wage for the under 21 year olds; and less affordable housing. All these factors structure a form of youth poverty that conditions less than conventional and, at times, criminogenic responses i.e. shoplifting, begging, drugs, and for young women in particular, prostitution (Carlen 1996). And whilst poverty, housing difficulties and drug problems are often cited as reasons for young people's involvement in prostitution, such involvement is also seen to bring about these problems (Melrose *et al* 1997). Thus, the very material and social conditions that structure some young people's choices also rapidly become the effects of involvement in prostitution (Phoenix 1999).

There is a worrying incongruence between the rationale of the DOH/HO guidance, the way in which the guidance flattens any distinctions between different categories of 'young people' and the age group most affected by the new reforms. The guidance makes specific provision for *all* young people involved in prostitution. It assumes that there are few differences in terms of 'need' and 'risk' between young women 16 and 17 years old and girls 10, 11 and 12 years old. In a strictly legal sense, this is correct because all individuals under the age of 18 are, in law, defined as children. The rationale for the DOH/HO guidance is the assumption that because young women are below the age of sexual consent they should not be criminalised for offences related to sex. But the age of the most commonly criminalised young prostitutes is above the age of consent. As

Table 4.1 indicates, in terms of proportions, the 'problem' of children and prostitution is a problem of older young people who fall outside the protective measures of lawful sex and age of consent legislation and for whom social services can do little. And, more importantly, this group of older young women is precisely the age group whose lives have been most profoundly torn apart by two decades of anti-youth social policies.

Research also details the widespread practice of extorting money from young people in prostitution via the use of threats, intimidation, violence or indeed through 'charm' (Phoenix 1999). The impact of such practices is profound. In addition to further diminishing the opportunities young people have for social and material security, the experience of violence can be extreme, devastating and lasting in its effects. Young people tell researchers of regular violent physical and sexual attacks resulting in hospitalisation, broken bones, bruises and burns (Barnardos 1998), of being kidnapped and raped (Melrose) and of having most (if not all) of their earnings taken from them by 'boyfriends', 'pimps' and other exploitative adults (Melrose *et al* 1999; Phoenix 1999). And the violence does not end there. Young people also experience violence from the police, from punters and harassment from neighbours (Phoenix 1999).

Recognition that young people are also victimised in prostitution and lead lives shattered by the aggregate effects of poverty is not the same as the constitution of them in policy as always and already victims of child (sexual) abuse and the violence of men. The concern in this chapter is

Table 4.1: Convictions of females from 1991–1999 for soliciting and loitering for the purposes of prostitution by age, England and Wales[4]

	10–14 yrs.	15–17 yrs.	18–20 yrs.	All ages
1991	3	318	2175	9559
1992	1	247	1616	8778
1993	0	105	1375	7348
1994	4	137	994	6574
1995	0	101	758	5512
1996	0	177	884	5312
1997	1	147	728	5509
1998	0	110	698	5118
1999	0	38	418	3288
Total	**9**	**1380**	**9646**	**56998**

Source: Crime and Criminal Justice Unit (RDS), Home Office 2001 (quoted with permission).

about the impact of incorporating an ideology of victimhood into youth prostitution policy on the population that the new policy is claiming to help. The argument is that such an ideology operates to erase the social and material specificity of young people's involvement in prostitution. By so doing, *Safeguarding Children* creates the conditions in which young people may be criminalised more (not less) and may experience a greater (not lesser) threat of 'protective' incarceration.

Safeguarding children

Safeguarding Children Involved in Prostitution is a jointly-issued Department of Health and Home Office (2000) appendix to the *Working Together to Safeguard Children* guidance. It advises local authorities, police authorities and all those who come into contact with children on the enactment and implementation of the Children Act 1989. In particular it advises welfare and criminal justice agencies about young people's involvement in prostitution. The specific advice aims to enable all the different agencies within a locality that work with children and young people:

- to provide an 'integrated' approach in order to both recognise the 'problem' and provide solutions;

- to treat young people as victims of abuse in the first instance;

- to safeguard children and promote their welfare;

- to work together and provide children and young people with 'exit strategies' in order that they might leave prostitution;

- to investigate and prosecute those who coerce, exploit and abuse young people in the course of their involvement in prostitution.

It has already been argued that the current reforms of youth prostitution policy are geared to changing the symbolic framework that shapes the practice of both statutory and voluntary welfare and criminal justice agencies. Those who are under 18 years old and involved in prostitution are to be defined, in the first instance, as 'children in need' and/or 'at risk of suffering significant harm' and, as such, entitled to the full protection of the state. Such redefinition is possible because the guidance collapses the distinction between youth prostitution and child (sexual) abuse and, in so doing, creates a legal framework that brings youth prostitution firmly within the ambit of child protection laws, rules, procedures and treatment.

The 'problem' the guidance addresses is not that young people are involved in prostitution *per se*, or the worrying social and material conditions which often drive young people into, and then justify involvement in, prostitution. Instead, the 'real' problem is the presence of those who abuse young girls: the boyfriends and adult men who entice, threaten or intimidate young people into prostitution, together with their profit from that involvement and those adult men who purchase unlawful sex from girls legally unable to offer consent. On these points, *Safeguarding Children* is replete with what have become depressingly familiar stories of predatory men who are quick to target and exploit possibly homeless, occasionally in care and certainly vulnerable, damaged youngsters for their own pecuniary gain.

> Vulnerability is identified and targeted by coercers [*sic*] whether a child is living with their own family, looked after away from home or has run away.
>
> (DOH/HO 2000: 15)

In a similar vein, *Safeguarding Children* gives very clear instructions about 'punters':

> 'Clients' who assume that payment buys them agreement of the child and puts them beyond the law are completely wrong ... they are child abusers.
>
> (DOH/HO 2000:16)[5]

Safeguarding Children invokes a particular model of causation in which young girls' involvement in prostitution occurs via a four stage 'process of control' (including 'ensnaring', 'creating dependency', 'taking control' and 'total dominance') in which an older 'boyfriend':

> ensures the girl becomes emotionally dependent on him, initiates her into sex and detaches her from other influences in her life ... using emotional and physical violence. This abuse progresses into the older man selling her for sex.
>
> (DOH/HO 2000:15)

The Government recognizes that the vast majority of children do not voluntarily enter prostitution: they are coerced, enticed or are utterly desperate. It is not a free economic or moral choice.

> (DOH/HO 2000:15)

In other words, young girls are forced into prostitution. Such a causal explanation is premised on a literal notion of 'free will' and a deterministic concept of force. Free will, here, is synonymous with 'voluntarism' and the capacity to make a different choice. Force, on the other hand, is the absence of free will: a lack of choice, a lack of 'voluntarism'. Within *Safeguarding Children*, some factor (usually a pimp or abusive adult) removes young women's ability to make *other* choices i.e. not to become involved in prostitution. This naïve understanding of both free will and force displaces discussion and recognition of how material and social conditions operate to funnel the choices that individuals have access to and impel them in their decision-making. In short, linking free will to 'voluntarism' and an individual's ability to make other choices erases the force of necessity.

Safeguarding whom from what? Erasing materiality

There are two specific consequences of making sense of youth prostitution as a form of child (sexual) abuse. Firstly, the linking of causation to an individual's status as 'victim' in a tautological explanatory model (i.e. young prostitutes are victims because they were coerced into prostitution and vice versa) paradoxically creates the conditions in which dominant understanding of prostitution as crime and prostitutes as offenders remains unchallenged. For, if individuals can be seen to have voluntarily entered prostitution, they are not, by definition, victims, as one defining element of victimhood is that it is a condition foisted upon the individual and not one chosen; if they are not victims, then they are offenders. It is important to note that the guidance does not render 'unspeakable' the possibility of voluntary involvement in prostitution: it merely transforms it back into a problem of crime.

> The entire emphasis of the Guidance is on diversion using a welfare-based approach to children and that it should be adopted *in all cases*. However, it would be wrong to say that a boy or girl under 18 never freely chooses to continue to solicit, loiter or importune in a public place for the purposes of prostitution, and does not knowingly and willingly break the law … The criminal justice process should only be considered if the child persistently and voluntarily continues to solicit, loiter or importune in a public place for the purposes of prostitution.
>
> (DOH/HO 2000:27–8)

Criminalisation remains an appropriate response but only for those young people who are deemed to be 'voluntarily and persistently' offending via their continued involvement in prostitution, despite the best efforts of those welfare-based organisations that are trying to 'exit' them from prostitution. Thus, *Safeguarding Children* formalises a distinction: between young people in prostitution who are the victims of predatory men and thus are deserving of care and protection; and those who are actively engaged in law breaking behaviour and thus legitimately subject to criminal justice intervention.[6] The irony, however, is that *Safeguarding Children* prompted a process in which the practice of giving prostitutes' cautions for young people formally has been abandoned. Young prostitutes are now to be dealt with under the provisions of the Crime and Disorder Act 1998 with the wider range of disposals available. Hence, the construction of young prostitutes as victims does not challenge the older, dominant construction of them as offenders; it simply smothers it.

Safeguarding Children is presented as an 'evidence-based' policy reform via the citation of research that claims to detail the 'real' causes of youth prostitution. Whilst it cannot be denied that much of it draws on detailed empirical studies, the key terms deployed within the document (i.e. 'children', 'sex', 'coercion', 'voluntarism', 'exploitation' and most importantly, 'prostitution') are little more than the 'common-sense' elements of a discourse of children as victims (cf. Burton and Carlen 1979). Underpinning the central assertions of *Safeguarding Children* is a symbolic landscape that presents children as innocent, asexual and pure *and* as corruptible and vulnerable. Such constructions position children as forever separated from the 'adult' realm of sex and sexuality. This understanding is not innovative or new. As Weeks (1981), Foucault (1981) and Evans (1993) have all noted, nineteenth century discussions of childhood masturbation, child prostitution and child labour have all constituted and re-constituted children as 'corruptible innocents'. Indeed, Foucault (1981), Evans (1993) and Donzelot (1979) have argued that it is this very construction that facilitates and makes possible the current techniques, strategies and organisation of protection that monitors and controls the lives of children. If children are innocent (i.e. non-sexual and/or ignorant and immature) and yet such innocence is corruptible by adults, then children must be protected from themselves (and the actions of others that would take advantage of their innocence) by a greater moral and social authority (i.e. the plethora of regulatory agencies such as the police, social services, teachers, health workers and so on). The power of such a discourse of childhood to render the socio-economic and material conditions structuring the experiences of young people irrelevant and to produce ever expanding webs of governance should not be underestimated. Over a century ago, in the late 1800s, the Maiden Tribute Scandal initiated a debate about the boundaries between childhood and sexuality that resulted in raising the age of consent for girls (only) from 13 to 16 years old, outlawing buggery, extending to the police greater power to regulate aspects of prostitution (such as brothels) and formalising parents' 'rights' to 'protect' their children from the corrupting influence of other, older men[7].

In millennium Britain, however, young people who are vulnerable and have low self-esteem have supplanted the impoverished working-class girls of London; pimps and child sex abusers have taken the symbolic place of 'white-slavers'. Indeed, a careful reading of *Safeguarding Children* reveals that without deploying archetypical images of essentialised masculine predatoriness and sexual violence the guidance makes little sense. It is arguable that the central subject of the new policy is not young people in prostitution at all, but the occasionally violent and at least potentially sexually abusive man – the pimp who targets, grooms and conditions vulnerable young people into denying their abuse, the punter who has a sexual appetite for younger and younger children, the 'network of abusers which may be operating across a number of Local Authority areas' (DOH/HO 2000:20).

In not demarcating involvement in prostitution from child (sexual) abuse, *Safeguarding Children* makes it near impossible to understand and treat young prostitutes who may be either voluntarily involved in prostitution *and* victimised or whose involvement does not follow the template set. Where voluntarism is evident (for instance, it is recommended that an absence of a third party coercer may be indicative of voluntarism), the young person is not experiencing child abuse, but rather is merely involved in prostitution (and thus a legitimate subject of criminal justice intervention). More importantly, the material realities experienced by young people in prostitution are erased in agency discourse in favour of a construction of them as victims to the sexual violence and exploitative behaviour of older men. Consequently, if they are victims of child sexual abuse for the agencies who deal with them, wider structural issues are not as pertinent as the young women's victimhood.

Safeguarding Children also renders the material and social conditions of youth prostitution less than relevant through conflation of the two sociologically distinct phenomena of child sexual abuse and youth prostitution. Specific prostitution-related relationships (such as between prostitute and police or prostitute and pimp) and experiences (such as violence from punters) are decontextualised and removed from their institutional and commercial context. Instead, these relationships and experiences are constituted as particularised, individual relationships between abuser, abused girl and exploitative adult.

Child (sexual) abuse usually occurs in the context of intimate and/or familial relationships. Whilst the abuse may occur over time, child (sexual) abuse is defined in relation to specific acts and/or activities that occur within the context of particular relationships (i.e. between adult and child). By contrast, the relationships and activities constituting the institution of prostitution have little meaning outside the context of the exchange of money (Phoenix 1999). Prostituting becomes something sociologically distinct because of the commercial context in which it occurs. Young people's involvement in prostitution does indeed expose them to being abused by adults, but it cannot be conflated with that abuse without erasing the wider material, economic and ideological processes that make either prostitution possible or people's involvement in it plausible. In short, the social institution of prostitution is constituted by and within the context of wider material, economic and ideological processes (and is thus shaped and influenced by those wider processes), but it is not reducible to either social relations outside of itself (i.e. gender, age and/or class) or the context in which it occurs.

Thus, and in summary, *Safeguarding Children* reconstructs the 'problem' of youth prostitution in a binary fashion: as child (sexual) abuse, except where voluntarism can be established in which case it is a crime problem. Such an oppositional construction has huge implications. If a young woman is seen as suffering abuse, she is entitled to state care and protection. If, on the other hand, a young woman is portrayed as being voluntarily engaged in prostitution, she is to be treated as a young offender and punished. What happens to her depends entirely on how the welfare and criminal justice agencies that come into contact with her assess her motivation and reason for engaging in prostitution. Hence, official attention is turned, not on the material realities of young people's involvement in prostitution, the specific social and economic context inhabited by the young person, but on her wider relationships, her behaviour and whether she is assessed as being willingly engaged in prostitution.

Professionals talking: young prostitutes as child victims

In the five different geographical areas where the research reported here was conducted, there was near universal acceptance amongst social services, voluntary organisations and the police that youth prostitution is child (sexual) abuse. Interestingly, many of the interviewees[8] struggled to articulate exactly why this might be, treating the claim to be self-evidently true.

> We want to use the phrase 'children abused through prostitution' and we want to raise the awareness about the fact that these children are being exploited by adults rather than peddling wares. Because that's what they are.
>
> (Police)

> What are we talking about here – I mean they are the same as any other children at risk from physical abuse and sexual abuse. It's exactly the same. **[Why?]** Because abuse is abuse is abuse no matter where it happens.
>
> (Police)

Others offered a more nuanced framework of meaning in which youth prostitution was conflated with child (sexual) abuse. Foremost was an understanding that youth prostitution was both symptomatic and the result of previous abuses experienced, because previous abuses effectively stopped the young person being able to resist the exploitation or coercion of others:

> You know, a lot of these kids, the abuse is in the background – they have absolutely awful backgrounds and anyway home's a terrible place and that's one of the reasons they start running in the first place and then it is a short trip from there to prostitution.
>
> (Social Services)

> A high proportion of them have been sexually abused in the past. Even if there is not a positively identified pimp, there's the use of drugs, a lot of men exploiting, you know what I mean. Their past makes them vulnerable, doesn't it?
>
> (Voluntary organisation worker)

Still others noted more specific reasons why young people involved in prostitution are victims; amongst these included specific dangers of the 'job' or a general concern about age.

> Another reason for me thinking it is another child protection issue is that while young people may choose to have unprotected sex, and while you know, I don't think you can legislate for that, I just think

firstly, the chances of being coerced into unsafe sex by a punter, is of course a high chance and then just statistically the more punters you have the more times you put yourself at risk.

(Voluntary organisation worker)

I think that the age of entry into selling sex is often a significant indicator of lots of other things and so yes, I think that's why we make interventions. It's about the entire package that somebody has brought with them in terms of why they're selling sex at that age.

(Voluntary organisation worker)

And, in keeping with *Safeguarding Children*, most of the interviewees wove a symbolic web in which voluntarism and consent became the crucial determinants in defining victimhood:

Where we come from, we would say that no boy or girl has ever made a positive choice to sell sex.

(Voluntary organisation worker)

Mostly for the young girls, she'll probably have somebody controlling her, she'll be pimped and probably work from an address.

(Police)

Our argument here is that nobody wakes up one morning and says, when I grow up I want to be a prostitute. There's no child involved voluntarily.

(Social Services)

Translating prostitution into child abuse: extending control and erasing poverty through protection

Discursive strategies used in the process of reform (i.e. the very act of making sense of a problem, the way that it is differentiated from other problems, the manner in which it is discussed) are constituted by and within the particular social, economic and ideological context in which they occur. For example, constructing young prostitutes as victims of child sexual abuse becomes difficult in a social and ideological context in which children are not positioned as vulnerable and adult male sexuality is not seen as dangerous. Importantly, these discursive strategies are also enabled (or disabled) by connecting institutional structures and techniques. Proceedings against young prostitutes as victims of child sexual abuse are enabled by a system of statutory and voluntary welfare agencies which focuses on 'child protection'. There is no necessary connection between the discursive reconstructions of a 'problem´ and the emergence of new ways of governing it; a specific dispersal of discipline and regulation is not inevitable or necessarily linear (Bottoms 1983; Nelken 1989). Hence, simply calling youth prostitution a problem of abuse does not mean that its solution either necessarily or solely inheres in the machinery and techniques used to deal with child abuse.

Yet, because the majority of workers did feel obliged by the 'guidance' to see prostitution as a problem of child abuse, they effectively erased the specificity of prostitution by re-focusing attention on the *entirety* of the young persons' lives, rather than just their lives within prostitution.

> Once we start looking at bringing in children in need because of the way they are being abused in prostitution we find their issues are very much more complex. We are looking at drug problems; we are looking at home and family life and housing problems. We are looking at sexual abuse in the past and so on.
>
> (Police)

> Of course prostitution is about exploitation and abuse, but the issues are much wider and we need to work with as many of them as we can in the life of any one young person.
>
> (Social Services)

In short, it is the *lives* of young prostitutes that have become the object of governance rather than their activities within prostitution. In this fashion, a seemingly benign reformation (such as the recognition that young prostitutes are victims) can have unexpected outcomes. When placed within a context of existing institutional structures and methods of work that are charged with governing troublesome youths and families (Parton 1991; Donzelot 1979; Rose 1999), the ideology of young prostitute victimhood results in a dissolution of the boundaries of the 'problem'. What started out as an issue of sexual abuse and exploitation of under-age prostitutes ends up as a concern about levels of 'vulnerability', risky sexuality and criminal survival strategies of a group of young girls.

> Very often the issues are different for young men in prostitution than the girls. Some will work for men, but there are many who will do it on a one-off basis and it's about finding out where they are themselves and this seems like a good enough way of earning

money as anything else. It's more like an issue of sexuality for men, whereas for the girls it's often about them being vulnerable generally and using their sexuality inappropriately.

(Voluntary organisation worker)

For the girls, there is a significant amount of violence all around them, whereas for the men, that kind of fabric of violence around them doesn't seem to be there, they're just isolated and even when they're working together. [pause] I mean it's poverty driven in the same way for the girls and boys, but the girls are more vulnerable. It's more risky for them.

(Police)

Benign interventions often produce controls that are more intrusive and less accountable than supposedly 'repressive', 'malign' interventions (Cohen 1985). In the context of youth prostitution policy reforms, the extension of social control (and, arguably, anti-social control) is noticeable by the way in which agencies discussed the benefits of a multi-agency format of working. Of particular benefit for police and social services were: a 'high level of information sharing' among agencies about specific girls; and that voluntary organisations could not use their guarantee of 'confidentiality' to resist requests for information. The point is that everything that can be known about a young person can, in fact, now be known, shared, discussed and actioned.

There were issues about whether all meetings were section 47 enquiries[9] under the Children Act or whether they weren't. Police were saying that they couldn't share information unless they were section 47, particularly the child protection teams because of the confidential nature of it. In the end we decided that we would take all the enquiries about children in prostitution under, or as reaching the threshold of, section 47, how we then chose to deal with it was different. But we label it as child protection and section 47 to get around the issue of confidentiality and sharing information between police, social services and the voluntary organisations we have here. Everyone has to share.

(Social Services)

We've actually all got our act together and we're all speaking to one another, which I think is really important and they're also talking to other voluntary organisations and getting them on board in terms of child protection and confidentiality and letting them know that sometimes there is a need that they ought to be talking to us.

(Social Services)

If they (voluntary organisations) work in isolation and they do not share information with the forum, then they may get a completely different picture of either what the risks are or what the protector factors are or how well that young person is coping. If they share it with other agencies and then you can figure out the total picture and know how to get the young person out of prostitution.

(Social Services)

Protection and punishment: protection against what? Punishing whom?

The degree to which young prostitutes are located as 'risky' children is reflected in the ways in which social services, voluntary organisations and the police discuss them as posing threats in the form of 'liability' to various agencies. A complex process of owning and disowning 'the problem' of youth prostitution characterised agency-discussions about when and against whom to take action. Like a game of pass-the-parcel, the 'problem' of any specific young prostitute was passed back and forth between agencies. Unlike the game, however, the objective was to ensure that the agency was not left holding the parcel by themselves when the music stopped. For the reforms have placed a legal burden of protection on agencies without also providing the means with which to achieve such protection (i.e. no additional resources were made available). Thus, whilst such an argument was repeated by all the professionals to whom I spoke, the game is also shaped by a legalism that structures a culture of blame within social work[10] (Parton 1991). Those most vulnerable to this threat were the voluntary organisations who did not have the juridico-legal power to exact co-operation from (or provide 'protection' for) the young people with whom they worked.

The protocols do mean, I don't know whether this is real or imagined, but it feels very often that we are carrying a lot of risk that maybe a statutory sector agency ought to be carrying.

(Voluntary organisation worker)

For me the reforms are all about making an agreement that we have a procedure by which agencies share the idea they're going to live

83

with the risk, so that we're not in a position that one agency is going to get shafted should things go wrong.

(Voluntary organisation worker)

The 'risk' posed by young prostitutes to social services was the direct threat that when that young person failed to leave prostitution, the social services would be blamed.

All this multi-agency work with young prostitutes is all about managing anxiety and managing risk between the different professional organisations. We call a child protection conference and regardless of the outcome, we can get on with the work because the risk is assumed by all the agencies sitting around a table and saying yes, this is how we're going to work with this young person.

(Social Services)

I'm not saying that child protection frameworks work all the time, they clearly don't. I'm not saying that child protection frameworks are always there for the benefit of the child, quite clearly they're for the protection of the professional as well sometimes. But it would be a very dark and dangerous place if we went in without those checks and balances.

(Social Services)

I think from an agency point of view you have to be seen to have acted appropriately irrespective of what the outcome of that is, providing we do what we do on a day to day basis, there's no problem.

(Social Services)

Within a context wherein working with young prostitutes is seen to be inherently dangerous, where the material realities experienced by young prostitutes are subsumed by a totalising oppositional construction of them as victims or offenders, the attention of police, social services and voluntary organisations is turned to the relatively small but extremely significant task of assessing motivation. For, if it can be shown that the girls are engaged in prostitution voluntarily, then it becomes a simple matter of dealing with them via the increased punitiveness permitted within the Crime and Disorder Act 1998.

We're also very well aware that the protocols don't say *never* arrest these young people. The protocols say don't arrest them as a first course. Find out what their lives are like first and why they are in prostitution.

(Social Services)

The protocols are very good, but in the end it doesn't say how hard you have to try before you can then treat them as an adult or how voluntary their involvement in prostitution should be; when you should get a psychiatrist report on how they have been affected by their past experience to be able to voluntarily make that choice to stay in or exit or whatever.

(Social Services)

The discretionary powers accorded to the police in terms of proceeding only against particular people, events, actions and behaviour is well known. In reference to young prostitutes, the police become one of the key gatekeepers by whom girls are either processed through the new protocols (i.e. as victims) or through the Crime and Disorder Act 1998 (i.e. as offenders). A combination of signifiers indicated whether any specific young girl picked up was voluntarily engaged in prostitution. Most important amongst these was age. The age of the girl often raised the question of whether she had made a life choice:

There's a dilemma here because if you have got a 17 year old, she may have made the life choice and that is the way she chooses to go on behalf of herself; then there has to be a point where you say, 'Well hang on a minute, this person is actually not a victim, this person is an offender' and we've got to be able to be very clear that we know where we stand with that because it is a problem.

(Police)

Many of the 16 and 17 years olds are making life choice decisions from their point of view about this and [they decide] that that is the way they want to go.

(Police)

Occasionally 'life choice' was inferred from other signs such as: whether the young person responded immediately to the efforts of the welfare agencies (i.e. persistence) and general 'demeanour' or 'behaviour' (i.e. did the young girls conform to stereotypes of being a 'victim' such as wanting help).

You know it happens once and they're treated in a certain way. It happens twice and they're treated in a certain way, but after a while you've got to say, hang on.

(Police)

The police are saying that we don't want to treat these young women as criminals, we want to treat them as victims, however when we've arrested them for the tenth time and when they're swearing and spitting and kicking us, when they're not co-operating with us, then when they do some criminal damage, etc., etc. they're going to get nicked.

(Voluntary organisation worker)

She would only be arrested if she continues to go back despite our best efforts to divert her and take her away from it. If she decided she wants a life of prostitution then she would get arrested irrespective of her age.

(Police)

If she doesn't want to comply, doesn't want to help herself or allow herself to be helped, then she'll just go back into the pot with the rest of them – a childhood prostitute.

(Police)

Once voluntarism has been established, young prostitutes are referred to Youth Offending Teams. Now that the system of administering prostitutes' cautions and subsequent convictions (for which the usual punishment was a fine) has been abolished for the under 18 year olds, Youth Offending Teams can recommend disposals ranging from reprimands, final warnings, anti-social behaviour orders, or fast-tracking through the courts and even custody. In other words, the very narrow range of punishments has been extended. Whilst it is too soon to assess the full impact of this, early signs would indicate a process of up-tariffing is taking place, not because of a desire to punish more, but rather to punish less. There is a general worry about the effects of fining young prostitutes and thus placing an unrealistic financial burden upon them.

We let the Youth Offending Teams make the decision about what to do with them. I mean, again, you go back to your vicious circle where you have the younger child who has persistently gone back to prostitution and then you've gone through the various reprimand and warning and then we go to the prosecution stage. Well, we can't really fine them anymore because if they have to pay fines, well they'll just go to prostitution for that, so we have to think of other ways of dealing with them. So we have talked about using anti-social behaviour orders banning them from particular areas of town.

(Police)

When protection becomes punishment

Agencies struggled with what to do with young prostitutes deemed to be in need of 'protection'. For the most part, social services were happy for whatever voluntary organisation that was in place in the locality to take the lead (typically these were either sexual health outreach projects or youth prostitution specialist projects). And, as noted above, many voluntary organisations were more than uncomfortable with this, feeling that it should be social services who took the lead and the risk. Nonetheless, there was widespread agreement that the most that could be done was to work where 'the young person is at'. What this meant in practice was to offer counselling for emotional traumas, work on building self-esteem and confidence and offer some type of inter-agency advocacy.

There are two strands to the work we do. We do counselling in an informal sense. Allowing young people to actually talk about what has happened to them in a more structured way. We do lots of stuff to get them to get in touch with their emotional self, because a lot of these kids have never cried before. We also make sure that we refer them on for other stuff.

(Voluntary organisation worker)

Such methods of work were shaped and influenced by the very ideology of victimhood that located the causation of youth prostitution as the vulnerability of certain young people to predatory adults and as a condition from their past abuses. Whilst there can be no doubt that young people in prostitution have multiple personal and psychological difficulties, the way in which this particular ideology operates is to obscure from vision (and thus action) the extreme poverty and social and material difficulties encountered by young prostitutes. Agencies were not unaware of this situation, but claimed they were unable to do anything about it.

Prostitution is one aspect of their problems. Quite often they will have drug problems and all those other things like homelessness. I mean if you look at these young people, they have really complex needs. They've had extreme abuse, emotionally, physically or sexually and we're looking at a highly vulnerable group. They are in an erratic emotional state. So you have to work with all those things. But, I suppose at the end of the day, if you can't get them benefits or help them to maintain their benefits, then there is less likelihood that they're going to withdraw from prostitution or exit no matter what you do.

(Voluntary organisation worker)

The exception to the method of 'working with where the young person is at' was when social services and the police felt the situation had become too risky and that the only recourse was a heavy intervention. What 'too risky' meant in practice was that there was the perception that the young girl was becoming further entrenched in prostitution. The 'heavy intervention', although drastic, was to lock up the young girl in secure accommodation.

In very high risk cases we might be looking to secure accommodation. But that is usually when there are heavy links with crack cocaine and drug dealers and violence and guns and stuff. So, really the prostitution is peripheral, but included in that. It's the whole of their life that is putting that person at increased risk.

(Social Services) [See also Hannah-Moffat chapter 11
on 'whole life' approaches to lawbreaking. Ed.]

You see this balancing act going on to the point where the only way ... is to secure them. We have avoided that at the moment, but I can see situations where we will end up having to use it. Maybe not because they are in prostitution, but because of something connected. Like this one young girl at the moment, really she was secured because her drinking had got so bad, she was gone for days at a time and in the end she was really, really vulnerable to being sexually abused by punters and being raped and stuff. Then there was this involvement with drugs. Really, she was secured because she was incapable of dealing with her life in prostitution because of her alcohol use.

(Social Services)

Most agencies discussed the difficulties they faced working to get young women out of prostitution because, in reality, there was very little that they could actually do. Thus, custody became the only 'real' option available to agencies who, nonetheless, also recognised that it did little or nothing to help the young women; that it was merely a strategy of blame avoidance.

In the past there has been a lot of battling and argument back and forth as to whether this is a social care problem or a mental health problem and who's going to lock this kid up so that we don't have to be worried anymore.

(Social Services)

Unfortunately there was one girl we secured and it didn't work because she still works as a prostitute. She drifted off into her old ways again. She's 16 and she is not in our children's home anymore. She has just been thrown out of her B&B accommodation because she had a punter in there. Secure is really a last resort. I am not in favour of it at all because what do you do afterwards? You're just putting the young person back in exactly the same environment, you haven't changed the environment at all. But when they are in real danger and when we can no longer protect her from her lifestyle, then there is no other option.

(Social Services)

The only way I can see anything getting done and having discussed it with various people is we've got to remove this girl from where she is. At first, they removed her to a B&B which just happens to be right in the middle of it and it just seemed a nonsense to me. So, we came to a decision yesterday. We argued over secure accommodation and that is what social services' advice for her is. (And it is through their bosses and legal department coz they've got to get funding and then they've got to find a bed and they were saying we haven't got anything, we've got no staff and no funding. But they found somewhere.) But in the interim, we're going to arrest her under police protection and then we've got 72 hours until the social services come in and of course we must hand her over to them. But at least we will see that she's OK and then social services can take it from there. We can only get 72 hours secure accommodation. Our job is only to pick her up, it's social services' job to do something with her. Social services can then go for 4 or 3 months of secure.

(Police)

> I mean the only sanction ... no, not sanction ... the only way of dealing with these girls is to lock them up. And that can't be right!
>
> (Police)

For service providers the purpose of secure accommodation was to contain the young girl so that more inclusive and deep reaching interventions could be made.

> We've moved on to thinking about locking this young girl up. I'm thinking she should be locked up so 'X' voluntary agency can go and talk to her – give her a bit of counselling, like. Also other various agencies can find out what is going on for her inside. Then, if they can get her off drugs what a wonderful thing that would be. Locking her up would save her.
>
> (Police)

> What's the point in giving a kid a prostitute fine? [Why not] drugs counselling, drugs support, and even imprisonment, well secure accommodation in certain circumstances. You get supervised. You get your drugs counselling. You try to get yourself sorted out with education and if you do all that then you won't have to work again. All the kids need is a little bit of persuasion.
>
> (Police)

The interesting twist that many agencies put on securing young prostitutes in 'protective custody' was that it is what the young person really wants.

> In the end we have secured two young women and on both occasions I have to say it was with the consent, well almost, of the young women concerned and followed a period of extensive close work to help them get to the point of saying, 'Please help, I can't do this anymore and no matter what you give to me it's not going to help me get out of prostitution. I'm scared and this is too heavy for me. I want to be out of the area and please put me somewhere that'll prevent me doing this'.
>
> (Social Services)

> The first time we secured her, she was a bit reluctant but I mean she saw what it was [pause]. She was a heroin user and we had major concerns about her health. She didn't resist strongly but she wasn't actually willing. She had about 3 months secure and really got

herself together. But within a matter of 9 months she was back on the scene again and then came back to us and said, 'I can't hack this, I need to go away. It was OK when I was locked up, can you do it again?'

(Social Services)

I think the thing for me is how much a young person is able to assist you when you physically lock them up either in secure accommodation or a safe place. I think if they can't say it directly to you, but their behaviour is saying, 'Do this for me please because I can't'. Then we can legitimise it for them. You know, they don't get the shit when they return [to the street] – it wasn't their choice.

(Social Services)

Secure accommodation may well remove the immediate risks of violence, exploitation, homelessness and so on facing young people (or the risk of liability facing agencies). However, the point of secure accommodation is to *secure* the young person; it is designed with incarceration in mind (Kelly 1992; Harris and Timms 1993). It may be possible to do many things with a young woman in secure accommodation, but the social and material privations structuring her involvement in prostitution will never be addressed. Sadly, there is every reason to assume that all that is actually achieved when using secure accommodation is a further obfuscation of the actual lack of alternatives for certain young people (Bullock *et al* 1998).

In summary, the unintended consequence of a reform process that explicitly 'renames the game' (i.e. prostitution is child abuse) is that more young people end up in custody, though, so the story goes, not as a punishment … but for their own (and the agencies!) protection.

Conclusion

The general argument of this chapter has been that policy innovations that socially decontextualise the subject of those innovations will always and already be limited. Specifically, it has been argued that the type of 'renaming game' played by the current Labour government is limited by its unintended consequences. The material realities (most especially the significant degree of poverty) that structure the lives of most young people in prostitution have been submerged by locating the 'problem' that needs addressing within a child protection framework. Child protection machinery and techniques are premised on an assumption that there is a need to *protect* a child from *specific* danger or threat (usually, though not always) embodied in a particular *person*. Child protection strategies are not ameliorative of social inequalities nor are they designed to counter the anti-social effects of anti-youth social policies that have fractured and torn apart the lives of 'marginalised', 'excluded' young people.

Current reforms have created the framework, mechanisms and techniques for a greater 'anti-social regulation' of young lives (Carlen 1995). This is not because *any* reform will always be incorporated by the tutelary complex and disciplinary mechanisms of the state but because these innovations are based upon a politically expedient ideology of victimhood that all but erases the wider social and material conditions that structure and make possible young people's entrance into, and continuation in, prostitution. The irony of current government innovations is that in one deft symbolic movement the carceral net has been cast that little bit wider and the mesh woven that little bit thinner. For, while we see the emergence in Britain of a new discourse on youth prostitution, it remains the same old story. Agency definitions of young women 'in need' are made officially meaningful by finely graded notions of risk and young women 'in need' soon become seen as young women 'at risk'. Once young women 'at risk' (to self) are given care by regulation as young women 'at risk' (to others), it is not long before they are in receipt of care by incarceration.

Notes

1   For the sake of consistency, the terms 'young' or 'younger' or 'children' are used to describe those individuals less than 18 years old.
2   This study was funded by the Nuffield Foundation (ref: SGS/00049/A) and sought to investigate and theorise how and under what conditions it is possible for criminal justice, statutory and voluntary welfare agencies to 'come together' to implement *Safeguarding Children*. Five very different types of local authorities were focused upon. Directors and workers within agencies responsible for drafting protocols and implementing innovations were interviewed. Whilst the specific mix of local agencies varied, the interviewees were mainly strategic directors and policy writers for social services, senior police personnel in either local divisions, vice squads and/or child protection teams and directors for voluntary organisations that dealt directly with young prostitutes or whose general work brought them into contact with young prostitutes. Typically, these voluntary organisations were either one of the big children's charities (such as the National Society for the Prevention of Cruelty to Children, Barnardos, National Children's

Homes, the Children's Society) or local sexual health outreach projects that worked with prostitutes more generally.

3   By anti-youth, I mean social policies that actively wither and diminish the possibilities of material and social stability for young people.

4   These statistics only show the numbers of girls and women that have come to police attention and for whom it was felt that criminalisation was appropriate. Furthermore, the actual ages of the young women may not be accurate as it is common practice for many younger girls to lie to the police about their age for fear that they will be returned to the families they have left or the local authority care they have rejected. For these reasons, these figures are given only for general illustration.

5   The guidance suggests that every effort should be made to initiate 'appropriate investigative action against those who may have coerced and abused them [i.e. children in prostitution]' (DOH/HO 2000:19) and then prosecute them. In the case of 'clients' this may mean investigating whether they are parents or carers of other children and assessing whether those children are at risk of, or are suffering, significant harm at the hands of these men.

6   There is nothing particularly new in this distinction: youth justice policies for the last two centuries have oscillated between constructions of young offenders as 'deprived' and/or 'depraved', as 'victims' and/or 'villains' (Muncie 1998).

7   'The Maiden Tribute of Modern Babylon' was a series of articles published in the *Pall Mall* in July 1885 that claimed to expose the trafficking of girls into prostitution in London. The final and most sensational article detailed the story of Lily who was sold into prostitution for the sum of £5. That these stories were later shown to be fabrications did not detract from the panic they fostered or the impact they had in terms of creating new machinery to police the boundaries of children and sex (cf. Walkowitz 1992 for a detailed account and analysis of the events).

8   Interviewees are identified only by their organisational location in what follows. Hence, 'Social Services' indicates that the person was either a social worker, a team leader, a service manager or policy writer for the social services, 'Voluntary organisation worker' indicates that they were a worker within, co-ordinator or director of a voluntary organisation and 'Police' indicates that the individual was either a member of a vice team, child protection team, local ward team or strategic officer charged with writing policy.

9   Section 47 of the Children Act pertains to the investigation and identification of 'children at risk of significant harm' and places a duty of care on all agencies.

10 Parton (1991) explains that within the last 20 years the 'central' role of social work has changed from one of providing 'care' to 'assessing risk' and that such assessments occur within an increasingly legalistic framework in which 'risks' are known only through the mediation of court-acceptable evidence and 'care' is transformed into legal liability.

Part Two
Practice

Chapter 5

A gender-wise prison? Opportunities for, and limits to, reform

Kate De Cou

Introduction

Traditionally, in the United States, men and women in the correctional system have been subjected to nearly the same standards of operational management. This is especially true of the 3,328 local jails and houses of correction (Bureau of Justice Statistics 1998). Only 18 are exclusively for women (Gray *et al* 1995); the remainder house both men and women within the same facility. Although most of the state prisons separate the sexes, the State Departments of Correction establish and maintain the same operating standards for all facilities. While the women's facilities are sometimes permitted some discretion regarding daily operational procedures, such discretion is generally minimal and must conform to the overall paradigm of power and control – most usually defined by male administrators.

In the 1990s there was an upsurge of research studies describing the characteristics of female crime and female offenders: crimes by women are less dangerous to society and women commit fewer violent crimes (Immarigeon and Chesney-Lind 1992); many women in custody have significant histories of physical and sexual abuse (Browne *et al* 1998); higher rates of mental illness are recorded for women in custody than for men (Teplin *et al* 1996); and women offenders frequently experience a tangle of personal and social deprivations (Owen 1998).

The problems confronting women and men in custody are very different. Females more often have sole responsibility for children, experience more problems acquiring adequate finances and housing, and usually have more serious physical and sexual abuse histories together with the accompanying mental problems. They have also usually had less education and significantly less work experience or preparation for employment.

These gender differences have implications for custodial regimes for women (Alamagno 2001; Covington 1999). Traditional male facilities in the United States have less privacy for toileting and hygiene than women have been brought up to expect; they also rely heavily on segregation in cells for punishment, and use physical restraints such as shackles for control (Jackson et al 1995a and 1995b; Veysey et al 1998) – all regime features that are inappropriate to women's life experiences. Similarly, whereas many programmes for males place an emphasis on anger management, it can be argued that, given their histories of victimisation, trauma and abuse management are more important for women. Finally, a major difference between male and female offenders is that women are more likely than men to have been themselves victims of crimes. Addressing the results of both crime victimisation and crime perpetration within programmes for women requires a special and gender-sensitive curriculum.

Now, there are certainly elements of control which are necessarily inherent in all custodial operations and which, therefore, must remain features of all custodial regimes, whether for men or for women [see also chapter 12. Ed.]. Secure perimeters and head counts which protect against escape, techniques for quelling disturbances, violence, or threats to staff, together with a level of control to ensure inmate responsiveness to officer commands, are key factors in sustaining a safe and secure environment. Additionally, procedures must be in place that: protect inmates from bullying or victimisation; segregate (where necessary) those prone to violence and destruction; prevent the introduction of contraband; and ensure that items which could be used either in a disturbance or for self-destruction are properly supervised or eliminated. None the less, the methods an institution uses for implementation of these control procedures may vary, and they should be constantly subject to a gender litmus test. For even necessary control principles are capable of varying operational interpretations as they are made more appropriate to the differing characteristics and life experiences of male and female populations – and without security being compromised.

Hampden County Correctional Center

The rest of this chapter describes a specific model of gender-sensitive responses to women inmates in one setting: Hampden County

Correctional Center in Massachusetts. The main argument is that regime innovations can be implemented without erosion of the necessary security controls common to all custodial settings and despite the further difficulties which seem perennially to occur when male and female prisoners share the same site and overall management structure.

The Hampden County model of regime innovation focuses on changing both staff and inmate attitudes to organisational and personal change. Staff reluctance to make changes and modify traditional management techniques is addressed by careful selection and retraining. Inmates are encouraged to make productive use of their time in the facility, learning not only life skills but also learning about themselves and how they make decisions. The Hampden County model further emphasises the maximum use of interpersonal communication skills and the application of programme material to daily living on the residential units. Control tactics by staff are shifted away from threat of the use of force and towards early recognition and intervention of stressful behaviours and circumstances. Thus, both inmates and staff are encouraged to embrace an understanding of the psychological implications of early abuse in creating current behavioural and emotional responses. When this occurs, control of inmates becomes part of a staff-inmate relationship in which inmates are encouraged to make specific behavioural choices with a clear awareness of the positive and negative consequences.

Hampden County Correctional Center (HCCC) is a large local facility supervising about 1800 inmates of which 200 are female at all security levels from maximum to community day reporting. The population includes pre-trial detainees and those with sentences of 2 ½ years or less. The average bed stay is 8.4 months. The general philosophy is to keep the sexes as separate as possible, though this brings its own problems, such as those connected with the allocation of limited resources, the scheduling and supervision of movement, and supervisory efforts to control the attempts between male and female inmates to communicate.

In 1992 a new facility was constructed for men and women as a result of overcrowding. The current facility is a state-of-the-art direct management style jail. Direct management refers to a physical design that permits many inmates to be supervised by one officer. It is popular in prison and jail construction because it is cost-effective in that more inmates can be supervised by fewer staff. In the Hampden County jail this means that 77 inmates are supervised in their living areas (pods) by one officer. Another main feature of this direct style of supervision is the increased reliance on the use of interpersonal communication skills as the key management tool, rather than any routine dependence upon threat of force. In Hampden County there was an opportunity to tailor the operational policies to the female population to maximise effective supervision, although the physical plant was the same throughout the complex.

It was known that 90% of Hampden County's female population are addicted to substances and were trauma survivors (Curran *et al* 2000). So, because of the pervasiveness of the co-occurrence of problems related to addiction and trauma histories, it was decided to integrate drug treatment and trauma treatment principles into a management style that would address both issues.

The women's unit retains the same management goals as those of the larger facility – to create a fair, firm, and secure environment where staff and inmates alike are treated humanely, safely, and with dignity. The ultimate objective in relation to male and female offenders is to combine rehabilitative programming with effective behavioural control in such a way that inmates learn new skills to redirect their lives when they return to the community. Because inmates are expected to be accountable and responsible for their own behaviour, the management style aims to go beyond warehousing, to productive engagement.

However, steps to accomplish productive engagement must be tailored to the population – and certain techniques, environmental features and approaches are more effective with females than are those traditionally employed in the management of male inmates. In both management techniques and rehabilitative programmes in Hampden County the aim is to empower women to become more aware of themselves – their strengths, resources, and options – so that they can make more personally and socially positive behavioural choices. [But see also chapter 11. Ed.]

All the inmates are introduced to the concept of personal empowerment early in their stay. They are shown that they may choose to participate in a variety of groups and activities that will help them understand both themselves and others' responses to them; and they are advised how best to enhance the quality of life during their incarceration. Certain behavioural choices will lead to more voice or power to exercise some control over their environment.

The written mission of the women's unit is:

- To house women inmates in a safe, secure, and orderly manner which ensures public safety and acknowledges women's developmental, experiential, and physical realities;

- To create an opportunity for personal growth through an environment that promotes education, gender-sensitive programmes, and greater connection to community resources;

- To empower women by helping them discover or restore for themselves a basic sense of self worth, dignity, and behavioural options that include clear boundaries and accountability.

A formula was created to implement this mission. This management formula is **Security + Programs + Milieu = Effective Management**. Each of the elements in this formula will be described in greater detail. First, though, the characteristics of the female population as well as certain guiding principles relating to trauma management will be outlined.

Profile of women offenders in Hampden County

A profile of the Hampden County women's population from a 1998 survey of 156 female inmates conducted for a National Institute of Corrections project on Women and Intermediate Sanctions (Curran *et al* 2000) revealed the following:

- 90% are addicted to drugs or alcohol

- 89% had multiple and often chronic experiences of physical and or sexual violence

- 85% are mothers (of these, 90% are single caretakers)

- 66% have an average of three children under age 16

- 80% have non-violent crimes, mostly drug offences, property offences, or prostitution

- 80% meet mental health criteria in DSM-IV for one or more disorders

- The Q5 (suicide alert code) status of females is three times higher than that of the male population

- 65% have work histories of three years or less (average age 32)

- The ethnic division is 1/3 each Latina, African-American, and Caucasian

- 68% request treatment for physical health problems

- One third state they are homeless and another third have unstable housing.

What leaps out from this statistical profile is the multiplicity of complex problems which characterises the lives of imprisoned women (cf

Covington 1999; Fletcher *et al* 1993; Owen 1998; Singer *et al* 1995). Significantly, women in custody themselves frequently indicate that they would appreciate help in addressing their problems.

Co-occurrence of addictions and trauma

The therapeutic model informing the regimes for women at Hampden County Correctional Center focuses on the co-occurrence of addiction and trauma, since both have implications for the custodial management and in-jail programmes for women. Generally the women acknowledge that they have addictions which led them to commit the crimes which brought them to jail. Our model therefore assumes that, in order to reduce the likelihood of women committing crimes in the future, both drug addiction and the conditions for recovery must be addressed.

Research on women's addictions reveals that many women abuse substances for two primary purposes in addition to a physiological predisposition: to mask severe emotional pain resulting from multiple experiences of violence and injury (Blume 1990; Herman 1992; Miller 1994), and either to stay connected to relationships or to avoid intimacy (Covington and Beckett 1988; Finkelstein and Piedade 1993). Therefore, the impact of the trauma must also be addressed, since it often underlies the addiction. Recent social service policy refers to this as 'trauma-informed' service delivery.

'Psychic trauma' occurs when a sudden, unexpected, overwhelmingly intense emotional blow or a series of blows assaults the person from outside. The sense of trauma is maximised whenever a person feels utterly helpless or powerless to control what is happening to them (Terr 1990). Yet the control paradigm of traditional corrections is designed to create the very conditions which effect inmate powerlessness! Moreover, because powerlessness is such a key element in traumatic responses, it is also critical to conditions which relate to trauma healing. This is why the Hampden County model encourages inmates to realise where they can have some real effect on their environmental conditions, what choices they realistically have, when their voices can be heard, and where absolute institutional control is unchangeable and inherent in the correctional model itself. An example: inmates learn in relationship violence groups about specific behaviours by partners which can be demeaning or limiting of their freedom. They are taught language and behaviours to help them insist on being treated with dignity and freedom to act without being punished. This is intended to apply to interpersonal partner-relationships in the community. However, sometimes inmates then complain about a particular officer's behaviour or commanding tone, and want to resist complying until their conditions of respect are met. In these cases, inmates are told not only that compliance to officers' commands is expected at all times but also that there is an approved procedure for making a complaint against an officer and that they should both comply with the officer's demands *and* use the grievance procedure.

The consequences of trauma are listed as: hyper-vigilance, violent outbursts, suicide ideation or attempts, self mutilation, dissociation, flashbacks, nightmares, eating disorders, and a high incidence of mood disorders, especially acute depression, anxiety, or bi-polar traits (Blume 1990; Herman 1992). These effects of traumatic stress require the cultivation of coping mechanisms to deal with threatening events. For example, if a person experiences an intense memory of an event, or if a condition in the environment bears some similarity to a past trauma, the coping behavioural characteristic, such as hyper-vigilance, can intensify. The similarity to past trauma in the environment is called a 'trigger' and the related coping behaviour is called a 'trigger-response'. Many elements of a jail or prison setting, such as locked doors, noises, invasions of privacy, and strip searches, serve as triggers to which previously abused inmates respond with distress (Bill 1998; Owen 1998; Veysey *et al* 1998).

Another consequence of trauma related to behavioural choices and change is the fear of taking risks and a hesitation to try new life alternatives (Terr 1990; Walker 2000). Since, therefore, traumatised women are likely to be hesitant about trying new behavioural options in order to protect themselves, the jail setting and the programmes must demonstrate that they can influence their immediate environment to bring about better and more positive consequences as a result of their new choices. For example: inmates in Hampden County can choose which groups to participate in and are informed about which activities or constructive behaviour will earn them an earlier release date. Inmate safety is also prioritised and an openly discussed condition of the environment.

In summary, with a trauma-informed perspective, a jail management system must: acknowledge the incidence of trauma symptoms; minimise as many trauma triggers as possible (such as excessive strip searches, or use of force); address inmate behavioural responses with an understanding of the automatic trauma responses and the need for emotional support; maximise inmate choices; and then demonstrate how employment of all these strategies can lead to effecting positive change. Finally, there must be an understanding and assurance of inmate safety from the broadened perspective of confidentiality; including not only the traditional correctional protection from physical injury, but additionally, protection from any verbally degrading comments (by either officers or inmates) which attack and erode self esteem. Overall, the emphasis is on the maximum use and development of interpersonal communication skills by both inmates and staff. These trauma-informed operational principles are integrated into each component of the Hampden County women's unit's management operations formula: Security + Programmes + Milieu = Effective Management.

Gender-responsive security strategies

In correctional operations total security can never be compromised. However, gender-responsive principles can inform security techniques. These include:

- Flexibility in the use of inmate segregation
- Balancing inmate isolation and stimulation
- Modifying forced-move techniques
- Maximising the use of communication skills
- Identifying and attending to issues of perceived inmate safety
- Minimising the use of invasive techniques (e.g. strip searches)

Inmates who are placed in segregation, and by definition *are* more isolated from the rest of the population, may experience heightened trauma symptoms, such as self-injury, poor impulse control, depression, and auditory or visual hallucinations. For some women, isolation in a small, contained area, such as a cell, may trigger memories of being locked in dark closets or simply memories of being overpowered and hurt by the adults around them. One way the Hampden County women's unit addresses these potential 'trigger-responses' in the jail setting is to utilise creatively the Special Management Classification System to formulate individualised behavioural regimens as indicated. Inmates who are guilty of frequent disruption to the living environment are given assignments, such as essay writing, or loss of privileges, but are never isolated in their rooms for long periods. Instead, they can still participate in group and other beneficial personal growth activities.

Gender-responsive programmes

Hampden County Correctional Center's women's unit staff have developed a comprehensive and gender-sensitive programme, called *women's V.O.I.C.E.S.*, that is designed to empower female inmates (De Cou and Van Wright, 2001). Each component has a written curriculum and pre- and post-tests and is implemented with attention to such key concepts as safety, confidentiality, and the relational model for women.

Relational theory states that relationships are central to core identity, functioning, and growth. The relational model of women's development and growth has been clearly articulated in the work of Jean Baker-Miller (1976) and Carol Gilligan (1982) and further developed at Wellesley College's Stone Center for Women. According to relational theory, women do not seek autonomy and separation as successful adult goals. Rather, their primary motivation is to build a sense of connection with others, traditionally with parents, families, children, and partners. Women's style of learning is more frequently experiential and characterised by much interpersonal dialogue and 'processing'.

The relational model (with its emphasis on interpersonal skills and learning) offers an alternative to the cognitive model (with its emphasis on individual reflexivity) and it is being successfully used in many women's treatment settings in the community. Addicts, in particular, need to cherish a sense of self and self worth through developing a sense of being valued by others (Covington 1999).

Five principles guide the *women's V.O.I.C.E.S.* programme: *empowerment*; *incremental* phase-oriented approach; *menu* of group offerings in key 'domains'; *programmes* that are structured with clear guidelines for accountability; and *staff* who are trained in both women-specific topics and professional group skills.

Empowerment

The empowerment principle aims to create expanded self-awareness. This helps women to formulate more detailed and specific post release plans so that they can succeed in making realistic and achievable changes when they return to the community. As inmates gain more information about their life issues, problem-solving skills, and community resources, and as they apply these to their life experiences, they develop more self-awareness and confidence to make more informed choices and have more control over their lives. The element of increased confidence to formulate and try new behavioural options is fundamental to empowerment.

Incremental phase-oriented approach

Because of the many life problems that female offenders experience, the programme is broad and incremental. Due to the profound emotional impact of many of the issues addressed in the programmes, participants need to be guided safely and slowly to describe their personal stories. To accomplish this, the learning format is unfolded in four gradual phases: *exploration, information, treatment* and *reintegration planning*. The first *exploration* phase is mainly introductory to the programme and to the inmates' issues, and it is implemented through brief two or four hour modules. Phase two, *information*, focuses on the provision of information and facts. This generally takes place in specific-topic, eight-session psycho-educational groups. In these groups participants are carefully guided to self disclose limited portions of potentially powerful details of their lives. Phase three, *treatment*, permits screened and selected inmates to become involved in therapeutic groups and the month-long addictions treatment component. The last phase, *reintegration planning*, actually occurs throughout the inmate's stay but becomes more specific as inmates near release. Here, participants are helped to apply the educational material to their lives as they develop written growth plans, referred to as *maps*.

Menu of group offerings in key domains

In each phase inmates are encouraged to explore many of the key life issues or 'domains' which are common to this population. The domains included in each phase are addictions, violence and trauma experiences, parenting, relationships, and life skills.

Structured and accountable programme design

There is a tight contract and accountability structure for the programme components. These help inmates to maintain clear boundaries and to experience positive or negative consequences for their specific behavioural choices. For example, being late for groups or having unexcused absences leads to termination from the group and being placed on the waiting list to re-enroll. Inmates select their interest in groups but must progress sequentially in the curriculum to afford protection from emotional overload. There are many related discussions regarding the effect of disciplinary incidents on group participation. Also, inmates must complete work assignments in the facility, such as completing a laundry contract for work in the central laundry or other institutional cleaning assignments. While these work loads are not staggering, there are several ways to assess women's ability to meet their many varied commitments in the outside world which presents similar challenges of balancing schedules and demonstrating accountability.

Inmates are highly motivated to participate in these programme activities and there are often 15 to 25 names on the waiting list of each offering. They show tremendous enthusiasm for the *V.O.I.C.E.S.* programme. As they progress through the phases, their energy becomes steadier and more consistent, and even on a daily basis, their behavioural choices demonstrate greater self control and awareness.

Staff – see next section below.

Milieu

The last part of the management formula is milieu. This refers to the actual setting where security and programming become integrated and jointly applied. The following are key principles inherent in this concept:

- Integration of security and programmes
- Learning laboratory – application of programme skills to daily behaviour
- Staff team work
- Emphasis on interpersonal communication skills

The inmates' living quarters are treated as an environmental learning laboratory. The skills learned in the programmes are actively used to solve daily problems as they arise. An example is the frequent use of mediations as a concrete tool to diffuse interpersonal stress. Inmates learn the techniques and communication skills to conduct mediations in Anger Management and Love and Violence Groups. If an officer observes tension building between women, a staff member is asked to oversee the mediation. Inmates are eager to practise their newly learned skills. These are effective in restoring harmony on the pods.

This learning laboratory is a dynamic environment and a team approach among staff members is essential. Staff present a united team presence and this is created by constant communication in several formal interdisciplinary meetings, informal interaction on the unit, and through popular team-building staff retreats conducted off-site. The multi-disciplinary staff team consists of correctional officers, supervisors, CCWs (correctional caseworkers), counsellors, a family services specialist, a nurse, and a forensic clinician. Each player performs their own specific role but must learn about the others' duties. Counsellors must graduate from the officers' training academy while correctional officers must learn about the programmes and how to encourage inmates to participate in these. Staff teach each other how best to use one anothers' skills and talents, and this interdisciplinary approach is often explored and developed further as new situations and problems arise. The team commitment to their own and the inmates' growth provides a positive environment to overcome the limits to gender-specific responses in women's correctional settings.

Education and vocational training

Very little has been said thus far about the role that formal education and vocational training plays in this programme. At Hampden County Correctional Center all inmates participate in education classes and vocational activities that are run by other departments. Legislation in Massachusetts requires that all offenders who do not have their high school equivalency certificate must be provided with tuition at their level of need. Hampden County offers a GED (General Education Equivalency) course in preparation to graduate from high school; ABE (Adult Basic Education) for inmates at more remedial learning levels; English as a second language; and some college courses for college credit. When female inmates showed limited interest in formal class work learning, the education staff developed a creative curriculum which integrated the life issues of most interest to the inmates (for example parenting). The staff emphasised experiential learning opportunities to adapt to the women's preferential style of learning, and also developed ways to address short attention spans. Through these staff efforts, attendance at education has increased to nearly 100 % with minimal absences. Vocational instruction in culinary skills, trades in prison industries, and graphic arts are additional opportunities offered to longer term inmates. And team work continues as educational staff, vocational staff, and unit counsellors discuss educational and vocational achievements of each inmate's individualised learning programme. Progress is recorded in writing in inmates' personal contracts and plans are made for continuation of educational or vocational activities in the local community at the end of their jail term.

Family services

Because at least 85% of Hampden County inmates are mothers with an average of three children who anticipate restoration of child custody in the community, Hampden County believes it is important to focus on the family unit as often as possible to support the maternal bond and enhance parental responsibility. There are visits each Saturday between mothers and their children only. Inmates may simply take the time for a quality discussion or they may choose to participate in a structured activity created by the educational department staff. Through a grant called 'Reading is Fundamental', jail staff can purchase and give a book to each child to take home each week. A creative play activity, such as a puppet show or a demonstration of an exotic animal from the zoo, enhance the visit and support the learning theme for the week. The children's play area is well-stocked with age-appropriate toys.

Films and discussions with inmates are related to pregnancy and child-birth preparation. In addition the Unit operates a PlayCare Project in which child-care supervision skills are taught in an advanced curriculum. Finally, special celebrations for mothers and children centre around such holidays as Christmas and Mother's Day. Inmates are allowed to have pictures taken which they can send home to their children. The most recent addition to mother/child activities is the Story Book Project through which inmates can create audiotapes of themselves reading a child's book. The book and tape are then sent home to the child.

Conclusion

This description of Hampden County's Correctional Unit for Women has aimed to show that a gender-sensitive management approach within women's prisons and jails is possible – even within the most secure and difficult settings. However, because of the entrenched culture and language of control in corrections, implementing gender-specific pro-grammes in US jails and prisons will remain a challenge for some time to come. To effect minimum standards for gender-sensitive management across the whole correctional system would necessitate legislative activity at federal and state levels. While this is not likely to occur in the near future, this chapter has set out to demonstrate that, in the meantime, individual innovative models – which recognise that the requirements of female prisoners are different to those of males – *can* be implemented and sustained within sympathetic correctional settings; and, moreover, that their continued development and debate is of the utmost importance in the struggle for gender-specific justice for women.

Chapter 6

Women-centred: the West Mercia community-based programme for women offenders

Jenny Roberts

For those who see justice and equality as identical, the issue of whether or not too many women are sent to prison is readily resolved by examining whether they are imprisoned in similar proportions to men, or for similar reasons. If the similarity test is satisfied, then that seems to be acceptable. [See also Worrall, chapter 3. Ed.] The origins of the groupwork pro-gramme for women offenders, established in the United Kingdom by the Hereford and Worcester Probation Service (now the West Mercia Area) in 1993, lay, in part, in similarly shallow ideas about there being 'too many' women on the service caseload.

This observation occurred in the context of the implementation of the 1991 Criminal Justice Act. This radical piece of legislation sought to base sentencing in the criminal courts on the principle of 'just deserts', which requires offenders to be sentenced for the seriousness of the offence, without mitigation for the personal circumstances of the offender or additional weighting for the offender's previous record. As the Act came into effect in late 1992, the effect on the sentencing of male offenders emerged as a marked reduction in use of both custodial and intrusive community sentences. Use of imprisonment for women offenders remained low, and use of probation orders in particular remained high. This was a cause for concern, because of the disproportionate demand on staffing of a large low risk caseload, and because the possibility of contributing indirectly to subsequent use of custody for such women could not be ignored. It also laid the service open to criticism about women offenders not being considered suitable for community service orders to the same extent as men, another possible indirect cause for use of custody.

The introduction of the groupwork programme was, however, primarily a logical continuation of local policy, to offer courts relevant alternative programmes for the main types of offenders who are sent to custody. Although numbers of women sent to custody were small (about 20 a year for the area), the policy was still relevant to those few. A strong commitment to such groupwork programmes had been established over the preceding ten years, following the introduction of a very successful programme for young adult male offenders in 1984 (Roberts 1987).

The importance of providing courts with useful solutions to sentencing problems is rarely discussed. When magistrates and judges are required to observe the principles of the prevalent sentencing framework, they also welcome the opportunity to do something positive about the circumstances of the individual offender, and especially about the factors that may have contributed to their offending. Even with a 'one size fits all' sentence like the community service order, sentencers express a hope that a work habit will be instilled, or skills learned, so that an offender will become more employable. The programme for women offenders was, from that perspective, one of a wide range developed for local courts to meet the sentencers' need for community-based provision relevant to the offenders they sentenced – thus programmes were developed for burglars, violent offenders, sex offenders, drink-drivers, and several other groups. We reasoned that, on the 'in-out line', the availability of a community sentence designed for that particular type of offender could tip the balance away from custody.

From the outset, and in line with the recommendations of HM Inspectorate of Probation (1991) it was agreed that the women's programme should be women-centred, and staffed only by women practitioners. Two staff with experience of working on men's programmes were designated to survey relevant provision elsewhere in the United Kingdom and design a programme for women. The programme they produced, with some further development especially as a result of being designated a pathfinder for the What Works initiative in 1998, has continued to run for nearly nine years.

Although women constitute half the population in the real world, in the world of criminal justice they are a small minority who pose little threat to public safety. The consequence is that the technology of criminal justice and penal sanctions is principally designed for men. Women's needs are identified *by comparison with those of men*. It is routine to see statistical analyses of the characteristics of women offenders set out alongside the equivalent information about male offenders, with the implication that, in order to meet their needs, provision for women can be adapted from that already available for men. During this early phase of developing the programme, the phrase 'through the men's window' was coined to express the pressure to view women offenders as a group to be compared with and treated like male offenders.

It seemed much more appropriate to develop provision relevant for women by looking 'through the women's window', that is by starting afresh and considering what kind of programme of supervision would be most likely to help women offenders to desist from offending. That would enable women offenders to be treated equally, by making available to the courts methods appropriate to women offenders. Applying sanctions designed for male offenders to a minority of women offenders is neither justice nor equality. It is likely to expose them to methods that are irrelevant to their needs, and unlikely therefore to be effective. Worse still, they may be expected to occupy a minority situation amongst men who are often deeply hostile to women, unable to relate to them other than as objects, and possibly serious abusers of women.

The introduction and development of the programme exposed those involved to challenges about the women-centred approach, challenges that took several forms:

• Why provide differently for women?
• Why provide separately for women?
• Why could male practitioners not work with women?

Over time those involved came to believe that these challenges were the product of deep-seated cultural attitudes towards women, and a good deal of determination and commitment to the value of a women-centred approach was needed in order to avoid being deflected.

Two elements encouraged continuation: the reactions of the women who participated in the programme, and the attitude of local courts. The feedback from women who had completed the programme was unusually enthusiastic, compared with comments normally received during such consumer surveys. The programme was described as 'life-changing', and all reactions were positive. Some, with previous experience of probation, reported that this was the first time they could recall supervision being relevant to their life and circumstances.

The willingness of local courts to use the programme, as a condition of a probation order, was welcome, but the differences in sentencing of men and women remained something of a puzzle, until the publication of an excellent study by Hedderman and Gelsthorpe (1997). This illustrated why it is particularly important to offer courts community sentences tailored to the needs of women offenders. A neat phrase is used to capture the way magistrates view the differences between male and female defendants: they see women offenders as 'more troubled than troublesome'.

Here are a few examples of differences perceived by magistrates, as reported in the study:

• perceived differences in motivation for offending
• women's offences seen as less reprehensible
• different sentences used to 'help' women compared with men
• the family is central to the sentencing of women
• the appearance of women usually favours them in court
• magistrates' tendency to deal differently with women is reinforced by a similar culture among court users

So courts are presented with a number of difficult dilemmas, when dealing with women offenders: the principles of sentencing require them to apply just deserts and to punish offenders, yet they view women differently, and their crimes often as less reprehensible. In England and Wales there are often no community-based sentences tailored to the needs of women, and if as a result women are required to undertake sentences designed for men, they will be a small minority receiving inappropriate provision. Sentencers may find this so unsatisfactory that they are discouraged from using a community sentence. Failure to acknowledge these dilemmas, and to provide courts with community sentences specifically for women, may contribute directly to the increasing size of the female prison population.

The publication of the Hedderman and Gelsthorpe (1997) study prompted a programme of presentations to local magistrates courts, about the findings of the study and about the groupwork programme. The aims were both to get sentencers to acknowledge and reduce any ambivalence about treating women differently, and to promote the women-centred programme. The reactions of magistrates to these presentations appeared to be very favourable.

The model of change

The groupwork programme established in 1993 was designed by staff with an open commission to find out what might be relevant to women, and what other programmes might offer. The evidence they accumulated about the needs of women offenders, supplemented in due course via consultancy and local research (Rumgay 1996), culminated in the development of a theory of offending by the kind of women most usually appearing before the courts. That theory was reflected in the design of the programme and subsequently, as a result of the demands of the programme accreditation process, was termed the model of change, explaining why the programme deals with and reduces offending behaviour.

The model explains offending by women as the product of:

- the breakdown of their ability to hold in balance (or manage) the demands upon them (deriving both from their position as women and from their specific circumstances)

- the external resources and legitimate opportunities available to them

- and their capacity/functioning (which is assumed in the model to be impaired usually as a result of their history and experiences).

In relation to demands, the programme aims are:

- to raise women participants' awareness of how these demands are constructed;

- to identify strategies for meeting them more effectively and constructively;

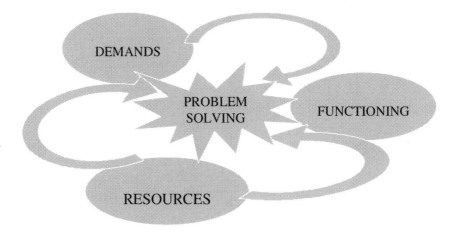

Figure 6.1   The Model of Change

- to acknowledge their power to manage demands upon them in legitimate ways.

In relation to resources, the aims are:

- to increase the capacity of participants to identify resources relevant to their needs and aspirations;
- to improve their ability to access and use those resources;
- to reverse the effects of earlier disadvantage, for example interrupted education or training.

In relation to function, the aims are:

- to increase participants' awareness and knowledge about problems of functioning;
- to reduce the effects of problems of functioning;
- to challenge beliefs that reduce their problem-solving capacity;
- to improve their self-esteem.

The relevance of the programme to the needs of women offenders was demonstrated by analysis of offending-related problems assessed by probation officers writing court reports and using the ACE (Assessment, Case management and Evaluation) system to locate such factors. In just under 200 such cases, these were rated as the top nine major or medium factors:

Finance	56%
Reasoning/thinking skills	56%
Stress management	55%
Responsibility, control	54%
Self-esteem	51%
Impulsiveness	50%
Personal relationships (all)	49%
Mental/emotional	48%
Drugs	45%

The close clustering of this range of factors, with quite similar levels, supports the view that an effective programme for women must be multi-modal, rather than a single mode programme, for example dealing only with thinking skills.

A similar analysis was undertaken more recently for the Probation Studies Unit (2001), and compares ACE scores from assessments on men and women in Hereford and Worcester. This analysis does not differentiate offending-related factors from others, and found higher levels of problems with employment, accommodation and health among women than among men. In other respects this analysis confirms the earlier findings but, in addition, found that women were more likely than men to accept responsibility for offending and to be concerned about the effect of their offending upon others, including victims.

Programme delivery

Some features of programme delivery are as important as the model of change itself, and in some instances equally controversial:

1. It is delivered in a safe, women only environment – i.e. all staff who work with women offenders are women, including staff from other agencies who assist with the programme. This recognises the high levels of victimisation and abuse at the hands of men that many participants disclose once they feel safe to do so. Once established, the importance of such an environment for effective work with women became clear. The detailed arrangements for participants (relating the timing to women's domestic responsibilities, provision of crèche, assistance with travel) and the content of the programme enabled practitioners to discover that women offenders, far from being more difficult or unreliable than male offenders, contributed considerable strengths to the process of supervision.
2. It can be delivered via closed groups, or one-to-one delivery. Group delivery is preferred, because women work well in groups. However, for those women who could not participate in a group, a one-to-one version is available.
3. In the local probation service, practitioners have been systematically trained in a number of techniques which support effective practice, and in particular in motivational work. This may help to explain the high attendance levels and completion rates, and the overall effectiveness of the programme.
4. It is supported by childcare facilities at the point of delivery, and by associated systems, e.g. communal lunch which provides an opportunity to model good diet, food preparation, managing children's meal arrangements, etc. These facilities in turn contribute to the group process, by encouraging bonding in the group in a way that

had not been anticipated, but that encouraged disclosure of important problems, and completion of the programme. The crèche worker can also assess any serious child health or care problems.

5. The model assumes women should wherever possible access community resources, so the programme is not treatment oriented. The expertise of the probation service is in relation to offending, and participants who need help with other issues are linked to agencies with relevant expertise. Some agencies participate directly in the programme, in order to explain provision to the participants, and encourage self-referral. The ideal is to deliver the programme within a separate women's centre, which is strongly linked to key agencies. Such a centre was established in Worcester from 1994 to 1997, and is about to be re-established with regional funding.

6. Participants are empowered, not pathologised. They often carry heavy responsibilities in difficult situations and with few resources to draw upon, and thus must have quite good levels of problem-solving capacity. Tests of problem-solving designed for male offenders were usually too basic, and a series designed for women has been adopted. The group is encouraged to be mutually supportive, drawing on the inherent capacity of women to work well in groups.

7. Consistent with treating participants as normal, capable people, the model of change is taught to them explicitly. They are introduced to it by the probation officer writing the report for court, who organises her information collection around the model. It is reintroduced in more detail at induction, and used to structure the programme sequencing and information exchanges between programme staff and supervising probation officers.

8. Links between the programme and outside agencies had the additional benefits of influencing the attitudes of those agencies towards women offenders, as well as enhancing their conceptions of how their provision might help women to be law-abiding in the future. The sequencing of the groupwork programme, which participants attend on one day per week for four hours (which includes a lunch break taken with those children of the participants who attend the crèche on the same premises) is shown in Figure 6.2.

Does it work?

The programme has now been running for over eight years, and attracts a completion rate of around 70%. Women who miss two of the 15 sessions are normally required to restart the programme, and many of them com-

1	Introductions	
2	Demands:	Women's issues
3		Why women offend (I)
4		Why women offend (II)
5		Relationships
6	Functioning:	Women's health
7		Assertiveness
8		Anger management
9		Stress management
10	Solving complex problems legitimately:	
		Doing it differently (I)
11		Doing it differently (II)
12	Community Resources:	
		Education, training and employment
13		Women and abuse
14		Substance misuse
15	Relapse Prevention:	
		Planning for the future

Figure 6.2 West Mercia programme for women offenders: sequencing of sessions

plete at their next attempt. Such a level of completion, especially considering the domestic pressures which many of the participants face, is itself a measure of the relevance of the programme to women offenders. In addition, consumer surveys usually reveal remarkable levels of enthusiasm from participants about the programme.

Although courts may include a special requirement in a probation order that women attend the programme, most have done so without such a special requirement. Courts use probation for women offenders, with or without the special requirement, very fully, and the number of women sent to custody by courts in Hereford and Worcester has remained very low since the programme was introduced. Women have also attended the programme following release from custody, sometimes after they had originally agreed to undertake it as an alternative to the prison sentence they actually served.

A rather crude evaluation done in 1998 showed that women who completed the programme were reconvicted at levels well below the rate predicted by use of the Offender Group Reconviction Score (OGRS1). This score uses static factors to predict the reconviction rate of groups of offenders with those factors. OGRS1 has since been revised, to become OGRS2.

A much more sophisticated evaluation, by the Probation Studies Unit at the University of Oxford (2000) as part of the pathfinder evaluation, looked at women who started and completed the programme over several years up to early 1999. The sample was therefore drawn before further improvements to the delivery of the programme of supervision and introduced in January 2000, as a result of the process of applying for accreditation. The outcomes shown in Figure 6.3 may therefore be capable of further improvement as a result of those changes, which integrated the entire process of supervision, from the collection of information for the pre-sentence report onwards, around the model of change. All women practitioners were fully trained in application of the model in their work with women offenders and referrals increased in line with the expectation that this was the intervention of choice for women under supervision.

Perhaps the most important aspect of the findings is the way the reconviction levels diverge over time. At six months, outcomes vary little, but after two years, women who served custodial sentences were reconvicted 14 percentage points more than those who completed the programme. This divergent effect will probably increase with longer follow up periods. With regard to individual sentence types: those who do not complete the programme do very much worse than those who do complete. Such failure to complete may have an adverse effect on self-

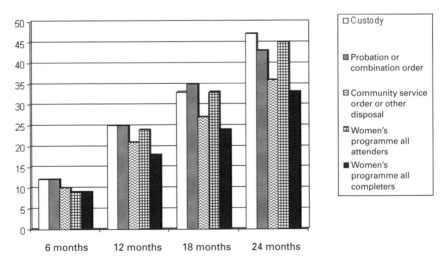

Figure 6.3   Proportion of 575 women offenders reconvicted over four time periods by the type of sentence, and attending or completing the women's programme

esteem. Secondly, women who complete community service do well in terms of lower reconvictions, too, and may be a lower risk group. That may be an indirect benefit of having a groupwork programme, that a larger proportion of women offenders have access to a sentence that is appropriate to them. Custody has the worst outcome. The poor outcomes for probation and combination orders where the programme was not used may very well be the result of a selection effect, with the best risks selected for the programme and community service. While that merits close attention with the aim of improving those outcomes too, the community-based sentences as a group still have better outcomes in terms of reconvictions than custody. This despite the fact that the custody group includes several women who undertook the programme following release and were not reconvicted in the follow up period.

Accreditation

In the context of the Home Office What Works initiative and the establishment of a joint prison/probation accreditation panel, the programme for women offenders was selected as one of two pathfinders in 1998.

Substantial work was undertaken to prepare the documentation for the application for accreditation, together with participation in the retrospective reconviction study described above. Not for the first time, the programme was refused accreditation, before the evaluation results had been reported. An earlier application to the Prison Service Accreditation Panel, to run the programme in a women's prison, had also been turned down.

Participating in the accreditation process brought some clear benefits for those involved in the programme. The requirement to describe the model of change and to specify in detail how the elements of the model were linked to offending and its prevention, resulted in a much clearer and better evidenced account of the programme. Key practitioners were gratified to discover how well the style and content of the programme were supported by the relevant literature. These benefits in turn considerably increased the confidence of those involved, to underpin the groupwork programme itself by embedding it in an integrated process of supervision, consistently based on the model of change. This integrated process of supervision, to which all women practitioners in the local service were inducted, went far beyond the requirements of the accreditation process.

The model was taught explicitly to programme participants, who appeared to use it with ease to organise their perceptions of their circumstances and experiences. A typology of cases was developed, from direct experience of working with women offenders, and used to illustrate the model and how it influenced different types of women. Use of the typology helped in turn to refine and test the model, as well as to illustrate it to various audiences.

Some of the requirements of the accreditation process were difficult or impossible to reconcile with the approach of the programme to women's offending. It proved very difficult to identify useful tests of intermediate forms of change, predictive of reduced offending. This problem was not unique to this particular programme, but had the added dimension that such tests were rarely designed with women in mind or validated for women participants. Ultimately, the SPSI-R (Social Problem-Solving Inventory/Revised), which is also used with accredited programmes for male offenders, was adopted and with the assistance of its designers, Chris and Art Nezu, a set of problem-solving tests has also been designed for work with women offenders and is now in use.

The main obstacle to accreditation appeared to relate to the requirement that accredited programmes deal primarily with cognitive-behavioural deficits which are effectively viewed as pathological. The women's programme by contrast is a multi-modal programme, which assumes a weakness or breakdown in capacity to meet demands, and which can be counteracted by a range of techniques very similar to those used in other programmes, but with an emphasis on empowerment, and on improving access to community resources. Alongside the general programme, an additional module dealing solely with offending behaviour was also designed, to meet the needs of the relatively small proportion of women offenders considered by local practitioners to have more substantial cognitive-behavioural problems. Given the dominance of forensic psychologists in the accreditation process, and the overwhelming preference for one particular approach to offending behaviour, the suspicion that programmes developed by probation officers were unlikely to be taken seriously by the panel was occasionally voiced. When Home Office officials stated, with apparent conviction, that it was preferable to offer women offenders programmes based on what was known to be effective (*sic*) with male offenders, than to pursue other options, we considered any reconciliation of views unlikely. [See also chapters 8 and 12. Ed.]

Such pronouncements may well be driven by the need to meet unrealistic targets set by the Home Office for tens of thousands of offenders to have completed accredited programmes by the end of 2003. This is possibly one of the most extreme examples of the counter-productive use of performance targets, inflicted on a service that has shown itself willing and able to rise to the challenge of performance targets for over ten years. The targets were set before any programme had been established long enough even to test the numerical feasibility of the target, let alone the usefulness of the programme in reducing offending.

It should be noted that there are as yet no published, peer-assessable results from any programme accredited by the current panel, and only one limited study showing a treatment effect from a prison-based programme. The results described earlier from the evaluation of the women's programme are therefore quite unusual, and the lack of interest in the reasons for these results calls into question the extent to which the Effective Practice Initiative is truly evidence-led.

Connecting women offenders with community resources

The importance of securing access to relevant community resources for offenders, as a key element in interventions designed to reduce offending, has long been recognised in probation work. In Hereford and Worcester the success of its earliest groupwork programme, the young offender project (Roberts 1987), was considered to be due in part at least to the emphasis placed on access to normal community resources, and to high quality outdoor pursuits facilities, alongside attention to basic skills. All subsequent programmes developed by the local service incorporated linkages to community resources, and in some cases were jointly developed and delivered with relevant agencies.

There was therefore a presumption in favour of such linkages when the programme for women offenders was designed and, as experience of their needs (as described earlier) began to accumulate, this came to occupy a central position in the model of change. Many participants had left school without qualifications, had typically acquired heavy domestic responsibilities without ever developing an employment record, and were isolated by poverty from real opportunities to change their situation. Family responsibilities were likely to determine their choices for some time to come, and their efforts were invested in coping on limited means. Older participants, whose children were no longer dependent, often appeared to find the transition to greater independence difficult, and were ill-equipped to make constructive choices about planning for their future. Younger and older women seemed to share a capacity to make things work, to deal with practical problems, a tendency to put up with whatever life threw at them, without seeking help. Some probation staff – women with successful careers – found this lack of aspiration disturbing, and noted in particular how exclusively the lives of many of the women were bound up with home/family and the care of others. The possibility of personal development, towards a future when childcare was no longer the central aim of their lives, was not a priority.

Locating the programme within a strong network of community resources relevant to the needs of women, and also in a safe environment for women, led naturally to the idea of the Asha Centre. A building leased between 1994 and 1997 offered scope to base other small key agencies alongside the probation staff responsible for the groupwork programme, such as a rape and sexual abuse counselling service. The building also contained a clothing store, a toy library service, a prayer room for Muslim women, and crèche and catering facilities. Vocational courses were provided by local colleges.

The Asha Centre lost its physical base when reductions in probation funding forced a rationalisation of premises in Worcester, but some key supporters of the concept established a charity (the Asha Trust) with the aim of developing a new base. Applications for funding to the Government Office for the West Midlands Region, under the Partnership Development Fund, were successful in attracting a small grant earlier in 2001, and a more substantial grant later that year, which will enable a new centre to be leased and staffed.

The committee set up by the Prison Reform Trust, and chaired by Professor Dorothy Wedderburn, to examine women's imprisonment, learned from evidence given by Dr Judith Rumgay about the aims and operation of the Asha Centre and the women's programme. A key recommendation of the Wedderburn Committee's report (Prison Reform Trust 2000) proposes the establishment of similar centres to promote diversion of women offenders from custody.

The new centre will again offer a base for small relevant organisations, space for workshops and seminars to introduce women to a range of community facilities and education and training opportunities, and a focal point for a range of services for disadvantaged and isolated women who are at risk of offending.

Conclusion

Feminism is the most revolutionary idea there has ever been. Equality for women demands a change in the human psyche more profound than anything Marx ever dreamed of.

(Polly Toynbee, *Guardian*, 19 Jan. 1987)

123

Others have described the Hereford and Worcester programme for women offenders as feminist, and those involved with running and managing the programme have routinely experienced the resistance, implicit in Polly Toynbee's comment, to the aims of the programme. We have preferred to describe it as women-centred, precisely to avoid the unproductive label of, and distracting debates about, feminism. We have, however, learned a great deal about attitudes to women and their position in society along the way, and those lessons have if anything increased our commitment to the women-centred approach. But the characteristics and eventual success of the programme, and the associated work with and support for other organisations with similar aims, have their origins in a concern for the relevance and effectiveness of provision for women, not in dogma. We sought to design and deliver provision that courts and women offenders found relevant, that a high proportion of participants completed satisfactorily, and that reduced their reconviction levels. Those are the criteria against which the programme should be judged.

Chapter 7

The Women at Risk programme

Sally Poteat

The Women at Risk programme is a comprehensive, community-based treatment alternative to prison, serving women in a four-county region of the State of North Carolina, in the United States of America. Women at Risk assists women to remain out of custody, to succeed on probation, and to recognise and change the self-destructive and abusive behaviours that brought them to the court's attention and the risk of imprisonment.

Issues leading to the need for the programme

The need for the Women at Risk programme grew out of several criminal justice policy changes over the last two decades that resulted in a rapidly growing women's population in state and federal prison facilities. The 'War on Drugs' and drug law enforcement led to the arrest and criminal conviction of increased numbers of women who were charged with buying and selling drugs, drug paraphernalia, or maintaining dwellings for the distribution of drugs. The plea bargain process reduced prison sentencing terms for many of the males arrested because they had information to share with prosecuting attorneys regarding the larger drug distribution networks. However, women typically did not have access to the same information and often faced longer sentences for less serious charges.

The second policy change affecting the numbers of women in prison, structured sentencing, grew out of the state's response to prison overcrowding and the threat of federal takeover of the state's prisons in the 1990s. In response to this threat, the State of North Carolina initiated a massive overhaul of its prison systems including the construction of new facilities designed to meet the growth in required bed space for inmates. Additionally, the State implemented a structured sentencing policy that mandated minimum sentencing requirements based on the offender's history and the current charges. Women now faced mandatory structured sentencing with no leeway given to judges and probation officers to consider individual needs and histories. It was not uncommon for a woman to be convicted of fraud and larceny charges and sentenced to active time in prison, without consideration of the offender's active sub-stance abuse and need for treatment underlying the presenting criminal behaviour.

The final trend impacting on criminal justice and social policies was the renewed demand on the part of lawmakers for both 'individual accountability' and for punishment. This demand was at the heart of initiatives such as structured sentencing and welfare reform. In both of these cases, women are being told to overcome huge obstacles and needs to meet the terms society established for them. However, community-based assistance in areas such as employment, housing, transportation and treatment needed to meet those terms and conditions is often not present. Consequently many women fail to meet the conditions established by the court and have their probation revoked.

The result of these policies is that women have become the fastest growing population nationally in prisons and in local jails. Between 1985 and 1995 the number of women in prisons and jails tripled from 40,500 to 113,100. At mid-year 1997, women accounted for 6.4% of all prisoners nationwide, up from 4.1% in 1980. The number of black women in custody increased by more than 800%. Seventy-five percent of the women incarcerated are serving sentences for non-violent offences or technical violations of probation. Two-thirds of the women incarcerated are mothers to dependent children. Fifty-four percent of the women nationally admit to active drug use at the time of imprisonment. More than 40% of the women nationally reported histories of physical or sexual abuse (Morash, Bynum and Koons 1998: 1).

Who are the women?

Jennifer is a typical Women at Risk client. Jennifer is 32 years old and lives with her boyfriend and six-month-old infant. She also has a twelve-year-old son who lives with her father. Jennifer is a high school graduate. However, Jennifer also has a history of physical abuse as a child and sexual abuse as a teenager. She has a history of drug addiction and involvement with the criminal justice system for worthless cheques and possession of drug paraphernalia. She is employed at a fast food restaurant and provides the primary income for her family. Her infant's father is disabled and unemployed.

Sixty percent of the clients in the Women at Risk programme are Caucasian, reflecting the racial composition in our geographic area, and are between the ages of 25 and 40. The majority of our clients did not complete a basic level of education and receive employment wages, usually in part-time service industries with no benefits such as health or life insurance. The majority also have between two and three dependent children. Eighty-one percent of the women served report a history of sexual abuse, physical abuse, and/or family domestic violence. An example would be Donna, who was molested between the ages of eight and 15 by her older brothers and currently has three children in the custody of the state.

Forty-two percent of the clients admit to a juvenile crime history. Many of the women have no support network in their family or community, having burned those bridges over the years or having families unable to provide needed support. Many of the Women at Risk clients are also likely to have physical health issues or neurological brain damage from drug use and lifestyles. An example here would be Diane, who is HIV positive and under a doctor's care for arthritis and ulcers. Diane has a long history of substance abuse with resulting diminished cognitive function.

The clients served by the Women at Risk programme have criminal offences that are typically drug charges or drug related. The largest number of offences include the possession of drugs and drug paraphernalia, motor vehicle offences such as driving while impaired or with licence revoked, fraud and forgery, probation violations usually resulting from dirty drug screens or technical violations, larceny, embezzlement and shoplifting, and soliciting and prostitution. Here, an example is Jamie who is 23 years old and a crack addict who began trading sex for cocaine at the age of 13. Jamie is a beautiful young woman who came to us after having been found under a bridge, cut repeatedly with a knife. Because of the extensive substance abuse damage to neurological functions, Jamie operates with core, survival brain functions and no long term reasoning skills.

The typical pattern for a woman involved in the criminal justice system goes something like this. The woman is convicted of a drug or drug related crime and, based on the structured sentencing guidelines, serves active prison time and/or receives time on probation. Because of the very limited treatment for substance abuse or physical/sexual abuse available for women in the corrections system, they do not receive the treatment and therapy needed to address the issues blocking successful completion of probation, skills development, or their ability to care for dependent children. With no access to a support network, the client fails to meet basic court requirements, typically resulting in dirty drug screens. The female offender returns to prison leaving her dependent children with family members and/or in state foster care. This is what happened to Kris, who had her probation revoked after failing three successive drug screens. While Kris had no new crimes, she was sent back to prison without any offer of drug treatment because her original charges were larceny and fraud. These were charges the court did not originally consider to be drug related, requiring drug treatment.

What was needed was a community-based solution, fostering long-term support networks. It needed to be treatment oriented and recognise both the impact of sexual/physical abuse and the recovery/relapse process in substance abuse treatment. Finally, any new response had to be cost effective compared with the minimum $20,000 US annual cost of custody per client plus the cost of child foster care.

Why do we focus on women with a gender specific programme? While male offenders also have a history of victimisation, they can usually physically grow out of it or have an easier time leaving the situation. Women tend to carry this pattern of victimisation from childhood into adult relationships and repeat the cycle with their own children. Women also tend to be more dependent on social systems and community, defined by relationships and interpersonal support. When a support network no longer exists, or was never there, women have a rougher time functioning. Finally, comprehensive, multi-faceted needs must be met concurrently for women to successfully meet the terms of probation or social service plans. The ability to meet probation and restitution requirements and be located by a probation officer is dependent on stable, affordable housing, employment, skills development, treatment, transportation and child care. Any one need left unmet is a major obstacle to successful completion of probation.

What is the Women at Risk programme?

The Women at Risk programme is a gender specific, community-based treatment programme designed to serve women who are considered 'at risk'. At risk behaviours may be related but not limited to criminal behaviour, family violence, substance abuse, histories of child abuse and neglect, and participation in family preservation programmes including possible removal of children from the home. Women at Risk is the community-based portion of a continuum of treatment services for female offenders and works as the treatment component of broader probation or social service plans. The programme works to reduce recidivism among female offenders, as well as the need to imprison them, by providing a treatment alternative to prison. Additionally, the programme offers intervention services to those women exhibiting 'at risk' behaviours typical of female offenders but who have not yet penetrated the judicial system.

The programme includes three major components. The first component is a 16-week group therapy component led by two masters' level clinical therapists with additional individual counselling as needed. The second component, case management, assists clients in developing the skills and support network they need to meet probation and social services requirements. Court advocacy, the third component, helps clients understand the legal process, the implications of decisions, and provides a supportive presence in court.

The programme serves four counties in western North Carolina. The community-based model was started in the early 1990s in Asheville, North Carolina by Ellen Clarke, executive director of Western Carolinians for Criminal Justice, an independent nonprofit criminal justice agency serving that area. The Asheville programme grew out of a prison-based treatment model developed by Dr. Faye Sultan, who worked with a group of long-term sentenced women at North Carolina Women's Prison who were convicted of murder. Dr. Sultan's work at North Carolina Women's Prison provided additional support for the growing body of knowledge linking histories of physical/sexual abuse with crime. Dr. Sultan used a group treatment approach combining group intervention and psychodidactic components designed to assist individuals sharing similar histories or difficult situations. Western Carolinians for Criminal Justice worked with Dr. Sultan to refine the treatment model for use in a community-based treatment programme, adding case management and court advocacy components.

The programme was expanded in 1997 to include the three-county judicial district served by Repay, Inc., another independent nonprofit criminal justice agency. Women at Risk is the only community-based comprehensive treatment alternative to prison in the State of North Carolina that is specific to the needs of female offenders. The programme provides a safe haven or sanctuary for women, allowing them to tell their stories, be heard, and have safe space to work on changes in their lives. Since 1997, the two agencies have opened 379 cases, and graduated or assisted 316 clients in making successful progress. Only 39 women have returned to custody in that time period, or ten percent of the cases opened. In comparison, the State's recidivism rate for community level offenders is 40% and jumps to 80% for intensive level probationers.

Additionally, in the last three years, the programme has expanded to serve women involved in civil court who were at risk of losing parental rights in family preservation proceedings. These clients exhibit the same behaviours as criminal court clients. Additionally, for many women, the loss of children is often the final step to removing barriers to behaviours penetrating the criminal court system. In 2001, the Women at Risk programme started two juvenile components. One component operated by Repay, Inc., called Just Girls, serves juvenile girls referred by the courts, school systems, parents, and child serving agencies with an early intervention programme. The juvenile component operated by Western Carolinians for Criminal Justice provides an adolescent therapy group for girls aged 16 to 19 who are facing prison sentences.

How does the programme work?

A woman can be referred to the programme through the judicial system network, other agencies, peers, and by self-referral. At intake, a psychosocial history is completed in addition to a mental health and substance abuse evaluation. Information may also be obtained from the Level of Service Inventory Revised tool developed for offender populations. Releases of information are signed for key collaborating agencies or relevant prior treatment providers. A full mental health assessment may be completed as needed. Intakes may be completed in the office, home, jail, other agencies or at residential treatment facilities.

Based on the woman's needs, the case manager will start working with the client on stabilisation issues such as housing, employment and substance abuse treatment, and the woman will be started into the group therapeutic process. If the client is not ready for group, she may be referred to individual counselling or a residential treatment programme. The groups are led by two masters' level clinicians and open once a month to receive new members. Case management is clinically directed. That is, the case manager's approach will vary from client to client based on the clinical needs of that client. It is very rare that a woman would not be accepted into the Women at Risk programme. A woman with diagnosis, behaviours or issues blocking the group process such as active multiple personalities, violent behaviour in the group or active substance abuse is not accepted until the behaviours can be controlled.

The case manager also reviews the probation plan and/or social services family preservation plan with the client, often times acting as a bridge between the client and multiple agencies to help form a common consensus on priorities. The case manager helps the client understand the terms and conditions of the plans and determines specific areas in which the client may need assistance to be successful.

The therapists and case manager maintain attendance records and group notes. Referring agencies receive a written monthly report as to the client's attendance and whether the client is making successful progress or not. Interim contacts provide coordination for the case manager and referring agent. As the client's case progresses in court, the case manager and court advocate provide a supportive presence, helping the client understand the legal process and the implications for her life.

The duration of services and contacts averages 18 months. Clients often have multiple starts before they successfully enter into the programme. Clients can also come back to the programme after they have completed activities. If a client feels that her life is becoming unstable and she needs help, she can always come back to the group with a minimum four-week expectation of attendance.

Terry's story

Terry is a 38-year-old African American woman who has been a Women at Risk client since March 2000. Terry has three children. Her eight-year-old son lives with her in a transitional housing programme. Her daughters, ages 20 and 24, are living with their grandmother. Terry frankly admits that she is a crack cocaine addict. She states that she had been using cocaine for over twelve years and using crack cocaine daily for the six months prior to entering Women at Risk. Because of her involvement with the criminal justice system and her addiction to cocaine, Terry had been unable to raise her daughters and voluntarily gave them to their grandmother for adoption. Terry's work record has been understandably sporadic. Before she made a decision to seek help, Terry was living with her son Fred in a motel known to be a thinly disguised 'crack house'. She states, 'I made a decision to change one day when I saw my son sitting on a box in that filthy place. I really want his life and my life to be better than that.'

Since she entered transitional housing, substance abuse treatment, and Women at Risk, Terry has made profound changes in her life. She has maintained sobriety and attends Narcotics Anonymous meetings on a daily basis. Terry has been working for five months in the furniture industry and is making enough money to support herself and her son.

Recently a service organisation assisted her in obtaining a restored automobile. For the first time Terry can drive herself to work! She is adhering to all the requirements of probation and is proud of the fact that she has paid back over $1,000 US which is all of the restitution owed for her past crimes.

Terry says that attending Women at Risk has provided her with the opportunity to look at her past history of abuse and addiction and move beyond that disabling history. She admits, 'I was never able to trust women in the past. I always felt they were my competition, not my friends.' Terry credits Women at Risk with making her conscious of the dysfunctional ways she was relating to her son, Fred. 'I never realised that I was just handing down that meanness just like my parents were mean to me. I want to stop that meanness before it becomes a part of my son.'

Shasta's story

In October 1999 Shasta was homeless, living on the streets and addicted to crack cocaine. Just six months earlier she served a month in jail because she had written a series of worthless cheques. A month later she was back in jail for soliciting on the streets. On both occasions she was supporting her drug habit. Shasta gave birth to a baby girl three months after her release from jail. When both mother and daughter tested positive for cocaine, the local department of social services stepped in and removed the baby from Shasta's custody. 'I feel so guilty', she states. 'I didn't know how much my cocaine use affected my daughter and I just couldn't stop.'

Following the advice of her social worker, Shasta entered the Women at Risk programme, went through a drug detoxification facility and began attending Narcotics Anonymous meetings. Shasta stated that Women at Risk group meetings helped her to look at her history and deal with the shame, anger and guilt she felt. As a result of her insight, Shasta decided that she was going to stop the cycle of drug abuse, physical abuse, and sexual abuse that had prevailed in her family. She was going to make her life different.

Shasta is now a graduate of Women at Risk. She has been grateful to learn that her daughter is developing normally. Shasta has remained sober for over one year and has not reoffended. With the support of her Women at Risk case manager, Shasta has located employment and is searching for an apartment suitable for herself and her daughter. Shasta knows she is still 'at risk' but she maintains telephone contact with Women at Risk and knows that she can return to the programme if problems arise.

How effectiveness is measured

Programme effectiveness is measured in a variety of ways. The first measurement yardstick is the recidivism rate of programme graduates versus those clients who did not successfully complete the programme. On 1 July 2000, Women at Risk conducted record checks on 95 programme graduates over a three-year period (from 7/1/97–6/30/00) and found that only six graduates had their probation revoked and an active sentence imposed. However, similar record checks on 167 unsuccessful programme terminations from that same time period indicated that 39 terminations violated probation and were serving an active sentence of at least one year. Women at Risk graduates are more than six times less likely to recidivate and serve active time upon successful completion of the program. Of total cases opened in the past three years, there was a ten percent rate of return to prison, and four percent for the past ten year period, compared to the 40-80% rates for similar probationers not enrolled in the programme.

Women at Risk also evaluates programme effectiveness in terms of stewardship of the public dollar. That is, how cost effectively is the programme able to develop and deliver services to our target population? And how do those programme costs compare with incarceration? On both levels, the Women at Risk programme is a bargain and a good example of a public-private partnership that works. Based on the year 2001 figures, the programme offers the following cost comparisons:

Annual cost per successful client with regular probation: $3,070
Annual cost per successful client with electronic house arrest: $4,719
Annual cost per successful client with intensive probation: $6,844
Annual cost of minimum custody confinement per inmate: $19,279
Average State cost of all adult confined custody types: $28,000

The community-based nature of the programme allows it to identify larger numbers of at-risk women and network them into treatment paths and community support at a higher rate.

Finally, the programme is evaluated by its ability to be replicated. The programme has standard operating procedures and programme components. Critical core staff positions have been identified over the tenure of the programme. Women at Risk also shows the same positive results in both urban and rural settings.

What makes the programme work?

A variety of factors come together to make the programme work for the clients involved. The programme design is flexible. [See also chapter 8. Ed.] It is not set in concrete. The design of programme services has evolved flexibly over the last ten years to grow and expand with additional information and with additional funding sources. The programme design has incorporated material from two National Institute of Corrections evaluations as well as client needs and outcomes.

The programme is multi-dimensional and deals with women's unique issues. The Women at Risk programme keeps victimisation and abuse related issues at the centre of programme planning, including topics such as self-esteem, relationships, physical health, sobriety, sexuality, mental health, pregnancy and parenting, decision-making skills, trauma from physical, sexual and emotional abuse, cultural awareness and sensitivity, and spirituality. The Women at Risk staff have a variety of backgrounds. Female staff bring skills from social work, mental health, substance abuse, public administration, education, anthropology, ministry, psychology, and personal history. This variety of skills and backgrounds fosters a multi-dimensional or multi-faceted approach to service delivery. The programme also works collaboratively with other agencies. When Women at Risk staff cannot deliver the services listed above, other providers such as psychiatric services, medical professionals and sub-stance abuse counsellors are formally attached to the programme.

The Women at Risk programme fosters the sense of relationship through the provision of sanctuary and the structure of service delivery. The tone and physical settings of the programme's offices provide a sense of sanctuary, safety, space to be heard, time for the telling and the hearing. The programme provides individualised clinical services and case management planning with the benefits of peer interaction in the group settings. Staff meet women 'where they are' both in the context of physical location and need. Staff may work with clients individually for months as they exit confinement or access individual substance abuse or psychological treatment prior to entering the Women at Risk group. The group provides the benefit of peer interaction. Staff then follow-up with clients as they complete their court process or need to touch base for support. The programme also provides transportation and childcare to promote accessibility to services.

The Women at Risk programme is designed to link the client with the community and foster the development of community-based support networks. Women at Risk is not a residential programme, nor is it a day reporting centre. The clients learn about community resources and how to access those resources effectively, increasing opportunities for long-term success.

The programme is linked with both the judicial system and social service providers. Referrals come from judges, probation officers, attorneys, jails, sentencing services staff, social workers, prison post-release planning, substance abuse treatment providers, and women's shelters. The programme is recognised and accepted as an effective part of the continuum of treatment services for female offenders.

Finally, programme funding is stable, or as stable as it can be in the nonprofit service sector. The programme started with soft money, grants and donations, limiting the core services that could be provided. In the late 1990s the North Carolina State Legislature significantly increased its support of the programme and currently funds 80% of the cost of service delivery, leaving only 20% of the funds to be raised from local donations and grants. The financial stability has provided stability within the organisations for programme service delivery and staff retention.

Who are the women who recidivate?

The Women at Risk programme is not successful with all women. Not everyone entering the programme is successful. Who are those who fail and what are the basic reasons for lack of success with Women at Risk? A review of case histories from the case files indicated that there are four primary reasons for unsuccessful termination. The first and primary reason for lack of success is substance abuse relapse and denial of a substance abuse problem. The second reason is client denial of the seriousness of the situation, a problem particularly apparent in cases of younger women. Lack of basic needs such as work, childcare or transportation can also block a client's ability to participate successfully in any treatment programme. Finally, a client's continuing involvement with negative male influences resulting in victimisation and substance abuse cycles will block successful completion of the programme.

Jamie's profile was presented earlier in this chapter. Jamie is a 23-year-old crack addict who had been severely injured while on the streets. Programme staff found Jamie a placement in a community-based transitional housing programme for recovering addicts until a bed in a residential treatment facility became available. Jamie told us earlier, 'I don't know if I can do this [stay clean and sober]. I want to, but every time I get out of jail my first thought is to get back on crack.' And that is exactly what Jamie did within 48 hours of placement in the transitional housing programme.

Overcoming difficulties in starting a community-based programme

There are four key elements for any successful community-based programme. The first element is that local correctional personnel and social service providers must accept the programme. Their buy-in to treatment as a part of the continuum of approaches to offenders is critical. Second, adequate and stable funding must be in place to secure and retain needed personnel. The Women at Risk programme is staff intensive and requires trained professionals in all of its programme components. Removing one of the components, or not having clinical oversight of programme components, will reduce the effectiveness of the programme. The high staff cost of this programme can be mitigated by the third element, which is to review the existing resources in your area in order to identify the most appropriate organisation for programme placement. An agency or organisation may have a portion of the staff or programme components in place, requiring a smaller investment in funds for programme start-up.

Finally, it is important to stop and identify the desired outcomes for the programme before it is started so resource allocation and measurement of outcomes can be coordinated from the beginning. While the Women at Risk programme uses recidivism as its primary outcome measure, there are other secondary outcomes that are tracked over time. These outcomes include the number of new, but reduced, charges for clients. A client may reoffend, but is the new charge of less weight than the original charges? The programme also tracks the numbers of women entering into more appropriate treatment, i.e. residential substance abuse or mental health treatment. Programme staff also evaluate the increased level of client knowledge about community resources and their ability to access those resources without staff assistance. Staff members track the number of contacts with women in local jails and the support and referral assistance for those women. The final outcome is the ability of the programme to break the inter-generational pattern of abuse and crime. What is happening with the teenage daughters of the women we serve? Are they involved in at risk behaviours or with juvenile court? Is the treatment and growth that the mother is receiving having a positive impact on the daughter?

Conclusion

The Women at Risk programme is a proven, successful, cost effective, community-based treatment alternative to custody for many women in our society. The programme also serves as a model of prevention for juvenile girls and for those adult women whose behaviours have not yet penetrated the criminal court system.

Chapter 8

Women's imprisonment: cross-national lessons

Pat Carlen

Despite the widespread international concern to develop and co-ordinate policies which might either slow down the rate of women's imprisonment or engender flexible custodial and non-custodial 'interventions'[1] successful in reducing the damaging time spent in custody, a recurring problem in several jurisdictions has been to develop effective projects which survive more than a year or two. The main reasons for individual project close-down (or change of role) are usually financial, though funding problems may sometimes mask a range of shortcomings (for example, change of objectives, poor or adverse publicity, loss of gender-specificity, non-use by the courts (see also chapter 6 this volume), and inappropriate expectations and/or evaluations by funders), for all of which reduced finance is only the presenting symptom.

Mindful of the short-lived nature of so many innovative criminal justice projects, one of the objectives of the author's cross-national research conducted during 2000–2001 was to investigate projects for female offenders which, while remaining true to gender-specific and reductionist objectives, continued to thrive two years (at least) from their inception. In interview, however, respondents, as well as talking about the operative features of their on-going projects, also wanted to talk about the more fundamental economic, ideological and political barriers to prison reform, barriers which they had had to confront daily. Many, indeed, are discussed in other chapters of this book (see chapters 1, 2, 9, 11, in particular). None the less, some of the less benign conditions in which the projects were operating will have to be considered also in this chapter, especially those quantitative and positivistic project evaluations which in several jurisdictions are frequently seen not only as being inappropriate, but also as being inimical to the effectiveness of projects, programmes and regimes addressing not only crime but also the social and psychological causes of crime.

The rest of the chapter is divided into five parts: lesson-drawing in penal justice; cross-national lessons for gender-specific projects; cross-national issues for gender-specific projects; exemplary lessons in gender-specific penality; and, fundamental lessons about the logic and legitimacy of penal incarceration and its alternatives.

Lesson-drawing in penal justice

According to Richard Rose (1993:27) the '[t]he process of drawing a lesson involves four analytically distinct stages': the search for satisfactory programmes; abstraction of a cause and effect model; creation of a lesson; and a prospective evaluation of the likely consequences of applying the lesson elsewhere in the future. Two problems[2] immediately arise for the researcher aspiring to draw lessons in penal justice, and both of them are definitional. First, there is the problem of what is meant by 'lesson'; and secondly there is the problem of 'what works?'

Richard Rose (1993:30) recognises that there are several alternative ways of drawing a lesson, and the methods chosen in the research reported here are closest to being an amalgam of what Rose calls 'synthesis' and 'inspiration'. Once projects had been chosen on the grounds that they had survived without compromising their foundational principles, they were then investigated so that their shared characteristics and operating conditions might be noted and their relationship to the effectiveness of the project discussed. But how were the projects chosen?

There may be areas of social policy where it is easier to talk about 'What works' than it is in relation to crime. But in the area of penal policy, it is notoriously difficult to get agreement as to the nature of the problem to be addressed, let alone the best ways of addressing 'it' and then assessing 'what works'. The 'hard evidence' preferred by governments would demonstrate a positive relationship between intervention and a reduction in recidivism, and though (given the financial incentives to produce it) such 'hard evidence' might appear to be forthcoming in relation to participants in a particular project, without detailed knowledge of the selection and characteristics of project members, together with information about the other influences on them at a particular time, it is usually difficult (if not impossible) to isolate any one factor as being solely responsible for any individual's desistance from crime – even if such a complex phenomenon were actually to be amenable to sensible assessment in the short-term. (See Carter *et al* 1992 discussed below.)

The favoured official modes for assessing project success often muddy the waters still further, especially when demands for quantitative assessments of policy 'successes' or 'failures' are being made in situations where such quantitative measures are either impossible to produce in any meaningful form or where they are simply inappropriate. For example, analysis of the anti-suicide policy at Cornton Vale women's prison in Scotland (Carlen 2001a) suggested that paper and other routine organisational outputs told nothing about either the quality, or the relative importance, of quantitatively audited activities in reducing the number of suicides in a prison. For example, does a 'near miss' (i.e. a 'prevented' suicide) indicate that the anti-suicide programme is a failure insofar as it is still not preventing suicidal despair? Or does it, rather, indicate a success insofar as a potential death has been averted?

Similarly, and in the same context, because of the small numbers and complex issues involved, it would be impossible for anyone ever to know to what extent a new culture and programme of care at Cornton Vale may have reduced the propensity of individual women to take (or wish to take) their own lives. For, in addition to compliance with base-line procedural performance indicators, the committed staff had to work in uncharted and more demanding areas according to principles relating to the humane but individualised treatment of women at risk of suicidal despair. Overall, the aim was to achieve quality of prison life rather than a tally of the 'reformed' or a justificatory procedural 'cover' for the institution.

With such definitional difficulties inherent in the research subject matter, the researcher decided to identify innovative projects in several jurisdictions and ask their leaders what, in their opinion, were the conditions conducive to running innovative, holistic and gender-specific programmes for women lawbreakers which might reduce their offending and increase their social options. The following innovative projects/ programmes/regimes/units were subsequently identified: Cornton Vale's anti-suicide regime in Scotland; the Prison Service's Women's Policy Group and the Hereford and Worcester Probation Service's Programme for Women Offenders, both in England (see chapter 6); the Women's Unit of the Hampden County Correctional Centre (see chapter 5) and Hart House, Tewkesbury, both in Massachusetts, USA; the Women at Risk Programme in North Carolina, USA (see chapter 7); the Israeli Rehabilitation of Prisoners Authority's employment unit for female ex-prisoners and hostel for ex-prisoner mothers and their babies in Jerusalem; and in New South Wales, Australia, the Parramatta

Transitional Prison, the Mother and Baby Programme and the Drugs Court.

The lessons I hoped to learn were: first, whether it was possible to identify any operational principles common to gender-specific interventions which survive; secondly, whether there were operational concerns common to all or a majority of them; thirdly, whether there were any schemes which could be described as exemplars of innovation; fourthly, what, if any, more fundamental or global criminal justice issues were troubling practitioners across jurisdictions, and, finally, what was the significance of these issues for future responses to women in trouble with the law?

Cross-national lessons for gender-specific interventions[3]

Interviews with the managers of a range of custodial and non-custodial gender-specific projects in US, UK, Scotland, Australia and Israel, suggested that in order to manage effective survival without loss of identity, integrity and effectiveness, gender-specific criminal justice projects for women should (ideally) have in common at least the seven operational principles outlined below.

1. Evolutionary and flexible organisation

All respondents were of the opinion that projects should constantly monitor the appropriateness of project provision to the varied or constantly changing situations of women actually attending the project at a particular time. Furthermore, they argued that organisational needs (such as maintaining credibility through compliance with inappropriate evaluative standards or rigid adherence to foundational structures), should (ideally) come second to participants' requirements, thereby ensuring that the form and structure of the organisation is appropriate to delivery of services tailored to those whom it was set up to serve (see also chapter 6).

2. Democratic ownership of innovation

The nurturing of staff identification with organisational goals was mentioned in varying types of project, and was seen to be especially important in custodial settings where disciplinary staff (guards) frequently feel excluded from the more innovative types of decision-making. A democratic mode of policy-formation was seen to be an essential prerequisite to high staff morale which, in turn, was seen to be essential for the success of project innovation and survival (see also chapter 5).

3. Holism – in relation to interagency working, women's requirements and the spatial proximity of multi-agency provison

An holistic approach to service delivery was seen as being desirable in both custodial and non-custodial settings, with successful inter-agency or multi-agency communication a priority. In custodial settings the stress was on building effective working relationships with agencies in the community, but always under the auspices of the holistic non-essentialising approach that sees project participants not as 'female offenders' but as 'women who break the law'. Relatedly, several of the most impressive project-managers pointed to the geographical clustering of multi-agency services as being integral to the success of their service delivery – in terms of ease of access for the women, and minimisation of both inter-professional distrust and accidental mutual subversion of one anothers' endeavours by agencies sharing the same clients. (But see chapters 11 and 12 for discussion of the uses and potential abuses of the 'holism' slogan.)

4. Insistence on a realistic approach to drugs rehabilitation

An insistence on sponsor or funder recognition of the realities of drugs rehabilitation was common to all projects. Although project workers were generally prepared to require project participants to be drug-free, they almost always insisted on giving relapsed participants 'as many chances as it took'. (This, however, resulted in the necessity of them calling for, and devising, much more sensitive and complex 'accountability' evaluations (see 'Cross-national issues' below.)

5. Resistance to the erosion of gender-specificity

Because of the relatively small numbers of females eligible to take part in some women-only non-custodial projects, there was often pressure to extend the facilities to men. This pressure was felt particularly in smaller jurisdictions where it was feared that spare capacity might result in loss of funding. However, there was general agreement that facilities for women had to be ring-fenced as such. Shared-site provision (however arranged) tends either to be under-used or (subsequent to its under-use) re-roled as a male-only facility. This is because women's histories of male physical and sexual abuse make them reluctant to put themselves at risk of male violence or harassment in mixed projects.

Similarly, workers insisted that programmes developed in other countries or for men (such as cognitive skills acquisition) were not to be parachuted into projects as prisoner-processing packages with a universal application; instead, they were to be gender-assessed and adapted to the very specific histories and attributes of the actual women currently attending the project.

6. *Vision based on explicit principles of how humans should be treated*

Despite the prevalent claim that a main concern was crime-reduction, all project leaders admitted to a more fundamental driving-force – a vision of how all human beings (including lawbreakers) should be treated. At the most fundamental level, therefore, they often saw the secret of a project's relative longevity as being dependent upon their continuing success at convincing courts, public, crime victims and criminal justice professionals of a congruity of interest in reducing the chances of project participants being in trouble again in the future, by improving the quality of their lives in the present. This commitment to leadership and vision usually led to the development of strong public relations policies.

7. *Excellent public relations*

The importance of 'educating the public, policy-makers and the courts' was taken seriously by all interviewees. Larger agencies employed specialist public relations officers, but innovative project directors – for example, sheriffs (in US), a prison governor (Scotland), Rehabilitation Authority officials (Israel), and drugs court officials and Transitional Prison Superintendent in Australia – all welcomed opportunities to address public fears about offending behaviours, project/programme risk, and to spread word about both the low risk presented by the majority of women who come before the courts and the often incredibly complex and gender-specific social and health issues which require address if the risk of the re-offending by project participants is to be reduced.

Cross-national issues for gender-specific interventions

In addition to the agreed survival strategies described above, there was discussion of three other survival strategies, around which there was much more ambivalence or unease. Two were mentioned again and again, whilst the third (discussed first below) was raised by this author.

Employment of ex-offenders or ex-drug users

All of the non-custodial projects visited cited the employment or other involvement of former drug users or lawbreakers as an organisational strength and, in some cases, as being in fulfilment of a funding stipulation. Yet, none of the projects had developed education, training or career plans for these 'non-professional' and non-salaried or low-paid helpers. However, as a result of conversations on this very issue with many ex-lawbreakers, I have two difficulties with the prevalent ideology that the employment of ex-offenders in rehabilitation projects is unambiguously to the benefit of all involved – though there is no doubt that, as the organisers claim, the projects *are* usually the beneficiaries of such authoritative, committed and cheap assistance.

First, although it is often claimed that the employment of ex-clients can confer a certain legitimacy on an organisation's claims to therapeutic authority, many drug users are initially wary of going to projects where some of the staff are ex-users, or, in the case of ex-prisoners, of living in hostels partly staffed by people who, they think, have been in much worse trouble than themselves.

The more serious issue, however, is whether it is desirable for rehabilitated ex-prisoners or drug-users to be encouraged to embrace the 'ex-offender' role, and most seriously of all, whether the goodwill and experience of those who have suffered multiple disadvantage should be exploited (outside a proper career and salary structure) in the service of professional counsellors and state officials. In raising this question, I am well aware that some of the most successful non-custodial projects for female offenders owe their existence and persistence to the vision and commitment of people who themselves were once addicts or prisoners. These visionary leaders, however, are exceptional and, even at the same time as exploiting it to benefit others, usually rise above the label 'ex-prisoner'. However, even in their case, there is no doubt that they should (but seldom do) receive proper recompense and recognition for their labours.

Protection by an umbrella organisation?

A majority of interviewees ruminated on the age-old question of the merits and demerits of charismatic leadership versus organisational stability. Most (whether part of a larger organisation or not) eventually concluded that their own projects would not have lasted so long had they not been blessed with some very strong campaigning leadership during the first few years when the necessity to establish the need for gender-specific women's projects was a recurring challenge. However, those who were part of a larger organisation also claimed that, *because the leadership of the parent organisation had been supportive in principle*, belonging to it had offered them a measure of protection against critics and funding problems.

A minority of the respondents cited their favourable position as part of larger service providers or members of an umbrella organisation as a main reason for their survival. However, when, at the same time they were part of an organisation (for example, a mixed prison site) where males were also catered for, they were continually having to fight for recognition of women's different requirements (see chapter 5).

All respondents, however, while pointing to the twofold need for committed, strong and innovative leadership *and* stability of established organisational structure, recognised that there were inevitable tensions between the two. It was therefore in order to cherish innovation, avoid organisational stagnation and protect leaders from burn-out, that there was a general insistence on the development of the evolutionary and democratic structures described above. None the less, it seemed to the researcher that, in every country visited, the most common threat to gender-specific projects in the early stages of their development was posed by the overlong hours worked by project leaders driven to deliver a holistic and very demanding service outside of any effective official recognition that the social, economic and health burdens of women in trouble with the law are, at the present time, usually much more complex than those of males.

Accountability, measurement or quality?

A constant issue for the project leaders and staff centred on the terms in which they should or could adequately account for their work, in such a way as to satisfy employers and/or funders that they were getting value for money. All recognised the moral obligation and practical necessity (in terms of project-survival) to be accountable for the money spent, yet all, without exception, felt that their funders/employers entertained un-realistic or inappropriate expectations of the job to be done and how it could be adequately assessed.

Funders' (including the general public's) *unrealistic* expectations were the easiest to deal with, and could gradually be changed in the appropriate direction by increase of information about the histories and experiences of the project-clients and the difficulties of rehabilitating women with a myriad of social and economic difficulties.

Expectations which project-workers thought to be *inappropriate* were generally related to notions that the quality of their work was amenable to quantitative measurement. However, because such expectations resulted in the annual reporting requirements primarily being comprised of measurements of output and performance upon which, in turn, the continuation of their funding/existence depended, they also exercised the minds and ingenuity of project leaders a great deal.

In their book *How Organizations Measure Success*, Carter *et al* (1992:14) point out that it is usually impossible to measure the impact on society of specific social policies for three main reasons: the problem of multiple objectives; the difficulties of specifying and understanding the relationships between intermediate outputs and output measures; and the inevitable time lag between input and impact, especially in programmes 'where the benefits only become fully apparent over decades'. Attempts to measure the outputs of many rehabilitation projects for women fall foul of all three strictures, while paper and other routine organisational outputs tell nothing about either the quality, or the relative importance, of their audited activities in reducing recidivism in the future or of improving the quality of life of project participants and their children (the latter, it was widely implied, being a good in itself).

Project leaders, however, had to meet the challenge of presenting their work in measurable form – and they did. The most favoured method was to compare the cost of custodial and non-custodial programmes for women, with especial emphasis on the hidden costs relating to childcare when a woman goes to gaol. The second method, especially popular with project leaders running innovative (and maybe comparatively costly) projects in custodial (or semi-custodial) settings, was to develop indicators demonstrating project members' increased 'accountability', 'self-knowledge' etc. – all put forward as factors conducive to reducing risk to the community in the future.

A third approach, however, took the line that it was necessary to be much more entrepreneurial about the type of assessment criteria thought to be relevant, and these more critical strategists set out to develop qualitative indices of (variously): the necessary conditions for maintaining client services; organisational strength in terms of staff recruitment, retention and qualifications; strength of community support in terms of relationships/interactions with other organisations, (especially the media and the formal criminal justice system), range of visitors, citations (academic and other); evidence of innovatory *qualitative* capacity – for example, the ability to meet the changing needs of clients and the criminal justice system; *qualitative* annual growth factors (already assessed numerically but now to be assessed in terms of *increased quality of service)* for example, more productive time spent with clients; and developed arguments about the amelioration of client need and community risk (though with an insistence that, although sometimes related, they are not same thing). In chapter 12 there is a discussion of the dangers of this approach. Readers will, however, already suspect that such strategies to meet funders' evaluation requirements may well be at odds with the first principle enunciated above – that of prioritising the needs of the women in the projects over organisational needs.

The limits to the quantification of qualitative measures, however, became most apparent when projects were explicitly committed to making, and sustaining, qualitative changes not amenable to measurement, and when the assessment of (at least some of) the success of those changes called for moral rather than quantitative evaluations. Many project workers expressed the view that when they are faced with women on the edge of despair or even death, one prerequisite for the preservation of life and the maintenance of staff morale is official recognition that, not only in life and death situations, but also in many of the other emotionally-draining experiences characteristic of work with women in trouble with the law, qualitative inputs are called-for, the value of which are not amenable to measurement as *performances*; and, moreover, that time-consuming but life-supporting responses (*inputs*) involving listening, kindness and comfort, together with other *non-programmable* therapies may be *good in themselves*. (See Carlen 2001a and chapter 12 of this volume.)

Exemplary lessons

Drugs court (or women's court?)

As part of the cross-national research programme I visited the New South Wales (NSW) Drugs Court which is for both male and female offenders.[4] It has four fundamental aspects (treatment, social support and the development of living skills, regular reports to the court and regular urine testing). It is a model which I think could be well-adapted to women offenders, including many who are not drug users or offenders – for the following reasons.

- It would divert women from custody at the same time as providing them with close support and supervision. In the NSW Drugs Court, programme participants return to court once a week and talk direct to the judge or magistrate without intervening counsel. Clapping is often heard in court as participants tell how they've addressed problems.

- It would provide a co-ordinated and specialised approach to provision for women's needs. In the NSW Court there is a team approach – and they have been especially successful in co-ordinating police activity in relation to prosecutions, referrals and warrants.

- It should result in one-stop provision of resources for women (for example, legal, medical, social, probation, child-minding).

- It would allow participants to follow individualised programmes tailored to their actual needs and circumstances – rather than women being forced into programmes developed primarily for men and in countries with entirely different cultural and social conditions.

Several different models of drugs courts are in use round the world, and some of them have very negative features (such as public shaming) and a great propensity for net-widening. However, given that it is now accepted that some of the needs of women lawbreakers are very different to those of men, it might be productive to explore further the concept of a specialist court for female offenders, at the same time, of course, as being especially wary of the traps of net-widening and the ever-present tendency to fit participants to programmes – rather than the reverse.

Parramatta Transitional Prison (New South Wales)

The Parramatta Transitional Centre, also in New South Wales, provides an impressive model for rehabilitating women serving long sentences.

The main objective of the Centre is to prepare prisoners for a crime-free life outside prison. It is made up of several small cottages and there are no fences, no institutional signs and no staff uniforms. Residents have to have achieved a low security rating in prison and are ideally between three and twelve months away from release. However, an evaluation completed in 2001 indicated that more and more risks were being taken in selecting residents, and that of 55 admissions made outside the selection criteria only six had 'been returned from the Transitional Centre to mainstream custody' (NSW Dept of Corrective Services 2001:1). The Centre was opened in September 1996 and the evaluation was also able to report that 'to date there have been no recorded instances of violence or self-harm' (NSW Dept of Corrective Service 2001:31).

Transitional Centre residents have to find (and all do find) full-time employment in the community, do all their own shopping, pay rent, and cover the cost of phone calls, education and all personal needs. Their children can stay with them full-time (and attend local day nurseries) or part-time at weekends or during school holidays. Residents link up with any community programmes or educational programmes as they see fit, open bank accounts and attend local medical practitioners. After they leave the Centre women can still visit or phone for support or just a chat. The main aim is to reduce the fear that many women serving a long sentence experience when they are released, a fear that can often atrophy their best attempts to lead law-abiding lives. The centre has recently been assessed as being *cost-efficient* and *effective* insofar as it has a low recidivism rate; and *appropriate* – in that offenders live, work and study in the community to which they will be released.

The Parramatta model is recommended because many women in prison have never had the opportunity to build their lives within a supportive and safe environments. The transitional prison model can provide them with the supportive and safe environments which for most people are prerequisites to law-abiding lives.

Fundamental lessons about penal incarceration and its alternatives

One of the major lessons to be learned from recent research into alternatives to prison for women and the reform of women's prison regimes is that, because of the essential nature both of imprisonment (that it has to control prisoners sufficiently to keep them *in* prison) and those punishments which are seen only as conditional alternatives to imprisonment, there are limits to prison reform. (See Hannah-Moffat and Shaw 2000; Hannah-Moffatt 2001; Carlen 2002a and 2002c. See also chapters 11 and 12 this volume.) For the extent to which custodial, semi-custodial and non-custodial interventive programmes are prepared either to accept or retain women as participants is dependent upon the women explicitly adopting the world-view of their mentors – or at least that part of it that assumes it is in the client's best interest to be drug-free and law-abiding. Yet whether or not the women do adopt the official view is likely to vary according to their past histories, their perception of their current social situations and their assessment of the extent to which their self-defined needs (rather than those defined by official report-writers) are likely to be improved by a change to non-criminal or non-addict lifestyles. Even if they do adopt the perspective of official counsellors, women offenders and/or drugs users may still reject their counsellors' therapeutic methods or take much longer than the counsellors are prepared to wait before their clients either choose, or are able, to see things their way.

When benign custodial or non-custodial intervention is officially defined as 'failing' because of client non-compliance there is likely to be a carceral clawback (see chapter 12). This means that if a convicted woman is already a prisoner she will be placed in a less benign regime; and if she is in a non-custodial project as an alternative to prison the original custodial sentence will be activated.

Most of the project leaders interviewed were very aware that because of the complex social problems in which a majority of female offenders and/or female addicts were enmeshed, they often required a long time and many attempts before they could take the first steps towards the attainment of non-criminal lifestyles. In the meantime, because of the nature of sentencing, probation or project sponsorship requirements, the threat of carceral clawback was a constant reminder to both project staff and participants that their relationship was (in many cases, though certainly not all) ultimately one of coercion (or at best, client acquiescence) rather than consent. While some staff and project clients would argue that an element of coercion can be a useful element in the early stages of drugs treatment, more of the interviewees were concerned to point out that many of the anomalies in the responses to offenders in general, and to female offenders in particular, inhere in the inappropriateness of responding to the material, social and psychological problems of female offenders with a psychologised, jurisprudential model which, while it refuses to call into question the taken-for-granted coupling of the concepts of punishment and incarceration, persistently conflates economic want and social injury (for example, various kinds of abuse) with psychological need and moral turpitude. (See also chapter 2 for discussion of the jurisprudential issues involved.) Under these circumstances, it seems that projects to reduce women's imprisonment and recidivism are unlikely to be more successful until appraisors, of both projects and their participants' progress, not only show a greater appreciation of the complex nature of the majority of female offenders' material needs and past histories, but also recognise that these complexities have considerable financial implications for the extent to which, and the pace at which, convicted women are likely to respond to innovatory projects designed to help them keep out of trouble in the future.

Notes

1   The research investigation actually involved 'programmes', 'projects', regimes and any other type of innovative action designed to reduce either women's imprisonment or its damaging effects, either by crime reduction strategies or by social and penal reform activity.

2   The problems are, of course, legion. Here I shall only discuss the two definitional issues most relevant to readers' understanding of what follows. For a more extensive listing of problems, see Rose (1993).

3   Some of the research findings and arguments contained in sections 2-5 were first published in Carlen (2001b).

4   The New South Wales Drugs Court began operation on a trial basis on 8 February 1999. A monitoring report in December 2000 indicated that in the first 17 months of operation 313 persons commenced the Drugs Court Programme, with 10 graduating and 133 being terminated from the programme (Briscoe and Coumarelos 2000).

Part Three
Critique

Chapter 9

Women's prisons in England: barriers to reform

Jackie Lowthian

The particular difficulties of women in prison rarely attract public attention. Women are a very small proportion of the prison population and therefore easily forgotten in a criminal justice system which is run, very largely, by men, to deal primarily with male offenders ... I hope that this report will help to ensure that women are not forgotten in the current debate about the future of our prison system and that the proposals put forward will be of assistance in planning a more humane and just system for men and women in prison.

(Nacro 1991:3)

The majority of women in prison are non-violent offenders, serving short sentences mostly for property related crimes. Women face a struggle after release even to get back to where they were before being imprisoned. It is little wonder that just over a third of women released from prison commit another crime within two years ... This is why a positive strategy for the resettlement of women ... is so badly needed. This report sets out what needs to be done.

(Nacro, 1993:4)

The women's prison population is at record levels and is rising ... Despite the rising population, relatively few women are serving sentences for very serious offences ... The recommendations in this report are ultimately about supporting women in their efforts to maintain their self-respect and rebuild their lives.

(Nacro 1996:3)

> ... after so much effort and so many practical recommendations about what needs to be done, why are we publishing (another report) in 2001?
>
> (Nacro 2001:3)

The above comments are taken from reports published by Nacro (a non-governmental organisation dedicated to reducing crime through services to individuals and other organisations, and through campaigning and seeking to influence changes in criminal justice policy) throughout the last decade on the subject of women's imprisonment. Prison reformers have long argued for the need for specific policies which will address gender specific issues relevant to women's offending. In addition to work by Nacro, many other organisations have conducted inquiries and published reports – The Howard League, the Prison Reform Trust, Women in Prison, the Catholic Agency for Social Concern, and The Women's National Commission. Many of these publications contain detailed analysis of the problems and set out practical recommendations for change. In addition to the reports cited, there is a considerable body of academic work which provides in-depth analysis and critique of the way the criminal justice system has failed to address the challenges presented by women's offending. In 1997 the then Chief Inspector of Prisons[1], Sir David Ramsbotham, published his wide-ranging *Thematic Review of Women's Imprisonment* and in 1998 the Scottish Office published *Women Offenders – A Safer Way: A Review of Community Disposals and the Use of Custody for Women Offenders in Scotland* (Social Work Services and Prisons Inspectorate for Scotland 1998). More recently, in 2000, the Prison Reform Trust published a substantial report by the Committee on the Imprisonment of Women, chaired by Dorothy Wedderburn, entitled *Justice For Women: the Need for Reform*. Taken together, this vast array of publications provides a considerable body of analysis of issues and recommendations for change on how the state might more effectively respond to women's law-breaking. How has the state received these calls for reform and how have government agencies used the information to implement change?

In October 2000 the Home Office finally published its own document on women, grandly entitled *The Government's Strategy for Women Offenders*. This publication described work of various government departments – the Home Office, the Youth Justice Board, the Probation Service and the Prison Service – in the context of what the report described as cross-departmental work to improve women's lives. The report made it clear that the best way to reduce offending by women was to improve women's access to services in the areas of health and well-being, drug dependency, family relationships, housing, social services and education, training and employment. There was recognition that

> The current system does impact differently on women and men, because women are usually the primary carers for their children, and because their small numbers in the system can mean prison places further from home.
>
> (Home Office 2000a:1)

There was also acknowledgement that, in the past, the factors leading to women's offending had been overlooked and there was a commitment to do things differently in future.

At last the arguments made by prison reformers appeared to have been heard. The Report drew on various research documents previously published by both the Home Office and the Prison Service and did a reasonable job in summarising the issues, providing some statistical analysis, describing some new initiatives across government departments and outlining how the Sentencing Review, being conducted by John Halliday, might produce better sentencing for women. Sadly, however, it did not go on to outline a strategy with action plans for change. Instead, the document stated the need for more research into ways of effectively addressing offending by women, and announced a consultation process through which those working with women offenders (in both government and non-government agencies) could respond to the Report. Whilst the opportunity to respond to the report was extremely welcome, it was particularly frustrating to find, yet again, that a report on women and criminal justice was published without any coherent plan for action likely to produce positive change in the immediate future.

Three regional consultation seminars were held and many individuals and organisations provided detailed written responses to the Report. For my own part, with a sense of *déjà vu* and more than a little frustration, I prepared a written response on behalf of Nacro.

In September 2001 (Home Office 2001b) another report was published. This document presented details of the feedback received through the consultation process and, importantly, clearly promised change. In his foreword to this publication Home Secretary, David Blunkett, announced his intention to 'strengthen the Government's resolve to reduce women's offending through a specialist programme of work'. He went on to say,

> I have charged Home Office staff with the task of co-ordinating the development of a cross-government, comprehensive, targeted and

measurable Women's Offending Reduction Programme. This will take effect in 2002 and conclude its first phase in 2005.

(Home Office 2001b:1)

Prison Minister Beverley Hughes' comments in the Introduction to the report indicate the extent to which messages about the reasons for women's offending appear to have been heard:

> Since taking up my post a couple of months ago I have been struck perhaps most of all by the alarming rise in women's offending and consequent rise in the number of women in prison. What is clear from even a cursory examination of the many reasons given for this trend is that women's offending is inextricably linked to their life experiences. Factors such as health, economic stability, level of education, employment and training opportunities, family and community ties and experience of abuse are widely accepted as criminogenic factors for women offenders.
>
> (Home Office, 2001b:6)

Over and over again, relentlessly, the same analysis of issues leading to the same cries for reform have echoed through the decade. Finally, Government appears to have heard the cries and is promising to deliver on change. What can we expect? Are we to anticipate great advances delivered through the Government's Women's *Offending Reduction Programme*? In order to assess the likely success of future reform it is important to explore what barriers exist and to identify what obstacles have prevented effective reform taking place in the past. What follows is a personal perspective, focused fairly narrowly on the issues related to resettlement.

I have worked in the area of women and imprisonment for some 15 years. Up until April 1999 my work focused primarily on managing and delivering resettlement projects run by Nacro and aimed specifically at addressing the many welfare, social and economic needs of women in custody. The longest standing of these projects, The Women Prisoners' Resource Centre (WPRC), operated between 1984 and 1999. A small staff team provided advice, information and support to individual women in custody – the only criterion set for access to the project was that women should be returning to live in London following release (criterion required by the funding body – the London Boroughs Grants Unit). Access to the project was by self-referral or referral by prison, probation or community agency. In practice, self-referral was the route by which the majority of women prisoners found their way to an appointment with a

WPRC Advice Worker. Our approach to the work was 'woman-centred': we listened, we heard, we treated women with respect, compassion and understanding, we enabled women to define their own needs and set their own goals. We had a policy of recruiting staff who had genuine understanding of how imprisonment impacts on women, some of whom had direct personal experience of living with criminal histories and emerging intact from experiences of incarceration. We understood the importance of being realistic about what could be achieved and, more importantly, we never undertook to deliver outcomes that were unlikely to be reached. We were clear about what actions we would take to assist a woman and clear about what she must do herself to contribute to the process. Above all, we did what we said we would do – too often we heard from women how they had been let down and disappointed by other agencies. Women felt confident in our service and demand always outstripped supply; we operated on minimal funding, and limited staffing resources. We were not unique in our approach – there were a small number of other voluntary agencies: Women in Prison, Creative and Supportive Trust, the Black Female Prisoners' Scheme, Hibiscus/Female Prisoners Welfare Project, all of which worked in the same way. We were not part of the enforcement process and our only agenda was to offer women practical support whilst campaigning for policy changes that would reduce the need for our own existence.

This experience of direct contact with many hundreds of incarcerated women gave us particular access to, and understanding of, the issues, concerns and experiences of women who were convicted of offences and sent to prison. Over the years the same issues, concerns and experiences confronted us again and again. Difficult, sometimes appalling, family circumstances, histories of neglect, abuse and sexual exploitation, poor health, lack of support, inadequate housing or homelessness, poverty and debt, and little expectation of change. However, recognition of the prevalence of such experiences should not lead anyone to assume that all, or even the majority of, women conform to a stereotype of downtrodden victim – certainly many women had been subject to various forms of victimisation and exploitation throughout their lives, but in the face of this, many of them had shown incredible resourcefulness, courage and strength in coping with these experiences and surviving. Also, we encountered many women who did not have the appalling life histories common to some – women who had ended up in custody following a first conviction, women who had previously held jobs, owned homes and were not previously damaged by the factors listed above. All of the women we encountered shared one particular experience, however: the experience of imprisonment and the consequent damage to well-being.

The damage and harm inflicted on women as a consequence of forced removal from family, home and community has been well-documented. As previously emphasised, there is no shortage of reports setting out recommendations for change that would, if implemented, repair the damage and reduce the risks of further harm. Both prison reformers and members of the establishment have concluded that change is essential. On commencing his role as Chief Inspector of Prisons, Sir David Ramsbotham very quickly saw the need to undertake a thematic review of women's imprisonment. This action was prompted by his suspension of an inspection of Holloway in London (England's largest prison for women) in 1995 due to the appalling conditions he witnessed. The report of the Inspectorate's *Thematic Review of Women's Imprisonment* was published in 1997 and this work was probably the most thorough and detailed blue-print for change ever produced. It contained clear analysis of the problems and set out detailed, specific recommendations for change under a range of different headings. The document was wide-ranging, covering all aspects of imprisonment; the recommendations set out specific actions. The report was widely welcomed by many inside and outside of the Prison Service and held out the hope of real change.

The Prison Service has gone some way to implementing some of the Inspectorate's recommendations and a recently published review of progress sets out the Inspectorate's analysis of the extent to which change has been achieved. As well as calls for change within policies, practice and regimes at individual prisons, the Thematic Review recommended key structural changes: primarily that women's prisons should be functionally managed by an operational head who would be accountable to the Director General rather than managed in geographical clusters with male prisons. The Prison Service responded to this recommendation and an Operational Manager for the female estate was appointed in 2000. Additionally, a Women's Policy Group had been established in 1998, and for the first time, this provided a mechanism through which gender-specific policy could be formulated. Those of us concerned with reform were hopeful that meaningful and lasting change would follow. Sadly, our hopes have not been fully realised and, it is my opinion, that the women's prison system is currently in danger of regressing rather than progressing.

In the Preface to his review document Sir David stresses the importance of these changes to the management of female prisons:

> The most important and positive developments ... have been the appointment ... of a Head of Women's Policy Group and later an Operational Manager of Women's Prisons. This was my first and

main recommendation in Women in Prison because … consistent improvement depends on there being someone responsible and accountable for it.

Sir David Ramsbotham (HM Inspectorate of Prisons 2001:3)

He goes on to commend the fact that many of the other recommendations in his original report have been implemented, and suggests that much of the credit for this must go to the Women's Policy Group. However, he cautions that

the good work will only be maintained if the number of outstanding recommendations from that report are actioned.

(HM Inspectorate of Prisons 2001:3)

The areas of outstanding concern relate to:

• The need for a strategic review of locations of women's prisons

• The need for improvements in the treatment of and conditions for girls under the age of 18

• The need to address some of the social and economic factors that play a part in women's offending e.g. low or medium level interventions geared towards tackling practical needs such as housing, education/employment, parenting and social skills rather than accredited offending behaviour programmes

• The need for suitable and suitably-trained staff and the resources to deliver this

• The need for a 'full, purposeful and active day' for all women prisoners which provides opportunities to develop personal responsibility.

Above all, Sir David stresses the need to achieve greater consistency across women's prisons. He points out that good practice exists in almost all areas of his recommendations and states that it is up to operational management to ensure that this good practice is delivered across the whole female estate.

I find myself largely in agreement with the conclusions reached by Sir David with regard to some of the positive changes to be found in some women's prisons. However, I do not have a great deal of faith in the likelihood of further change in the future. Below I set out what I consider to be some of the key barriers to further reform.

Key barriers to reform

Sentencing and the rising women's prison population

The numbers of women being sent to prison by the courts, both under sentence and on remand, have increased dramatically, and continue to rise inexorably. Reasons for this increase have been put forward by various commentators – the Home Office view is that women are committing more crimes, more serious crimes and are receiving longer sentences. However, a significant proportion of women in custody are held on remand, 23% in 1999 (Home Office 2000b) and roughly only one third of them (35% in 1999) receive custodial sentences when their cases are finally heard at court. This suggests that courts are taking account of time on remand and awarding sentences that reflect this – thus, the crimes committed are not deemed serious enough to warrant anything other than short periods of custody. The fact that women are committing more crimes suggests that these short periods of custody do nothing to deter or prevent re-offending. However, short periods in custody have a very damaging impact on women's lives and can result in making existing social, personal and economic problems worse.

One major concern is that women's involvement in drug-related crime is increasing and that this area of activity accounts for a significant proportion of the overall increase in the female prison population. On 30 June 1999 36% of the female sentenced prison population were convicted of drugs offences. However, the figure for receptions into custody under sentence throughout the year was 14% (the greatest category of offence being theft and handling (39%)). The difference is accounted for by differences in sentence length. What this means of course is that women serving sentences for drugs offences will spend longer in prison and therefore the numbers on any one day are likely to be higher. More women are sentenced for convictions of theft and handling; and they are received into custody more frequently and for shorter periods.

The Sentencing Review (Halliday *et al* 2001) has recently reported and some of the thinking behind the recommendations appears to suggest that those committing less serious offences should be offered community sentences, and for those committing more serious offences custody should be kept to a minimum with additional periods of supervision in the community. If accepted and acted upon by Government these changes could, theoretically, lead to fewer women being sent to prison and mandatory post-release supervision for those who are.

In order to deal with the increased demands for supervision the National Probation Service would require a huge injection of finance to provide the increased staffing resources necessary to meet this need. One assumes that 'supervision' will also generate the additional support that women require in order to address the personal, social and economic problems that contribute to an offending lifestyle. However, conversations with field Probation Officers indicate that the enforcement role within supervision, and the way in which this is monitored to deliver targets, leaves little time or inclination for over-stretched Probation Officers to provide additional 'support'. One cannot, therefore, assume that additional post-release supervision periods will generate the kind of interventions that address the factors referred to in the recent Government Strategy document. Indeed, the requirement that all periods in custody are followed by supervision in the community is potentially a mechanism for increasing the female prison population further. The licence period will be governed by strict conditions and failure to comply with these licence conditions will result in breach action and a return to custody. Probation Officers have told me that for women currently released on licence, breaching is increasingly common as the conditions imposed are unrealistic and likely to generate failure, thus resulting in greater numbers of women being returned to custody.

Recent political developments in relation to world events mean that Government will have less time to focus attention on domestic matters and the necessary scrutiny of Halliday's report is likely to be postponed. In any event, parliamentary time will be severely limited and any legislative changes are unlikely to be achieved in the short-term. In the meantime, we must hope that proper analysis of the potential impact of Halliday's recommendations on women is undertaken and that more effective ways of implementing change can be established.

The rapid expansion of the numbers of women being sent to prison has, of course, created an urgent need for more available places. The Prison Service has responded to the need for more places for women by an arbitrary and piecemeal process of 're-roling' establishments – turning prisons for men into prisons for women. This process appears to have been largely haphazard without any clear planning or lead-in time. In some instances, prisoners were placed within the newly designated female prisons without adequate time for staff to receive training or for regimes to be appropriately designed. Some of these 're-roled' prisons have been successful in creating positive regimes and in some cases innovative practice has been established to address women's needs. The problem, as ever, is the lack of consistency across the female prison estate as a whole. Variations in practice from one establishment to another create frustrations for prisoners when being transferred and do not facilitate effective delivery of sentence plans.

Most worryingly, the Prison Service has commissioned the building by the private sector of two new prisons for women which will create a further 800 places at two establishments. The creation of two large prisons for women is completely opposed to the accepted view that women should, where possible, be held in small units as close to home as possible – the question must be asked: do we really need more large prisons for women? The creation of these two large prisons for women represents one of the most significant barriers to reform; the resources being spent on these projects could far better have been directed into the provision of smaller units across the country, giving a better spread of places and thus enabling women to be imprisoned nearer to their home areas and local communities.

The failure to grasp the opportunity to channel resources into new and innovative penal practice for women indicates a disregard for meaningful change and unwillingness to genuinely foster new approaches. The Home Office and the Prison Service is awash with 'What Works?' rhetoric. 'Research, research, research' is the cry, and resources are being poured into numerous research projects to further analyse that which, in the case of women, has already been well documented. Surely some of these resources could have been directed at new approaches which take account of all the existing information referred to earlier in this chapter?

A further consequence of the increase in numbers is the demands placed upon staffing in female prisons. Managing increased numbers places a strain upon staffing and stretches human resources. London's Holloway, in particular, is experiencing extreme difficulties. Like many other public service employers, the Prison Service faces real challenges in recruitment and retention of suitable staff – the cost of living and, in particular, the cost of housing are cited as the main reason that Holloway finds it difficult to retain staff. The increased demands placed upon existing staff create higher than usual levels of stress which lower morale and lead to increased levels of sickness absence. Obviously, staffing problems have a direct impact on the quality of regimes and the availability of 'purposeful activity'; in some prisons staff shortages result in women not being unlocked for long periods and therefore unable to attend education or offending behaviour courses, or to meet with help agencies for individual appointments.

Clearly, the rising population of women prisoners is in itself a major barrier to effective reform. Steps must be taken to ensure that Halliday's recommendations for community punishments for less serious offenders are properly scrutinised and that credible and useful alternatives to custody for women are implemented. Sentencers must be made to respond more appropriately to those women appearing before them and custody must be seen as a last resort.

Gap between policy and practice

The Women's Policy Group (WPG), established at Prison Service Head-quarters in 1998, was the mechanism through which policy for women's prisons would be created from a sound base of knowledge and expertise on gender issues and an understanding of the ways in which women's law breaking could be more effectively addressed. Those of us who had been calling over many years for this very basic reform were delighted with this development and felt that, at long last, there was hope of real and meaningful change. Policies which took account of the realities of women's lives and the impact of imprisonment upon their lives could now be produced and practice within prisons could be adapted to respond more effectively and fairly to needs. We looked forward to the opportunity to engage with WPG and to lobby for the kind of changes we felt were appropriate. Yet, whilst there can be little doubt that WPG has been a central focus for the discussion of issues pertaining to women, and that the profile of women's needs has been raised, it is doubtful whether the extent of change hoped for has been delivered. I suggest a number of reasons for this.

Firstly, for much of the first year of its existence WPG appeared to be going through a process of undertaking a 'learning exercise' in 'women's issues'. The Head of the Group, a Chief Probation Officer with many years experience, seconded to the Prison Service to lead on policy for women, was clearly very experienced in managing corporate change. However, expertise in relation to women was rather less evident. Those of us within the field of penal reform were astonished to find that her primary task for the first year was to develop her knowledge on gender issues and to begin to gain an understanding of the subject. Whilst we appreciated her need to undergo a period of induction in a new role within a different agency, it seemed odd that someone without an established understanding of the issues and a track record in policy for women could have been appointed to such a key role. There were many women within the criminal justice field who had extensive knowledge and expertise in the area of gender and justice and it seemed a terrible waste not to have appointed someone with that particular background. However, we in the voluntary sector, ever ready to offer up our collective knowledge, were ready to work with WPG and were pleased to discover that a consultative approach was adopted. Built in to this approach was a recognition on the part of WPG that the voluntary sector had a valuable role to play and, indeed, an acknowledgement of the fact that it was the voluntary agencies who had, over the years, developed the expertise in working constructively with women in prison. A demonstration of WPG's commitment to working collaboratively with colleagues in the voluntary sector was the early acknowledgement of this expertise; two consultative forums were quickly established – one, the Women and Criminal Justice Liaison Forum, was to look broadly at all issues to do with women and criminal policy, and the second, the Resettlement Working Group, was to help produce a resettlement strategy for women. Nacro was invited to sit on both forums; I joined the Resettlement Working Group and the then Director of Prisons and Resettlement at Nacro joined the Liaison Forum. The majority of voluntary agencies active in the field of women and criminal justice were invited to participate in these fora and it seemed that there was hope for genuine consultation leading to real change.

The first meeting of the resettlement forum brought together a huge number of people with a wide range of expertise in the specific area of women and imprisonment. A great deal of debate and discussion ensued and it was agreed that a sub-group be established to take forward the task of drafting sections of a strategy. The sub-group was led by a member of the WPG and, ultimately, he would be responsible for pulling the draft together and preparing the strategy document. We duly met and agreed roles and drafting tasks, others outside the group were to be commissioned to write pieces. I personally undertook to produce the section on addressing housing needs and duly carried out work to complete this task. A number of further meetings took place and drafts were circulated. Some months later members of the group were informed that the WPG lead civil servant had moved on to another department. Work on the resettlement strategy would be postponed until a replacement was appointed. Nearly three years later (late 2001) a new Resettlement Strategy Group has just been set up and the task begins again from scratch! The drafts of the previous group have sat in a filing cabinet gathering dust and it is only to be hoped that the efforts of the new group do not meet with the same fate.

I relate this sorry tale to demonstrate how the workings of civil service machinery, even when set up with the best of intentions, actually thwart the achievement of change; and also to demonstrate how non-governmental agencies can be drawn-in and subverted by a process of consultation which metamorphoses into collusion with the status quo. [See also chapters 1,11,12. Ed.] Recent developments in relation to the resettlement strategy for women are actually very encouraging. The person currently tasked with preparing the strategy is a senior manager/practitioner with several years' experience as Throughcare Manager at a women's prison. She has the knowledge, experience and ability appropriate to the task and, importantly, is deeply committed to ensuring that the document is a meaningful tool to assist governors to improve resettlement activities in their prisons. She is determined that the strategy will be an informed blueprint for action and that it will not languish unread in filing cabinets throughout the female estate. She has established a small reference group to assist with the work and, crucially, she has arranged a programme of on-site prisoner consultation exercises. Having recently participated in one such consultation I am heartened by the openness and genuine desire to listen embodied in this approach. Through a process of talking to women prisoners, asking them to define their own needs and suggest useful approaches to tackling their problems, the strategy is likely to contain measures which are relevant and of practical value to the women towards whom they will be directed. On being asked to talk about their needs, the women were initially reticent and a little surprised: 'Nobody has ever asked us what we need before' was one revealing comment. By the end of the session we had heard a great deal from women and, although there were no surprises in the issues raised (housing, families, drugs, health, money, education, training and work) we were deeply saddened to find that the majority of women had received little or no help to address these needs.

The kind of help women suggested they needed was hardly rocket science:

- Support to deal with housing benefit applications and housing application forms

- Direct contact with housing departments in their home areas or someone to liaise on their behalf

- Better information on support services in their home areas

- More contact from home probation officers and/or social workers

- Someone to talk to

- Counselling services, particularly in relation to emotional distress linked to separation from children

- Use of temporary release to spend time at home in order to prepare for discharge.

All of these are measures which have long been advocated by those of us in regular contact with women prisoners and, if the political will and the resources were made available, all are measures that could so easily be implemented. It is to be hoped that the drive, commitment and genuine desire to produce a meaningful strategy for change embodied by the WPG lead on resettlement will be backed by the availability of resources to implement that strategy once finalised.

WPG have expended a great deal of energy on seeking out voluntary agencies and developing dialogues. They have performed a useful function in disseminating information about innovative practice, particularly those projects which are run in partnership between women's prisons and community agencies. They have worked collaboratively with the voluntary sector to move the debate forward and have sought to keep governors of women's prisons informed of opportunities for collaboration. Additionally, WPG have certainly created numerous new policy initiatives intended to bring about positive change within women's prisons – for example, improved policies on Mother and Baby Units have been introduced, and new pilot programmes on offending behaviour have been run in various prisons. However, the question remains, to what extent have these new policies been implemented? And to what extent has positive change within women's prisons been achieved?

One of the major barriers to reform appears to be the lack of connection between policy and practice. The WPG can initiate new policies which may or may not be approved by the Prison Service Board. Only through the granting of this approval can these policy initiatives be translated into Prison Service Orders – the administrative mechanism which gives policies meaning and ensures that prison managers are expected to put policies into practice. As far as I can see, WPG have little influence in relation to whether or not their policies result in changes in practice. Indeed, the former head of the group has argued that their role is to write policy not to implement it. Implementation is the responsibility of operational managers. Where is the link between policy and operation?

Prior to the implementation of the Chief Inspector's recommendation that a single operational manager should take responsibility for women's prisons, they were managed in geographical clusters alongside male prisons and Young Offender Institutions (YOIs). This meant that often a cluster or area contained only one female prison. Area managers were responsible for all the prisons in their area and, consequently, the particular needs of women and gender differences were not effectively addressed. Importantly, there were few opportunities for female prison governors to come together; and communication structures, based on areas, did not facilitate sharing of good practice, dissemination of ideas or discussion of shared problems specific to prisons for women. This ensured that there was little hope of achieving consistency between regimes and practice, and few opportunities to develop practice based specifically on a recognition of gender differences.

The acceptance of Sir David Ramsbotham's recommendation that women's prisons should be managed functionally as a group, and the implementation of this recommendation by the Prison Service in 2000, suggested that at last a mechanism to promote effective practice and consistency between regimes had arrived. We in the prison reform movement were hopeful that positive change would result and quickly. Our hopes have not been realised and indeed our hopes were dramatically dashed at a Prison Service conference in October 2000. Women's Policy Group hosted this conference and it was intended as a means of communicating to prison managers, probation managers and managers within certain voluntary agencies, what plans WPG had for reforming the women's prison system and introducing new policies. In her speech, the then Head of WPG outlined a whole range of policy initiatives – some already completed and some planned for the future:

- Research into criminogenic needs of women

- Offending behaviour programmes designed specifically for women

- National Drug Strategy leading to improved detoxification facilities within prisons, two residential drug rehabilitation centres for prisoners and plans for two prison based therapeutic communities

- Improved system for access to Mother and Baby Units and development of child centred approach to care

- Two new Mother and Baby Units to increase capacity to meet demand

- Two new-build women's prisons.

Most of these planned changes are either complete or in the process of implementation. However, welcome as some of these initiatives are, there has been enormous financial pressures on governors throughout the past year, making it difficult for them even to meet the day to day needs of the prisoners in their care. Warning of these likely pressures was given at the same conference in October 2000, when the Operational Manager followed the Head of Women's Policy Group and announced that his primary task for the coming year was to reduce the unacceptable level of overspend across the female estate and ensure that expenditure was within budget. This would mean, inevitably, that costs would have to be reduced and savings achieved. The options for governors were stark: cut staff ? cut overtime ? cut regimes ?

The Operational Manager expected that a short-term reduction in the quality of regimes was likely with a view to working towards a time when finances were back within budgets and long-term improvements could be delivered through meeting KPIs and working closely in partnership with Women's Policy Group.

The impression was that governors would be hard pressed to maintain existing levels of service, let alone develop new initiatives and improve regimes for women. Governors in the hall were left with little doubt as to the role of the Operational Manager, and those of us hoping for immediate change were left reeling. The aspirations of the WPG to lead on developing new policies for women were clearly undermined by the financial constraints imposed by the Operational Manager.

Performance targets and bureaucracy

According to one governor of a female prison, the greatest obstacle to implementing positive change is Prison Service bureaucracy 'being buried under mountains of paper – Prison Service Standards, Prison Service Instructions, Prison Service Orders (PSOs), Key Performance Indicators (KPIs), many of which run to several volumes'. He expressed the view that the time spent in attempting to read, digest, inform staff and keep abreast of paperwork tasks intended to ensure that positive change takes place actually has the effect of reducing his capacity to implement change in a meaningful way. Looking at the volumes of paper he held up as an example it was very easy to see his point and sympathise. However, another view was offered by a fellow governor; whilst he also felt frustrated by the sheer weight of bureaucracy, he supported the need for standards, KPIs, orders and instructions in order to ensure that those governors who were not so motivated towards positive change were required to implement new policies and measure performance against targets. My own view is somewhere between the two – I agree in principle for the need to set targets and measure achievement, but, and it is a significant but, I have serious concerns about the extent to which paper monitoring can divert time away from quality work with prisoners and, more worrying still, the trend to monitor quantitatively rather than qualitatively. An example I offer from first hand experience is that of the CARATS (Counselling, Assessment, Referral, Advice/Information and Throughcare Services) programme.

Introduced in 1999, and intended to provide comprehensive assessment, treatment and referral services for all prisoners with drug misuse issues, the CARATS programme is being evaluated for effectiveness and implementation. Contracts with a range of providers (commissioned through competitive tender) have been agreed in all areas of the country. The CARATS Service Specification is nationally applied and all providers are intended to deliver the same quality of service, measured by a uniform set of performance standards. Nacro, in partnership with RAPt (The Rehabilitation of Addicted Prisoners Trust), is contracted as a provider to four Prison Service clusters. I have management responsibilities in relation to some of this work and have first hand experience of how monitoring and performance measurement activity can impact negatively on the quality of service prisoners actually receive. The thrust of the monitoring is to numerically measure the extent to which the service is delivered – numbers of prisoners receiving initial assessments, numbers receiving full assessments, numbers receiving information/advice, numbers referred into treatment, numbers receiving counselling/groupwork in prison, numbers linked with community drugs agency for post-release support, etc. All these new measures have been implemented in order to ascertain the extent to which the service is being delivered. However, the staff time required to deliver the numbers and record the information which demonstrates this delivery is such that the quality of work, i.e. quality of assessments and interventions, can be undermined. Work is target driven and it is sheer throughput of numbers that governs the 'success' or otherwise of the delivery. In my opinion this can impact negatively on the extent to which meaningful interventions can be offered to prisoners.

A particular concern is the lack of scope within the programme for meaningful resettlement support. In theory the CARATS programme entails an element of post-release support; the service specification states that CARATS staff must ensure that prisoners are put in touch with an appropriate community based drugs treatment agency in their home area, and if this proves not to be possible then direct post-release support should be provided by the CARATS team for a period of up to eight weeks. Within the RAPt/Nacro Partnership a Nacro Resettlement Worker has specific responsibility for addressing resettlement needs; drugs workers refer clients to the Nacro worker for resettlement support and the release planning takes account of a whole range of needs, not just those specific to drug misuse. In practice this means action-planning to address housing needs, debt problems, money management, family problems, education/training/employment needs and wider health issues. However, the monitoring and evaluation framework only takes account of whether or not the prisoner is provided with an appointment at a community based drugs treatment facility, and whether or not this appointment is kept. Quality work to address all of the other needs is not contractually required and positive outcomes in relation to all of this other work are not part of the monitoring process. Thus, there is little incentive among CARATS providers to undertake the resettlement task in full. The measure of success lies in the throughput of numbers, and the target is to maximise the number of prisoners being offered an appointment with a drugs agency on release. This means that there is pressure on the resettlement worker to concentrate on this aspect of the work and ignore other needs.

For providers that operate CARATS services without a specialist resettlement worker as part of the team there is no incentive to undertake the broad range of resettlement tasks since the contract can be adequately delivered by ensuring that the optimum number of prisoners are given appointments with community drugs agencies on release. It seems fairly obvious that to offer someone an appointment for drugs treatment in the community when that person has no accommodation, no money and no access to other support is rather short-sighted and unlikely to provide a route out of drug dependency and offending. The inclusion of a Resettlement Worker as part of the CARATS teams within the RAPt/Nacro Partnership ensures that there are at least some resources focusing specifically on addressing resettlement needs. Other contractors are under no obligation to provide this level of resettlement support and since the measures of success take no account of this it is doubtful as to what extent any meaningful resettlement work will form part of the CARATS service. This reveals the bankruptcy of a programme intended to reduce reoffending by offering assessment and treatment to drug misusing prisoners, but which does not recognise the importance of tackling the whole range of resettlement issues in order to ensure that the good work undertaken during custody and any progress made is maintained after discharge. Those providers who wish to deliver a high quality effective service will strive to build in the necessary elements of proper support but the bureaucratic monitoring and evaluation framework does nothing to support this approach and, with regard to the pressure to deliver on numbers, may serve to actively discourage providers from delivering a quality service. The same may well be argued with regard to other initiatives intended to improve the quality of regimes and tackle prisoners' needs. Sentence-planning is another example that comes to mind. I have often asked women prisoners about their sentence plans and in some cases have been met with blank stares or queries such as 'what's that?' In cases where women have been involved in sentence planning and are aware that a plan has been agreed they very often comment that they are unaware of what elements of the sentence plan have been undertaken and have no sense of how the sentence plan is intended to operate. Regular Sentence Plan reviews should provide a mechanism for tracking progress and identifying further work but again many women state that their sentence plans are not reviewed. In the same prisons, however, monitoring will reflect that a certain number of sentenced plans have been delivered – there will be no mechanism for monitoring the quality of these plans or measuring their effectiveness in tackling prisoners' needs.

I am concerned that resettlement KPIs may be delivered in much the same way – a great deal of staff and management time will be taken up with recording processes and completing paperwork to demonstrate compliance with policies but less time will be devoted to meaningful inter-actions with prisoners in order to offer them the practical support required to effectively address resettlement needs. Thus, the very policies that are intended to promote positive change and bring about reform can effectively stifle the prison's capacity to deliver change in a meaningful way. [See also chapter 6. Ed.] I believe that setting targets is an important mechanism for driving change and that measuring the extent to which targets are achieved is paramount to the delivery of change. However, the targets set must be the right ones and the information gathered to assess achievement must be qualitative as well as quantitative. [See also chapters 8 and 12. Ed.] Equally important is the need to ensure that appropriate resourcing is attached to all targets.

Resources

Reference has already been made to the problems that are linked to staffing shortfalls in some prisons. The question of adequate resources is an issue that creates barriers to reform. Those of us who have long argued that women's prisons should more effectively address resettlement needs (housing, money, health, education, training, employment) and help pre-pare women more appropriately for release have been heartened and encouraged by the recent policy changes in this area. The Prison Service has recognised the importance of tackling these needs in the interest of reducing further offending and this recognition has been translated into KPIs, Standards and Prison Service Orders. The PSO on resettlement is detailed and well–researched. The guidance and requirements set out in the order are extremely important and welcome. For the first time, prison governors are required to address prisoners' housing and employment needs, and to achieve targets related to meeting these. This is especially important for women. However, these changes are deemed to be 'resource-neutral' – i.e., requiring no additional finance. This presents an immediate barrier to implementation. For example, if the task of assisting prisoners with housing needs is to be delivered effectively, staff time must be designated specifically towards this task. Staff training and material resources and equipment will also be necessary. We know from our own experiences of delivering resettlement support to women prisoners that the process is time-consuming, requires specific knowledge and expertise and access to appropriate tools for the job. These requirements are not 'resource-neutral' and without additional funding are unlikely to be effectively delivered.

The establishment of the Custody to Work Unit (C2W) and the Government's commitment to double the number of prisoners taking up employment on release have brought increased resources into the resettlement arena. As yet, though, it is not clear how women prisoners will benefit from C2W initiatives. A significant proportion of the C2W budget was earmarked for targeted initiatives at ten key prisons and YOIs identified as 'failing' – not one of these prisons is a women's establishment. Further, the issue of employment is not so clear-cut for women as it is for men; many women are primary carers and will need to address rebuilding family ties and resuming responsibility for children before even thinking about employment as an option. The need for appropriate and affordable childcare will also impact on women's ability to take up employment. So although new resources are being made available to address resettlement needs these resources are directed at addressing the issue of employment and, consequently, it is not clear how far women's specific needs will be considered and provided for within this new policy framework.

The whole question of appropriate resourcing represents an obvious barrier to achieving reform. The requirements on governors to operate restricted budgets and continually to cut costs clearly makes it difficult for them to implement change. Where change has been implemented effectively it is usually the case that specific resources have been directed towards this – for example, Low Newton and Winchester have received additional funding to develop and run a drug rehabilitation programme and a therapeutic community. In general, the changes required to meet the new statutory regulations relating to young offenders and juveniles have been delivered and new funding has been made available to ensure that this happens.

The question of funding affects all areas of public service and, of course, the Prison Service is no different from any other public body in so far as it has to exist on limited funding and demonstrate 'best value'. However, if the Government is to deliver its manifesto promises on crime reduction it is short-sighted not to put additional resources into constructive work in prisons to tackle offenders' needs. The failure to do so will only translate into further offending and further costs on the public purse – expenditure on other parts of the criminal justice system (police, courts, Crown Prosecution Service, probation), and health and social services will inevitably increase. These costs are likely to be far greater than the costs of providing services that meet prisoners' resettlement needs and reduce the likelihood of them committing further crimes on release.

Gap between custody and community

Finally, regardless of how many improvements to regimes are achieved, we cannot expect the Prison Service alone to address the lifetime of problems faced by individual prisoners. There have been serious failures by other public services – education, health, housing, and social services – long before a prisoner reaches the prison cell. In order for any good work undertaken in custody not to be undermined by lack of support once the prisoner is released (and to retain the benefits of any progress made, for example, on detoxing from drug dependency or an improvement in basic skills) it is crucial that appropriate support is made available to women in their home communities after release. We know that the vast majority of women spend short periods in custody, either on remand or serving sentences of less than 12 months. Consequently they are released without any form of on-going contact with any of the statutory agencies. The opportunity to provide on-going support is thus lost. We know that the Sentencing Review (Halliday *et al* 2001) suggests that this situation may change and I have already referred to the problems in assuming that post-release *supervision* will offer a means of providing post-release *support*. However, only through the provision of effective post-release support can we hope to ensure that gains made through improvements in prison regimes for women are not lost following discharge from custody.

Other public services must be made to take account of the needs of released prisoners – on the basis of crime reduction arguments if nothing else; and women released from prison must receive help to negotiate their way around these services. Partnership working between all agencies at a local level is fundamental to offering appropriate services and ensuring that a holistic approach to need is taken. Models of good practice exist: the Resettlement Pathfinder project operating a partnership arrangement between Low Newton Prison and Durham Probation Area and due for closure in March 2002 is one such; Back on Track, a multi-agency partnership project operated by Nacro in West Yorkshire between 1997–1999, is another.

Currently the Benefits Agency is providing pilot advice services to prisoners in some prisons to try and ensure that benefit entitlements are explained and claims submitted appropriately before and shortly after release. Schemes like this must be expanded.

All the prisons which offer extended family visits for those with primary carer responsibilities are providing a vital mechanism for women to maintain appropriate contact with children during their imprisonment. However, what support is available to help families after release? Women have told me on many occasions that there are all kinds of difficulties to contend with in resuming parenting roles and responsibilities after a period in prison, and rarely, if ever, are appropriate support services available. Local public services – education, housing, health, social services – must begin to accept that they have a role to play in crime reduction and a responsibility to provide appropriate levels of service to discharged prisoners. Criminal justice agencies must work towards partnership arrangements with other statutory and voluntary agencies and should strive to encourage joint working.

Overview of the current situation

It is clear that budgetary constraints, coupled with the need to accommodate ever-increasing numbers of women, have made it difficult, if not impossible, to achieve significant improvements consistently across the female estate. Some prisons, notably Low Newton, Drake Hall and Send among the closed establishments, have certainly created regimes which contain many elements worthy of praise; Askham Grange and East Sutton Park, the two open prisons for women, continue to offer women excellent opportunities to address needs and develop skills, knowledge and confidence. However, staffing constraints can impact negatively on the capacity prisons have to maintain improvements and I know of examples where positive initiatives, such as the housing advice service at Low Newton, have been curtailed due to staffing difficulties. Some prisons, notably Holloway, Eastwood Park, New Hall and Styal (most closely equated with male 'local' prisons, i.e. serving the courts by taking remand and newly sentenced prisoners for allocation), appear to have moved backwards rather than forwards. The pressures of taking many short-term and remand prisoners, whilst also accommodating young prisoners, lifers and longer-term prisoners, in addition to operating Mother and Baby Units, have resulted in conditions for women at these prisons not improving and, in some areas, worsening. One is left with a sense of decline. The picture is not uniform but the same concerns are raised frequently:

- Deterioration in standards of healthcare and hygiene

- Pressures related to staffing shortages resulting in non-mandatory tasks (e.g. housing and resettlement support) being dropped in order to ensure that statutory functions (e.g. security and discipline) are carried out

- Inappropriate allocation of prisoners due to the inexorable demand for places, resulting in open or 'training' prisons receiving inmates who are not likely to benefit from the regimes, and closed, 'local' prisons holding those serving longer sentences and thus not accessing the regime elements geared towards meeting their needs

- Staffing shortages resulting in the failure to maintain adequate standards of care and thus increasing the risk of bullying, self-harm and suicide

- Staffing shortages reducing cover to the extent that regime activities and education are curtailed since women cannot be unlocked

- Field probation role being one of enforcement rather than support and home probation officers having little time or resources to spare to see women in prison, or to offer voluntary aftercare post-release

- Focus on offending behaviour and other accredited cognitive behavioural programmes resulting in a lack of holistic, needs based programmes for women.

Elsewhere in this book detailed analyses of the problems associated with the obsession with accreditation are provided [chapters 6 and 12. Ed.]. The failure to allow for programmes that do not meet accreditation criteria to be tested is a serious obstruction to delivering holistic needs based interventions for women. Programmes such as those developed and delivered by the London Area Probation Service (Women's Probation Centre) and the former Hereford and Worcester Probation Service (now West Mercia Area of the National Probation Service [see chapter 6. Ed]) along with services provided by voluntary agencies like Nacro and Women in Prison[2] have offered women offenders something which is widely accepted by those who work with women to be of value. However, such services and programmes fail to attract funding as they fall outside the narrow, prescriptive limitations required for accreditation.

Research carried out to test the impact of programmes delivered by the London Women's Probation Centre shows that they are successful. The Centre takes a holistic approach that rewards efforts and progress.

Programmes are offered in a safe and welcoming environment and solution-focused methods of work are employed to help women resolve difficulties and undertake personal development. Research in the US by Dowden and Andrews (1999:438–452) has shown that this kind of programme is more effective in reducing offending by women than the cognitive behavioural models favoured through accreditation.

The picture is not totally bleak and good practice can be found throughout the women's prison system, for example:

- Therapeutic drug rehabilitation units at some women's prisons

- First Night in Custody project run by the Bourne Trust at Holloway Prison

- Improved facilities for visitors at Holloway Prison

- The Resettlement Pathfinder project delivered jointly by prison and probation staff at Low Newton (but due for closure in March 2002)

- A holistic, needs based skills training and resettlement programme run by Foundation Training at Highpoint

- An excellent employment project run by SOVA at Askham Grange

- Housing advice services at Low Newton and Drake Hall

- Better assessments of basic skills needs and improvements in the provision of basic education in order to raise standards of literacy and numeracy

- Provision of work opportunities for vulnerable prisoners at Bullwood Hall

- Opportunities for community work and, in some cases, proper paid external employment at the two open prisons and at Drake Hall (semi-open), and Send (closed)

- Workshops in several prisons which enable women to develop skills in areas like fashion design, dressmaking and hairdressing (sometimes derided as being stereotypically female and declared 'sexist' but in fact incredibly useful in offering women opportunities for self employment or other work on release, and especially important for foreign nationals returning to developing countries).

Indeed, there are many more examples that could be cited and there is no doubt that there has been an improvement in the extent to which prison managers are committed to delivering improved regimes for women. However, a key issue is the *maintenance of existing good practice, and the dissemination and expansion of good practice across all regimes*. There is currently no consistency and no general standard of provision which all prisons are required to meet. Variations in practice create inequalities across the system and make it very difficult for proper sentence planning to take effect.

The recent issue of a Prison Service Order on resettlement will, for the first time, impose a mandatory duty on governors to achieve targets in the areas of housing and employment for prisoners. All prisons will be required to have a Resettlement Policy Committee and all Prison Service Areas will be required to have a Resettlement Strategy. However, real concerns remain as to how effective such strategies will be and how targets will be met. The Prison Service Order should be the key mechanism that transforms 'policy' into practice. The requirement for governors and area managers to deliver targets and for performance against these targets to be measured should deliver change but, as we have seen, there are serious drawbacks to assessing change by quantitative measures alone.

Lessons for the future

The Home Secretary has declared his intention to ensure that positive change in the area of women and criminal justice is achieved. The establishment of a Women's Policy Team within the Home Office Correctional Policy Unit provides a mechanism through which, potentially, change can be achieved. The success or failure of this mechanism in driving change forward will depend upon the extent to which the barriers outlined above can be overcome.

Firstly, and above all else, there must be a commitment to action. As outlined in the opening section of this chapter, there are already a body of research and a profusion of reports containing recommendations for change. This existing knowledge must be used as a basis for new policies. As a matter of urgency, a means of reducing the numbers of women being sent to prison must be implemented. The Wedderburn Report (Prison Reform Trust 2000) suggests that a National Women's Justice Board (similar to the Youth Justice Board) might be established in order to get courts to adopt more appropriate sentencing for women. There are examples of good practice in numerous women's prisons and in certain probation areas there are models of effective work with women which could be used more widely. The Home Office Policy Team must ensure that these existing good models are replicated across the system and that structural changes in criminal justice policy for women, as recommended by many organisations and individuals, are implemented without delay.

Secondly, the ways in which policy and practice link across the women's prison system must be improved. It may be that the existing arrangement, of having separate policy and operational management should be re-examined. At the very least, there must be improved communication and more 'joined-up working' between the policy and operational management teams.

Thirdly, the need to evaluate work and demonstrate effectiveness must not work against the delivery of effective interventions. Targets must be appropriate and realistic and resources to assist with delivery must be made available. Consideration must be given as to how to evaluate qualitatively rather than just quantitatively.

Fourthly, if the Prison Service and the National Probation Service are to deliver positive change, the appropriate level of resourcing must be made available.

Finally, improved access to services in the community must be made available both to women on release from prison and to those serving community penalties. We must recognise that criminal justice agencies alone cannot repair the damaged lives of those women who fall foul of the law. Time and time again, women have been failed by other public services and we need to ensure that this failure is not repeated. Services like CARATS (the comprehensive service for drugs misusers referred to earlier) have begun (in a very limited way) to try and bridge the gap between custody and community. The Resettlement Pathfinder at Low Newton Prison demonstrates the value of offering women on-going support in their home communities after release. Mainstream statutory providers of health, housing and social services must be made to work in partnership with prisons, probation and voluntary agencies and to recognise that responding appropriately to the needs of women prisoners will work towards meeting crime reduction targets.

We have all the research and experience we require in order to respond more effectively to women who break the law; the time has come to cease discussing these matters, to overcome the barriers and to act to bring about change.

Notes

1   *Her Majesty's Inspectorate of Prisons* is an independent body which was established in 1980 to inspect prisons and make recommendations to the Home Secretary.
2   A small independent organisation that provides support to individual women prisoners and campaigns for policy changes.

Chapter 10

Time to think again about cognitive behavioural programmes

Kathleen Kendall

Introduction

As I was putting the finishing touches to this chapter, the British press announced that the number of women in prison had reached an all-time high of 4,045. This figure amounts to a 20% increase over the previous year, or a 33% increase across the last decade. The Government's short-term response to this dramatic and disturbing growth has been to convert the infrastructure of male prisons to accommodate females. In the longer term, there are plans to open two new women's prisons (Ford 2001: 1).

At the same time, implementation has begun on the Government's Strategy for Women Offenders, supposedly the first comprehensive, co-ordinated and coherent effort to govern female criminals. A joint venture between the Prison and Probation services, the overall aims of the Strategy are 'to protect the public and reduce re-offending' (Home Office 2000b:1). Such goals are to be achieved largely through 'offending behaviour' programmes. These programmes are purportedly based upon solid research evidence about the causes of female crime and 'what works' to prevent recidivism. Essentially, it is maintained that women offenders (and male offenders) lack certain cognitive skills which put them at greater risk of criminality. Programmes, therefore, are designed to teach offenders these skills. Once learned, criminals are rehabilitated and set to live a law-abiding life.

On the face of it, these two developments appear incongruous. The first is a policy of incapacitation, where prisoners are warehoused. This practice is justified on the grounds that people do not have the opportunity to offend while they are locked up. As Carrabine, Lee and South (2000) suggest, since the purpose of warehousing is simply to contain, neither people's characters nor their reasons for offending need to be considered. In contrast, policies claiming to 'rehabilitate' offenders rely upon detailed knowledge of individual personalities as a precursor to change.

In this chapter I will argue that the model underpinning offending behaviour programmes, cognitive behaviouralism, actually bridges these two seemingly contradictory policies. It does so by promoting the view that crime is almost entirely caused by character deficits or defaults in particular individuals. By situating offenders as 'troublesome others' – dangerous and inherently different to non-criminals – such a belief may be mobilised to legitimate both containment and programmatic inter-vention. As innumerable wars have shown, the creation of social distance between 'us' and 'them' not only encourages moral indifference but may further facilitate the commission of atrocities (Glover 1999).

It is therefore unsurprising that cognitive behaviouralism exists alongside a new punitiveness, exemplified by dedicated search teams, mandatory drug testing, handcuffing, and mass imprisonment (Carlen 1998). More fundamentally, it supports the political rationalities of advanced neo-liberal democracies, by embodying both notions of social authoritarianism (repression, punishment and order) and free-market individualism (choice, autonomy, and responsibility). On the one hand, offenders are denied volition through coercion and force. On the other, they are regarded as active agents, responsible for their criminal actions and their own reformation. Both strategies individualise crime and punishment by denying the structural inequalities and oppressions within which offenders are situated. They are thus in keeping with the dismantling of the welfare state and denial of citizenship rights to the socially excluded occurring across both sides of the Atlantic (Carrabine *et al* 2000). In this sense, cognitive behaviouralism may be conceptualised as a type of governmental technology or way of regulating people's conduct that is in keeping with the current political climate (Hannah-Moffat 2001; Rose and Miller 1992).

Antecedents to offending behaviour programmes

The popular science fiction serial, *Dr Who*, featured a story entitled 'The Mind of Evil' in which the eponymous hero investigates a revolutionary new way of treating criminals. A machine has been invented which literally sucks the perceived evil or criminal thoughts out of prisoners' brains. The Doctor, however, discovers that exposure to the machine leaves prisoners with no personality at all (BBC 1971).

Unfortunately, the use of technology to alter the criminal mind is not simply the stuff of science fiction. For example, in 1970, a professor of psychology at the University of Michigan proposed radical experimental treatment in a paper entitled 'Criminals Can Be Brainwashed – Now'. Dr James McConnell wrote:

> I believe the day has come when we can combine sensory deprivation with drugs, hypnosis, and astute manipulation of reward and punishment to gain almost absolute control over an individual's behaviour ... We'd assume that a felony was clear evidence that the criminal had somehow acquired full-blown social neurosis and needed to be cured, not punished ... We'd probably have to restructure his entire personality.
>
> (McConnell cited in Mitford 1974: 125)

McConnell never actually implemented his full proposal, but the kind of techniques he advocates have been employed by others in attempts to rehabilitate offenders on both sides of the Atlantic. Interventions have variously included, for example: drug therapy, electroshock, aversion therapy, psychosurgery, sensory deprivation, antabuse, operant conditioning, positive reinforcement, negative reinforcement, token economies, individual counselling, group counselling, and therapeutic communities. Although the use of these methods has not yet been fully documented, they appear to have been more vigorously applied in North America than in Britain (Kendall and Proctor 2001).

In Canada, the legacy of such practices is currently receiving attention through a statement of claim made against the federal government and former correctional employees by ex-prisoner, Dorothy Proctor. Ms Proctor alleges that, while incarcerated at the Prison for Women in the early 1960s, she was subjected to LSD experimentation. Evidence supports her assertions and further indicates that at least 23 other women were similarly experimented upon (Correctional Service of Canada 1998; Gilmore and Somerville 1998; Somerville and Gilmore 2000).

The psychologist conducting the experiment believed that criminals had unique defence mechanisms in their psyche, causing them to repress traumatic events. Such repression was considered to be the root cause of offending and pathology. LSD, it was hypothesised, would break down individual defence mechanisms, and thereby force prisoners to relive incidents they were repressing. In the process, prisoners would be cured of their criminality. LSD also had the effect of isolating prisoners from one another by encouraging them to withdraw into themselves. Since offending behaviour was thought to be fostered by criminal associations, LSD was a useful tool in breaking down the group influence. Those participating in the experiments were offered incentives such as early parole and better accommodation (Eveson 1964; Blanchfield and Bronskill 1998; Correctional Service of Canada 1998; Gilmore and Somerville 1998; Somerville and Gilmore 2000; Kendall and Proctor 2001). Although the case is still pending, in April 2001 the Canadian Government and psychologist Mark Eveson confessed to battery and negligence (Bronskill and Blanchfield 2001).

Following Ms Proctor's legal action, two male prisoners from Oak Ridge Institution, Canada, filed a similar statement of claim. They allege that from the mid 1960s through to the early 1980s, they were used as experimental fodder in attempts to reconstruct their personalities. Psychiatrist Eliot Barker led a number of experiments designed to force prisoners into abandoning their psychological defences through a combination of sensory deprivation, hallucinatory drugs, electroshock, force, restraint and humiliation. Prisoners furthermore served as therapists for one another, deciding when their fellow inmates should be disciplined, medicated and released. In fact, there is no doubt that such experimentation occurred, since the research was published in a number of academic journals, and even featured in a television documentary (Barker and Buck 1977; Barker and Mason 1968a, 1968b; Barker et al 1969).

Such experimentation marked the zenith of rehabilitation. The rehabilitative ideal was informed by the medical model. Scientific medicine, it was argued, could be employed to combat 'moral disease' or criminal behaviour in the same way that doctors cared for illnesses. Implicit was the assumption that offenders were either innately criminal or had a predisposition towards criminality. Under certain circumstances, such as trauma, the underlying disorder could be triggered, resulting in criminal behaviour. Offenders were therefore not responsible for their actions and deserved treatment rather than punishment. Since the problem lay within individuals, so too did the cure. Intervention was typically carried out by scientific experts with the requisite skills and knowledge (Moran 1992).

As Johnstone (1996) argues, medicine is not a monolith but consists of different philosophies and practices. Therefore, the medicalisation of crime has unfolded unevenly and adopted different forms. Within corrections, Johnstone suggests, psychiatry has been the most influential medical sub-discipline. Here, two distinctive methods are apparent: a medical-somatic approach and a social-psychological one. The first assumes the existence of an organic-based disorder typically located in the brain. Treatment is closely modelled on physical medicine: drugs are administered or surgery performed. Experts must be medically trained and they are highly active. Patients, conversely, are generally passive, 'Treatment is something done *to* the patient *by* medical professions' (emphasis in original) (Johnstone 1996: 20).

In contrast, the psycho-social approach presumes that persons are physically healthy, becoming disordered only in response to their environment. From such a perspective, deviant behaviour is typically perceived to be the consequence of psychological or emotional damage caused by neglect, abuse or some other trauma. Since the disorder is manifested subjectively or within a person's psyche, they are expected to take an active part in their treatment. Medical expertise is not mandatory and treatment is therefore provided by a range of experts and non-experts, including: psychiatrists, psychologists, social workers, psychotherapists, occupational therapists, religious instructors, reformers, and prison guards (Johnstone 1996; Hannah-Moffat 2001).

Johnstone's distinction between these two medical approaches provides us with a much more nuanced understanding of therapeutic interventions with offenders. Correctional rehabilitation is not monolithic, but consists of multiple, varied, and often seemingly contradictory practices. As Hannah-Moffat (2001) argues, we should apply a similarly complex analysis to the gendered nature of therapeutic correctional techniques. Thus, although the medical model has generally been more vigorously applied to females, different elements within it have been invoked variously across time and place. Within Britain, the starkest example is the aborted plan, dating from the late 1960s, to turn Holloway prison into a special hospital for women (Hayman 2000; Rock 1996).

Johnstone (1996) argues that although the medical-somatic approach is still in evidence, the psycho-social one currently dominates. This method of treatment, which presupposes active agency, is consistent with the emphasis on free will, individuality, choice and responsibility within neo-liberal societies. Indeed, as Rose (1999, 1996) states, psycho-social practices are now employed in the governance of entire populations. This occurs as people are encouraged to voluntarily examine and reshape their own subjectivities with the promise of self-actualisation and successful citizenship.

Thus, people become self-policing as they freely enter therapy, attend self-help groups and monitor their own appearance, thinking and emotions. The 'self' that is constructed and reconstructed through these processes is informed by dominant conceptions of who to be and how to behave. This is not to suggest that people are simply 'brainwashed' by prevailing discourses. We are neither discursive dopes nor empty vessels – we can and do resist power in varying ways. However, we are also situated within gendered, racialised, sexualised and economic networks of power. Our ability and desire to resist, manipulate or internalise constructions of the self reflect these. Crucially, they have real consequences, such as exclusion and criminalisation.

Both the medical-somatic and social-psychological approaches individualise social problems. Additionally, each claims to be benevolent or 'for prisoners' own good'. Whether the cause of crime is located in the mind or the body, whether individuals are held responsible or not, and coerced or bribed into treatment, the focus is on the individual rather than the social structure. Although perhaps less apparent in the social-psychological approach because of its recognition of the environment, the fault is ultimately conceptualised as lying within an individual's flawed mental and emotional capacity to withstand hardship or take advantage of the opportunities provided. Thus, while the two approaches may on the surface seem at odds, they are both rooted within the medical model and actually reinforce one another. It is therefore unsurprising that they co-exist or that particular strategies, such as the Canadian experiments described earlier, include elements of each. Cognitive behaviouralism, discussed below, fits closely with the social-psychological approach.

Cognitive behaviouralism

Cognitive behaviouralism is a term applied to a range of interventions derived from three psychological theories: social learning, cognitive theory and behaviourism (Vennard *et al* 1997). In the 1970s, these were combined into cognitive behaviouralism, 'a new approach to understanding the "complex dynamic relationships between thoughts, feelings and behaviour"' (McGuire cited in Vennard *et al* 1997: 4).

The cognitive behavioural model informing correctional policy and programming is best described by Don Andrews and James Bonta in their book entitled *The Psychology of Criminal Conduct* (1998). The authors claim that because they adopt the tenets of the scientific method, their own research is neutral, generalisable, empirical, rational and objective. They privilege quantitative methods and regard meta-analysis (discussed below) as the gold standard. In comparison, sociological research is thought to be unscientific, qualitative, ungeneralisable, non-empirical, value-laden and irrational.

On the basis of their research, Andrews and Bonta claim to have discovered a criminal personality which typifies all offenders regardless of gender, class, race or ethnicity. These criminal personalities are characterised by cognitive deficits or thinking errors which cause them to commit crime. Offenders fail to learn particular cognitive skills as a consequence of the interplay between problematic psychological and environmental factors. Treatment therefore should aim to provide them with these skills by teaching criminals how to think.

Andrews and Bonta (1998: 363) furthermore insist that it is a waste of time to address social-structural and systemic issues, warning: 'Do not get trapped in arguments with primary prevention advocates who believe that a society-wide focus on unemployment, sexism or racism will eliminate crime'. They promote the 'destruction' or 'neutralisation' of such explanations. At the same time, they accuse dissenters of being engaged in 'knowledge destruction' and of operating from professional, personal and/or ideological bias.

In sum, correctional cognitive behaviouralism assumes that offenders have failed to learn particular cognitive skills in their development. Treatment, therefore, should be focused upon teaching them these abilities. Despite its blatant individualisation of crime through its outright dismissal of structural factors, Andrews and Bonta argue that the accuracy of their model is overwhelmingly supported by research. However, their claims are in fact highly contested and at the centre of the 'what works' debate, discussed next.

The 'what works' debate

In the early 1970s, penal rehabilitation came under fire in both North America and Britain. Theoretically, it was criticised for its myopic focus upon individuals at the expense of society. Ethically, it was challenged not only for its intrusive nature but also because it was used as justification for indeterminate sentencing (Crow 2001). Additionally, American prisoners began to take legal action for being subjected to experimentation (Mitford 1974; Hornblum 1998; Harkness 1996). At the same time, the efficacy of interventions was challenged by a wave of evaluation studies which seemed to demonstrate that no one type of correctional programming was more effective than any other (Robinson and Smith 1971; Logan 1972; Greenberg 1975; Lipton *et al* 1975; Brody 1976; Folkard *et al* 1976). Most famously, Martinson's (1974) examination of 231 studies led him to the broad conclusion that 'nothing worked' to reduce offending.

The claims made by Martinson and others were challenged on various methodological grounds. Perhaps most importantly he was criticised for relying upon recidivism (reconviction) as a measure of programme effectiveness. As Hudson (1987) argues, the use of recidivism as a measure is misguided and inadequate. Should recidivism be established by arrests, convictions or actual offences? People may re-offend but not get caught, yet they would be counted as examples of programme success. Furthermore, someone may offend less or less seriously than they did before. Does this not count as some kind of success? Programmes that fail to reduce offending may still have some value to the participants, but their worth is not captured in the calculations. Finally, many law-abiding ex-offenders live in poor circumstances. Non-recidivism tells us nothing about their quality of life (Kendall 1998).

Taken together, these theoretical, ethical and empirical claims contributed to a pessimism around the notion that offenders could be rehabilitated. The effect of such scepticism arguably fell hardest upon the United States. Although Vanstone (2000) maintains that in Britain the impact was greater at the policy level than in actual practice, Crow (2001) contends that both levels were influenced considerably. Mair (1997) suggests that the election of Margaret Thatcher in 1979 was a greater influence on the decline of rehabilitation. The Conservative government she ushered in emphasised cost-efficiency, management, responsibility and individualism. A 'just deserts' model appeared to fit such a philosophy much more closely than a rehabilitative one.

In Canada, however, the reaction was quite different. Here, a group of psychologists affiliated with the Correctional Service of Canada undertook their own studies. Their research relied heavily upon meta-analysis, a statistical technique which codes various programmatic features and compares them according to their impact upon recidivism (see, for example, Gendreau et al 1996; Gendreau and Ross 1987, 1979; Andrews, Bonta and Hoge 1990; Andrews et al 1990; Andrews 1989). Based upon this method they concluded that interventions employing the following four key principles reduced recidivism:

1. *The risk principle*: Effective treatment programmes should match programme intensity to the risk of re-offending. Those at greater risk require more intensive programmes, while programmes delivered to those least at risk may actually increase recidivism. Therefore, it is essential that reliable risk assessments are undertaken.

2. *The need principle*: Two types of needs are identified, criminogenic and non-criminogenic. Criminogenic needs are those characteristics statistically associated with recidivism. This association is determined

through meta-analysis. Criminogenic needs include: pro-criminal attitudes, criminal associates, action-orientation, impulsivity, concrete thinking, rigid thinking, difficulties with interpersonal problem solving, lack of self-control, egocentricity, a tendency to blame others, external locus of control, and low levels of educational and/or vocational achievement. When programmes target these features, recidivism will be reduced. Non-criminal needs include: self-esteem, anxiety, depression, a history of abuse or victimisation, gender, race and class. These factors are not statistically associated with recidivism and therefore it is argued that addressing them is largely an ineffective use of programme time. Programmes using a cognitive behavioural model are the most effective at addressing criminogenic needs.

3. *Responsivity principle*: The delivery approach should match the learning styles of offenders. Offenders are thought to be characterised by particular learning styles, regulated by the following factors: poor social skills, inadequate problem-solving skills, concrete thinking, little motivation to change and poor verbal skills. Treatment programmes which set clear behavioural goals and tasks are the most effective. In this regard, cognitive behavioural programmes are the most responsive. Programmes which rely upon case-work, counselling and are insight-oriented, psychodynamic or nondirective are less responsive.

4. *Programme integrity principle*: Treatment should be conducted in a structured way with strict adherence to the programme manual, and delivered by enthusiastic and dedicated staff according to the principles outlined above. Pro-social modelling is encouraged. Here, programme deliverers serve as role-models by rewarding progress and exhibiting positive behaviours for offenders to mirror.

In sum, the principles recommend interventions which are highly structured and rooted in a cognitive behavioural model. They also insist upon the necessity of risk assessments. The research upon which these bold assertions rest has been challenged largely upon methodological grounds. For example, meta-analysis depends upon recidivism as a measure of programme success and excludes small-scale as well as qualitative studies (see, for example, Gorman 2001; Lab and Whitehead 1990; Mair 1997). More recently, the research has been criticised for its bias in sample selection, since it relies heavily upon studies with young American males. As such, it does not consider gender, nor does it distinguish 'race' or ethnicity (Hannah-Moffat and Shaw 2000a; Shaw and Hannah-Moffat 2000; Worrall 2000c; Rex 2000; Covington and Bloom 1999; McMahon 1998; Shaw 1997).

As Hannah-Moffat and Shaw (2000a) argue, research intentionally excluded by meta-analysis reaches quite different conclusions. For example, qualitative studies privileging women's own understandings of their lives have found that women's needs and their pathways into crime are in fact different from men's. This body of research also highlights the structural inequalities implicated in crime and criminalisation such as racism, sexism, classism and heterosexism. Furthermore, when asked, women prisoners prefer individual, client-centred counselling, the treatment approach rejected by the responsivity factor. Although Dowden and Andrews (1999) have recently attempted to assess the effectiveness of programmes specific to women, their work relies upon meta-analysis and 'is particularly problematic given the broad cultural variations and difficulties of measuring the impact of programmes on small and diverse populations' (Shaw and Hannah-Moffat 2000a: 168).

The contested effectiveness of rehabilitative programmes is at the core of the 'what works' debate. Less often considered, but arguably most important, are the epistemological underpinnings of the debate: assumptions about what counts as knowledge which inform both the research method (the techniques used in the conduct of research such as interviews, surveys or meta-analysis) and the research methodology (the theory or perspective and analysis followed in the research process). The 'what works' research is informed by an epistemology rooted in traditional notions of the scientific method which devalues subjectivity, assumes a linear causality and emphasises universality (Shaw 1997; Kendall 1998). The dangers of this model will become more apparent in the subsequent examination of cognitive behavioural programmes.

Cognitive behavioural programmes

Somewhat predictably, cognitive behavioural programmes have been designed by many of the same Canadian researchers involved in studies proving their effectiveness. This is true for the Reasoning and Re-habilitation (R&R) Programme, developed by Robert Ross and Elizabeth Fabiano, one of the first correctional cognitive behavioural programmes (Ross and Ross 1995; Fabiano *et al* 1990; Ross *et al* 1988; Ross and Fabiano 1985; Fabiano and Ross 1983). The course manual has been translated into at least five different languages and the programme delivered globally, including in the following places: Canada, England, Scotland, Wales, the United States, New Zealand, Australia, Estonia, Venezuela, Spain,

Denmark and Sweden (Ross and Ross 1995). It could be argued that the R&R programme stimulated an industry that continues to expand through off-shoot programmes, manuals, videos, course materials, training sessions, and so on.

The inspiration for the R&R programme was Robert Ross's work with female adolescent offenders at Grandview Training School for Girls in Ontario during the 1970s. Employed as a psychologist, Ross implemented various types of behaviour modification with the school's inmates, many of whom self-injured. After numerous unsuccessful attempts, he finally found a method that appeared to work, a technique he called co-opting. Aptly named, the programme persuaded the girls to coerce one another into the desired behaviour through peer pressure. The girls were trained in the principles of reinforcement therapy and encouraged to act as therapists for one another (Ross and McKay 1979, 1976).

In 1976 there was an investigation into the school which eventually led to its closure. Unfortunately the subsequent report was never released. More recently, eight former employees, including Ross, were accused of physical, sexual and psychological abuse against ex-prisoners. While Ross was acquitted of some of the charges, and others were withdrawn, eleven remain stayed. However, two guards were convicted and the Ontario government delivered a formal apology in 1999 as a part of a compensation package to former prisoners (*Globe and Mail* 1999; Laframboise 1997; Grandview Agreement Between the Grandview Survivors Support Group and the Government of Ontario, June 30, 1994).

Ironically, Ross and his colleague Elizabeth Fabiano (1986) were responsible for producing one of the earliest comprehensive overviews of programmes for female offenders. They brought attention to correctional sexism and concluded that women and girls were 'correctional after-thoughts', provided with poor quality services designed for males. However, they also recommended that female offenders be provided with 'time to think'. That is, cognitive behavioural programmes designed to teach them how 'to learn to stop, think and analyze consequences before taking actions' (Ross and Fabiano 1986).

The history of correctional cognitive behaviouralism is important to acknowledge. Not only does it situate the model upon a rocky foundation, it raises questions about the evidence for its stated success. If Ross's research findings were incorporated into a meta-analysis, the programme would be considered a success. However, the context within which it was delivered would never have been captured. Most crucially, the girls were never given the opportunity to tell about their experiences. The epistemological assumptions underlying cognitive behaviouralism foreclose even such a possibility.

Furthermore, the derogatory nature of cognitive behaviouralism is very worrisome. Offenders are conceptualised as being very different to law-abiding citizens. For example, in bragging about the success of cognitive skills training, the Canadian Commissioner of Corrections, Lucie McClung, recently remarked: 'The criminal mind ... does not operate like yours and mine. What would work for you in terms of deterrence will not work for the offender' (Stewart 2001: 38). Such an emphasis upon 'otherness' works to dehumanise prisoners, making it easier to strip them of rights and tolerate their oppression.

The revival of rehabilitation, therefore, may be cause for concern. As was discussed earlier, during the heyday of rehabilitation various abuses were carried out against offenders on treatment grounds. This was perhaps best illustrated by experiments designed to alter the criminal mind. Arguably, the methods employed at this time were mostly rooted in a medical-somatic approach modelled closely upon physical medicine. In contrast, it might be suggested that new rehabilitative models pose less harm since they rely on a social-psychological approach which acknowledges environmental influences and involves prisoners in their own treatment. However, as stated earlier, the root problem is still ultimately regarded to be lying within the individual and they become the focus of intervention rather than the social structure. As in the past, rehabilitation is focused upon altering the criminal mind.

An important question to consider is who decides how and what to think? The programmes and model upon which they are based are largely designed by white, middle-class men. It is likely the case that their own norms and values, as well as those of corrections, will be reflected in the research and in the programmes. Indeed, Hannah-Moffat and Shaw (2001) have shown that Correctional Service of Canada programmatic tools, manuals and instruments are replete with moral judgments and incorporate class, race, ethnic and gender biases.

In her observation of an American cognitive behavioural programme designed for violent offenders, Fox (2001) concluded that the programmatic goal was to bribe prisoners into internalising notions of a criminal identity. Similarly, it would appear that the aim of cognitive behavioural programmes is to induce prisoners into believing that they are criminals, characterised by cognitive deficits. Once this is achieved, it is then possible for prisoners to undergo the process of self-recovery. Not unlike earlier attempts to break down a person's defence mechanisms, the overall intent is to build a new personality. Although some prisoners may benefit from the programme and others resist it, the general effect is to hold individual women responsible for their own oppression.

Despite the many limitations and hazards associated with cognitive behaviouralism it continues to gain influence. How can this be accounted for? I think one important factor is the consistency between cognitive behaviouralism and the current political climate within which it is deployed. As stated earlier, the techniques it incorporates are used more broadly to govern entire populations. Furthermore, they both hold people responsible for the predicaments they find themselves in through an emphasis upon individuality, free will and choice. Rhetorically, although not in practice, prisoners are not forced into change but given the opportunity to choose a programme which will assist them to rehabilitate themselves. They are expected to take an active part in their own treatment so that ultimately they become self-governing. Finally, each emphasises the 'otherness' of individuals who become marginalised and/or criminalised and thus encourage their further exclusion. The specific impact of cognitive behaviouralism upon British women offenders will be discussed in the final section.

The new government strategy for women offenders in England and Wales

At the turn of the millennium, the British government introduced a new proposal for dealing with women offenders. The strategy is the product of a combined effort between the Prison and Probation services. Overall, the aim is to protect the public and reduce re-offending through programmes based upon solid research evidence as to 'what works' in preventing women from recidivating. Cognitive behaviouralism is thus at the very heart of this proposal and is apparent in the following quote:

> This Government promised to be tough on crime and its causes. There is no excuse for crime, whatever a person's background or experience. However, the characteristics of women prisoners suggest that experiences such as poverty, abuse and drug addiction lead some women to believe that their options are limited. Many offending behaviour programmes are designed to help offenders see that there are always positive choices open to them that do not involve crime.
>
> (Home Office, 2000a:7)

The hard-line law-and-order position of the Government appears to be legitimated here by the suggestion that women's options are not *actually* limited, women only *believe* them to be. This is an incredible denial of systemic inequalities and oppression which is then justified by cognitive behaviouralism. Presumably, offending behaviour programmes will teach women that their poverty, drug addiction and abuse are simply the result of their own deficit thinking. As they acquire the requisite cognitive skills through programmes they will be equipped to choose from a range of pro-social alternatives available to them. These assumptions do not fit with a growing body of literature which takes seriously women's own accounts of their pathways to imprisonment (for example, Bosworth 1999; Carlen 1998; Devlin 1998; Eaton and Humphries 1996; Eaton 1993; Morris *et al* 1995). These studies emphasise the very real structural barriers which contribute to re-offending.

Despite such research, the Strategy document states, 'There are a great many gaps in the research evidence about women offenders' (p. 4). It is clear that this gap refers to research specifically constructed to identify criminogenic factors. It appears, therefore, that the existing qualitative studies are considered less valuable than quantitative research such as meta-analysis. The epistemological privileging of expert knowledge over the women prisoners' own knowledge is apparent here.

In fact, the Prison Service has begun to examine the criminogenic needs of women offenders (Clark and Howden-Windell 2000; Howden-Windell and Clark 1999). This research concluded

> that many of the major criminogenic needs for both sexes are the same. This would suggest that approaches which have been developed to tackle these criminogenic factors in male offenders should work with female offenders. This does not of course rule out the importance of making offending programmes responsive to female offenders in the way they are delivered. But, indicating that treatment targets will often be the same, and theoretical approaches used with males are valid.
>
> (Clark and Howden-Windell, 2000: 18)

Again, this is inconsistent with research findings informed by women's own accounts.

Despite all of its problems the correctional cognitive behavioural model is becoming instituted through the Strategy and the accreditation process. This process will determine which programmes will be allowed to operate, both in prison and probation. As Mair (2000) argues, only those programmes which adhere to the cognitive behavioural model will be granted accreditation. [See also chapters 6 and 12. Ed.] Even the recent review of the sentencing framework for England and Wales embodies this model, as evidenced in the title of the review report, *Making Punishments Work*. In these ways, the central role of cognitive behaviouralism within corrections has become a *fait accompli*. Therefore, it is hard to take seriously the Home Secretary's assertion that the 'correctional policy must be seen in the context of wider Government initiatives to tackle poverty, social exclusion, and to bring about a fair society' (Home Office, 2000a: 1).

The primacy of cognitive behaviouralism is already visible in the programmes offered. For example, in April 2001, 68% of adult females were enrolled in either the R&R programme or the Enhanced Thinking Skills (ETS) skills programme, both cognitive behavioural models. The R&R programme comprises 38 sessions, each lasting 2.5 hours. The cost of this course is £2500 per participant. The ETS programme runs at a cost of £2000 per individual and consists of 21 sessions, each running for 2.5 hours (Women's Policy Group 2001). I can't help but wonder what might be accomplished if this money were used to assist women with other matters such as housing and employment.

Furthermore, these programmes claim to be generic or suitable for everyone. While some adaptations are made to suit the participant profile, these are merely cosmetic changes and draw upon sexist stereotypes. For example, gender-appropriate language is incorporated (changing 'he' to 'she') and seemingly more relevant examples employed to illustrate concepts (in using a case study, the person's occupation is 'secretary' instead of 'builder'). Nonetheless, the programmes were originally designed for a white male population and the fundamental assumptions underlying cognitive behaviouralism remain intact. No amount of tinkering will alter this.

Although gender-specific programmes are currently under development these too are rooted in a cognitive behavioural framework. They include separate programmes for women convicted of violent offences, acquisitive crimes and sex offences. Additionally, the feasibility of using Dialectical Behavioural Therapy, designed to treat women with borderline personality disorders, is being undertaken. I have critiqued this last programme elsewhere, arguing that its implementation in Canada pathologises women prisoners and poses other potential harms (Kendall and Pollack forthcoming). Fundamentally where cognitive behavioural programmes recognise women's differences they do so by drawing on traditional notions of women's madness. That is, females are regarded as inherently more prone to mental illnesses than males and this assumption is embedded into the programmes. The overall effect remains: women are encouraged to internalise their own oppression.

In December 1995, Chief Inspector Sir David Ramsbotham walked out of Holloway prison in protest against the appalling conditions. The experience encouraged him to carry out a thematic review of women in prison (HM Inspectorate of Prisons 1997). The resulting report contained a series of recommendations. Since then, he has written a follow-up report (HM Inspectorate of Prisons 2001). Unfortunately, this report places much importance upon and faith in offending behaviour programmes. Elsewhere, however, Sir David notes that in direct contrast to his recommendations, security has been intensified – with the number of women in open prisons actually reduced while overall numbers increased – and overuse of control and restraint actually continued. In fact, he states that they appear to be strengthening. This suggests that a punitive penal environment still prevails. [See also chapters 11 and 12. Ed.] The growing population is likely to exacerbate this situation.

Another thematic review, jointly conducted by the Prison and Probation Services, found that cognitive behavioural programmes were often not supported by the general prison milieu (HM Inspectorates of Prisons and Probation 2001). Some prisoners refused to attend treatment sessions on the grounds that they did not want to make themselves vulnerable within a non-supportive environment. [See also chapter 1 on 'rights' to refuse 'treatment'. Ed.] This is the crux of the matter. Prisons, by their very nature, are not safe places. They are founded upon unequal relationships and extreme control. Inmates are not allowed to make even the most basic decisions such as 'when to get up and go to sleep, when and what to eat, and when and whom to visit' (Hannah-Moffat 2001:196).

Yet, offending behaviour programmes emphasise individual responsibility. How can prisoners be expected to act responsibly when the institution makes this impossible? While there have been recent efforts to place greater responsibility upon prisoners it is not likely that prisoners will actually be given greater control over their own lives (see, for example, Pryor 2001). Rather it is a responsibilisation technique, whereby individuals are conceptualised as active agents who are able to make their own choices, exercise free will, and thus be held accountable for the decisions they make. This presupposes a level playing field and denies structural barriers. Although notions of 'choices', 'agency' and 'free will' are more apparent than real, the charge of responsibility remains. Ultimately, responsibilisation governs through the individualisation of social problems, victim-blaming and self-regulation (Hannah-Moffat 2001; Garland 1996).

Through a similar process of individualisation, cognitive behaviouralism obfuscates organisational, institutional and social problems. By insisting that the problem of crime inheres in cognitive deficits, the focus of intervention remains at the level of the individual. Thus, social inequalities and oppressions need not be addressed. Furthermore, by emphasising prisoners' differences from other citizens, the concept of cognitive deficiency ensures that all prisoners are situated as trouble-some and potentially dangerous. The curtailment of their rights, their containment and the programmatic interventions are thus legitimated. Ultimately, cognitive behaviouralism is a governmental technology which obscures the pains of social exclusion and imprisonment.

Chapter 11

Creating choices: reflecting on choices

Kelly Hannah-Moffat

While the capacity to reform the prison should indeed be distrusted, it is foolhardy to dismiss it entirely.

(Cohen 1985: 35)

An answer is only seen to be right if it sustains the institutional thinking that is already in the minds of individuals as they try to decide.

(Douglas 1986:4)

Creating choices? Reflecting on the choices

Ten years ago, the Canadian federal government made a long overdue commitment to reform the federal[1] women's penal system and to the implementation of the recommendations contained in the 1990 Report of the Task Force on Federally Sentenced Women – *Creating Choices*. This unique report proposed the development of a culturally appropriate, woman centred model of corrections that attempted to address the longstanding concerns of women prisoners, Aboriginal women, feminist reformers, advocates[2], femocrats and bureaucrats. Many regarded this initiative to be an example of innovative progressive corrections, and few questioned the compatibility of feminist and Aboriginal ideals with the institutional practice of imprisonment. Notwithstanding the by now well-established history of failed attempts of benevolent penal reform (see Rothman 1980; Cohen and Scull 1983; Cohen 1985), the men and women involved in this reform were cautiously committed to a tenuous process that they believed would redress a long history of inequity, by giving priority to gender. What emerged from this process was a feminist and Aboriginal inspired vision of woman-centred corrections. Advocates, bureaucrats, and prisoners alike were optimistic and sincerely believed that this effort would create the conditions for meaningful change and that the implementation of these recommendations would reconfigure and transform women's prisons.

With the benefit of ten years' hindsight, it is clear that, like many other 'innovative penal reforms', the ideals embodied in *Creating Choices* were not effortlessly translated into policy. Instead, these ideals were re-configured and adapted by organisational politics inherent to large correctional bureaucracies and the experiences of incarceration. Many of these eroded ideals are now in danger of being abandoned. While women's regimes changed because of the efforts, the changes were not aligned with many of the reformers' aspirations. This is an increasingly familiar pattern, repeatedly documented in institutional historiographies which have shown that 'reforms are not to be taken at face value; they do not necessarily lead to progress; often they can lead to further repression' (Chan 1992: 4).

Rather than spending the little time here on documenting the predictable and ever-increasing gaps between what reformers intended versus what occurred (Hannah-Moffat 2001; Hannah-Moffat and Shaw 2001; Hayman 2000; Monture 2001), this chapter discusses the certainty of this 'gap' occurring by examining some features of the structures and logics supporting modern forms of punishment. The argument is not meant to discredit the efforts of those who are tirelessly engaged in the necessary ongoing process of improving conditions of confinement. Instead, it reflects on systemic problems and on organisational dynamics of institutional reform, on the ability of the prison to absorb and adapt to critical discourses and on how a particular reform initiative (the con-struction of woman-centred prisons) is unsurprisingly diluted by over-arching managerial and pragmatic goals. The chapter reflects not on individual failures but on some of the bigger ideological and systemic problems that consistently plague our attempts to reform the prisons and, in particular, women's prisons.

The analysis is organised around four themes: carceral 'pragmatism'; appropriation and redefinition; empowering or controlling; and en-croachment and erosion. These themes capture some of the conceptual and organisational limits of this reform effort. Perhaps ironically, the chapter concludes by reflecting on the lessons that can be learned from the Canadian experience in terms of future initiatives. While I will provide a somewhat functionalist analysis of penal reform, it is also prudent to recognise that prisons are likely to persist and thus the conditions of confinement and nature of the regime remain important sites of concern and advocacy. From this standpoint, I favour the adoption of reflexive and strategic reforms that focuses on structural changes that decentre the prison, 'truth in punishment', and individual advocacy directed at situational or specific problems encountered collectively or individually by women prisoners.

Creating choices

In the late 1980s the federal Commissioner for Corrections, who has jurisdiction over all prisoners serving sentences of greater than two years, established the Task Force on Federally Sentenced Women. Its mandate was to develop a comprehensive strategy for the management of women offenders. The composition of the Task Force was unique and unlike any other that preceded it – in that it was not constituted simply of government officials but also included advocates, feminist and aboriginal reformers, women prisoners and members of the 'correctional community'. The Task Force was meant to address the longstanding and historically entrenched problems that plagued the Prison for Women (P4W), which until recently was the only federal penitentiary for women in the country. Some of these problems included: geographical isolation (many women were incarcerated far away from their families, friends, and communities); the absence of gender specific programmes attentive to women's needs and experiences; the failure to adequately address the cultural and spiritual needs of Aboriginal offenders; an absence of programmes and services for French-speaking prisoners; over classification[3] – in that all women were housed in a multi-level facility, whereas federally sentenced men had greater choices; and gaps in community programmes to facilitate release and reintegration. These problems were well documented in several government taskforces and commissions of inquiry (Hannah-Moffat 2001; Cooper 1987).

Briefly, the report of the task force, *Creating Choices*, outlined a women-centred strategy for reform founded on the following five principles: empowerment; meaningful and responsible choices; respect and dignity; supportive environments; shared responsibility. It was accepted that women prisoners were different from men prisoners and clearly stated that women in prison had more in common with other women than with imprisoned men, in terms of their vulnerabilities to male violence, their marginal socio-economic statuses, and their histories of discriminatory treatment and oppression. It was further argued and accepted that women prisoners were not particularly risky – but were instead high need and thus in need of a more supportive and empowering environment rather than the punitive or security-oriented environments that typically characterised imprisonment.

The central recommendations included:

- the closure of Prison for Women;

- the construction of four regional women's facilities and an Aboriginal healing lodge (all to be structured in accordance with community-style living environments and non-traditional penal architectures);

- the development of women-centred programmes, including survivors of abuse, substance abuse and mother-child programming; cognitive skills

- the establishment of a community strategy to expand and strengthen residential and non-residential programmemes and services for women offenders who are conditionally released.

The acceptance and implementation of these recommendations re-defined the future of women's imprisonment. In formulating its recom-mendations and in envisioning the guiding principles the Task Force drew heavily on feminist and aboriginal knowledges. The report addressed many of the concerns of penal critics.

What happened

While the recommendations of *Creating Choices* were fully endorsed by the federal government shortly after its release, the vision did not materialise as many involved in the process had hoped. Many fear that the new prisons are beginning to replicate the very problems they sought to resolve. Indeed the one Prison for Women closed in the spring of 2000, and in its place we have four new regional prisons for women and an Aboriginal prison (or healing lodge). Additionally (to the horror of many) we have three newly established, but 'temporary' segregated maximum security facilities for 'difficult' women in men's penitentiaries which have little to no programming. These units are expected to close once maximum-security units for women are built in the grounds of the new prisons.

The new prisons are overcrowded – there are increases to federal terms of imprisonment, in part due to women's requests[4] for such sentences (greater than two years) and partly due to judges' sentencing rationales (both punitive and benevolent). Prison capacity has been expanded and the proposed community strategy has not been implemented. Non-custodial alternatives for women are sparse, under-funded and over-subscribed. The only minimum-security accommodation for women, Isabel MacNeill House, is scheduled to close. The closure of this facility will mean that minimum security women will remain in the regional facilities, thus re-creating the overly secure and inequitable conditions of confinement for minimum security women. Only some Aboriginal women who are at the appropriate security level are eligible for admission to the healing lodge.

Although the Prison for Women was closed, the legacy of P4W continues to haunt Canadian women's corrections. Without doubt, penal governance changed following the tabling of *Creating Choices* but not in the ways envisioned by the task force or reformers. While Correctional Service of Canada (CSC) adopted a more feminised penal discourse and improved the material conditions of confinement for some women, the more oppressive and sinister elements of incarceration persist. These elements have systematically undermined attempts at reform. This well-intentioned reform initiative inadvertently reinforces traditional conceptualisations of punishment and further entrenches our reliance on the prison (or in this case more 'women-centred' prisons[5]) as a solution.

Explaining the widening gap

A major barrier to the realisation of the woman-centred ideal (whether it is based on maternalism, *'carceral pragmatism'* or feminist principles) or any meaningful structural reform or shift is its denial of the material and legal reality of carceral relations embodied in the prison. There is general failure to clearly recognise the limits of punishment, the problems associated with the confinement of an involuntary population, and the cultural and socio-political significance of the prison. The criminal justice system is perhaps the quintessential arena in which the state applies coercive measures against its citizens (Hannah-Moffat and Singh 1996: 6). The use of incarceration in a liberal state assumes the loss of certain rights and freedoms. The explicit intention of imprisonment is to punish and to limit the freedom and autonomy of individuals subject to this sanction. As Scull (1984:178) notes 'prisoners are not clients, and pain, privation, and suffering are seen by many as their just deserts'.

Woman-centred ideals of reform once integrated into penal discourse and popular cultures tend to obscure and to some extent silence or minimise the oppressive aspects of prisons and the unequal relations of power that characterise this sanction. Prisons are governed by material structures, cultural sensibilities and mentalities that limit the extent to which the content of a regime can be changed. Regardless of the form and content of a women-centred regime, it is still, in many respects, about punishment, security and discipline.

The prison is tied into wider networks of social action and meaning (Garland 1990). Simply changing the content of a penal regime to reflect a woman-centred approach leaves the wider institutional framework unchallenged. Currently, the way we think about and define punishment is derived from the wider criminal justice context. The limits of the current direction of 'woman-centred' reforms are perhaps most clearly reflected in the findings of the 1996 Arbour Commission. The report was written by the Honourable Madame Justice Louise Arbour following an alleged riot and escape attempt that occurred four years after the acceptance of the recommendations of the Task Force on Federally Sentenced Women.

The findings of the Arbour Report vividly document the violation of prisoners' rights and abuses of power that occurred at the Prison for Women in April of 1994. Based on the evidence presented at commission hearings, Justice Arbour indicated that the Correctional Service had exhibited a disturbing lack of commitment to the ideals of justice and the rule of law (Arbour 1996: 198). The inquiry revealed that women prisoners had been denied a number of basic rights including access to legal counsel, shower, clothing and bedding, and that several institutional directives were violated (i.e. involuntary transfer to a men's prison). While the behaviour of the prisoners was also clearly seen as problematic by the commission, the response of the Correctional Service was both inhumane and illegal and it violated laws and policies. The handling of this situation was in stark contrast to the guiding principles outlined in *Creating Choices*, which were meant to be shaping and reconfiguring managerial practices in women's prisons at the same time as these events were taking place.

Post-liberal reform strategies like those central to the woman-centred ideal (i.e. 'empowerment', respect and dignity, 'choice' and 'healing') require and assume that women in prison already enjoy certain rights. Justice Arbour's (1996) report raised serious questions about the potential of a repressive state to 'empower' individuals who are not even deemed by that state to be legitimate recipients of the most basic of human rights. The irony of the situation was reflected in the report and in Justice Arbour's recommendations that attempted on some level to grapple with difficult questions of administrative accountability and the preservation of a newly configured model of women's imprisonment.

'Appropriation and redefinition'

Cohen (1985: 35) has argued that 'entirely opposed groups deliver the same message, [and] entirely opposed messages will be delivered by the same group'. This localised discussion of appropriation and redefinition of reformers' well-intentioned and critical ideals is a reflection of a wider problem endemic to penal reform in general and the prison in particular: that is, the ability of institutions like the prison to absorb, integrate and temporarily silence critical discourses, thus creating an illusion of change. Perhaps it is this feature of the prison that contributes to its continuance as a viable punishment despite its well-documented failures. Critical reform discourses can be appropriated, redefined and adapted to concur with the managerial and political priorities of an organisation.

The critical feminist and aboriginal discourses and the elusive concept of 'woman-centred' corrections that shaped the Canadian reforms have been used to feminise the discourse of imprisonment and to obscure the realities of punishment and the complexities of women's differences. Good example of this is how terms like empowerment and healing have come to define women's penal discourse. *Empowerment* is a common term that can assume multiple meanings depending on how they are used and by whom.[6] Iris Young (1994: 49), in her article on the treatment and punishment of female drug addicts, notes that 'empowerment is like democracy: everyone is for it, but rarely do they mean the same thing by it'. Young's comments capture some of the difficulties associated with the current emphasis placed on empowerment in women's penal and treatment regimes. In this context, at least two interpretations of empowerment can be identified. For feminists, empowerment (ideologically, politically, and economically) is traditionally embraced as a way of transforming the lives of women by limiting gender oppression through a restructuring of power relations that allow women to make choices and regain control of their lives.

'Empowerment', in *Creating Choices* (TFFSW 1990: 105–106), is meant to highlight that the structural inequities experienced by women prisoners are similar to broader gender inequalities. It is noted that the 'research and the words of federally sentenced women have repeatedly stressed the connections between women's involvement in the criminal justice system and the inequalities, hardships, and suffering experienced by women in our society'.

The Task Force locates the disempowerment of women in two sites: in the structural arrangements of society and in the woman herself, with an emphasis on the latter. This understanding led the Task Force to argue for a

> holistic understanding of women's experiences and needs which encompasses physical, emotional, psychological, spiritual and material needs, as well as a need for relationships and connectedness to families. If needs are not understood in the context of past, present, and future life experiences, if a woman is not seen and treated as a *total person*, programs and policies designed for federally sentenced women will continue to be inadequate and dehumanizing.
>
> (TFSW 1990: 61).[See chapter 12 for discussion of the different uses to which the term 'holism' has been put in UK. Ed.]

Thus it is argued that women's needs cannot be dealt with in isolation and that the interrelationship between needs and opportunities is essential to effectively addressing women's problems.

Feminist and Aboriginal knowledges are selectively used to support an empowering-responsibilisation strategy. Not surprisingly, however, feminist and Aboriginal understandings of women's disempowerment and its remedy are *not* neatly incorporated into correctional narratives and practices. Quite independently, the Correctional Service of Canada has redefined and constructed empowerment and holistic notions of shared responsibility so that they are compatible with its own independent strategy of penal government. Contrary to the Task Force's support for reforms that extended beyond the narrow parameters the 'problem of federally sentenced women in corrections', the operationalisation of the report is narrowly configured within 'corrections'(TFFSW 1990:61).

Strategies of empowerment tend to resonate with multiple and conflicting objectives. While the strategy of empowerment coincides with the above-stated feminist objectives and intentions of the reformers, it is also compatible with the long-standing goals and objectives of correctional officials. Empowerment alternatively is defined by Corrections Canada as 'the process through which women gain insight into their situation, identify their strengths, and are supported and challenged to take positive action to gain control of their lives' (CSC 1994: 9). Empowerment in this context has a different meaning from empowerment in feminist reform narrative. Corrections Canada further indicates that their empowering process 'acknowledges and holds FSW (federally sentenced women) *accountable for their actions*, but also recognises their actions in a wider social context' (CSC 1994: 9). This definition of empowerment stresses responsibility and accountability, not structural relations of power or inequity. While it acknowledges the wider social structure, it is essentially about making the offender responsible. While previous welfare penal strategies of rehabilitation view the state as responsible for the offender's reformation, this empowerment strategy makes the offender responsible for her own rehabilitation. Predictably the correctional emphasis is on the individual, who must learn how to cope within the broader context of social inequality, sexism and racism. The responsibility of corrections is to facilitate this learning through programmes that teach women how to make 'responsible' non-criminal (pro-social) choices. This analysis fails to challenge existing structural relations in which *Creating Choices* and broader feminist narratives situate their analyses.

New strategies of responsibilisation appear to be less intrusive and less regulatory, and therefore reformers do not usually contest them. The offender, in this new correctional framework, is responsible for her own self-governance and for the minimisation and management of her needs and risk to the public or self. Empowerment in the prison context becomes a technology of self-governance which requires the woman to take responsibility for her actions in order to satisfy the objectives of the authorities and not her own. The choices women are empowered to make are censored and predetermined by the wider penal structure. Women in prison are only allowed limited choices that are deemed by the administration as meaningful and responsible and not necessarily the prisoner. Empowerment for Corrections Canada is clearly about responsibilisation and accountability. Having offenders take responsibility for, or ownership of, their actions is a paramount concern for correctional institutions. It is a concern that coincides with feminist demands for the integration of women's experiences and a feminist strategy of empowerment, which after all does not imply or necessitate the displacement of offender accountability or 'agency'.

Empowerment for the Correctional Service of Canada is not about a fundamental restructuring of relations of disciplinary power in the prison, but rather about adding a new dimension to existing relations by using empowerment strategies to responsibilise. Notions of holistic programming extend to the state the right and the ability to probe all aspects of a woman's life. It is no longer about simply punishing the offender. It permits a more totalising intervention in the name of empowerment. With respect to the woman-centred prison, it is increasingly unclear as to who is being empowered: the prison or the prisoner? However, what is clear is that the state now claims it offers women programmes and services that provide them with the opportunity of empowerment. It becomes more difficult for advocates and reformers to show how the state is negligent, in terms of its recognition of the programming needs of women.

'Empowering or controlling'[7]

Those working with women offenders are engaged in a power relationship with women prisoners. There is a tendency to view the empowering well-meaning woman-centred prisons as a liberated space free from the surveillance and restriction of the prison. These relations of power between the prisoner and the 'empowering guard' are most clearly visible in the management of the 'problem prisoner – or the 'unempowerable'.

A fundamental assumption that underscores the logic of the woman-centred reform is the notion that the prisoners are generally non-violent women who pose more of a threat to themselves than to others. As Shaw (2001) has observed, this woman-centred reform initiative, similar to wider feminist discourses on the female offender, ignored women's capacity for violence and resistance (also see Allen 1987a). Rather than being high risk, women were seen to be high need, and thus traditional punitive and static security measures were not required. However, a series of highly sensationalised events which occurred in the mid 1990s led to a gradual recasting of some woman prisoners as difficult to manage and as a danger to other prisoners, correctional staff and the public. Some of these events included: escapes and murder of a prisoner in the newly opened Edmonton prison; an alleged escape, riot, and stabbing of a guard with a needle in 1994 that resulted in the Arbour Commission, and increased public concern about women's and girls' violence and their involvement in serious violent incidents – most notable being the case of Karla Homolka.[8] The avoidance of these issues and the absence of discussion and acknowledgement of such events by the Task Force meant that when faced with a 'legitimacy crisis' and backlash for the public and correctional staff[9], the Correctional Service resorted to traditional discursive tactics and conventional methods of managing prison violence and 'violent prisoners'.

Given that the Task Force's construction of women prisoners did not include a discussion of the management of women defined as 'difficult to manage' for various reasons, when presented with organisational pressures to respond to anomalous incidents like those of April 1994 and at Edmonton and mounting concerns about 'maximum security women', solutions were structured along narrowly formulated institutional channels. The contested image of the unempowerable-violent women was used to legitimate the intensification of static security measures at all of the regional prisons and the re-entrenchment of punitive isolation strategies namely – 'special handling units' for women.

CSC stated: 'in 1996 shortly after the opening of the first regional facilities for women offenders, it became evident that a small number of women (about 15% of the population) were unable to function in the community styled living environment'. As an interim strategy CSC transferred all maximum-security women who reportedly required a greater degree of structure and control to three segregated units inside men's prisons and women with acute mental health needs were transferred to a psychiatric prison. Some of these women are still in these units five years later. More recently the government has decided that the new empowering regional prisons need to be modified to accommodate maximum-security women – so new secure units are being built and the capacity of each prison is being expanded. It is hoped that these new units will result in the closing of the segregated units in men's facilities.[10]

The responsibilisation of women through benevolence of empowerment and healing, or alternatively through scapegoating, has the effect of de-responsibilising the institutional structure. The woman-centred empowerment model of punishment has feminised the discourses and practices of punishment without fundamentally challenging or restructuring the disciplinary relations of power in prisons. In short, the concept of empowering healing prisons obscures the fundamental limits imposed by the 'historical, material and legal reality of imprisonment'. After all, what does it mean to create choice in prison – or to empower in a fundamentally disempowering place? How does one erase or set aside the imbalances of power inherent in the practices of confining involuntary populations to embark on a meaningful project of empowerment? Organisational politics contribute to the shaping of policies and in this case the reshaping of key reform principles such as empowerment.

It was clear from the outset that the Task Force on Federally Sentenced Women comprised a unique mix of bureaucrats, advocates, community partners and women prisoners (Shaw 1993) that had distinctive but overlapping agendas and standpoints. This combination contained several power imbalances, and while individuals may have respected one anothers' views, at the point of implementation the existing organisational structures of the correctional service prevailed. Others were excluded, or withdrew, from the process. Here Chan's observations on the process of policy implementation have much currency. She argues that at the implementation stage contestations of control over the 'life-chances of the reform proposal' emerge, and involve 'a complex series of bargaining, persuasion and manoeuvering under certain conditions, that is through politics or "games" played out within government bureaucracies, between levels of government and between government and outside groups' (Chan 1992:189). Given that the Correctional Service had the daunting task of constructing an empowering woman-centred *prison*, it is not at all surprising that ideals like empowerment were redefined and aligned with wider organisational logics (i.e. individual responsibility and accountability).

'Encroachment and erosion'

As Douglas (1986:92) has observed:

> institutions systematically direct individual memory and channel our perceptions into forms compatible with the relations they authorize [...] any problems we try to think about are automatically transformed into their own organizational problems. The solutions they proffer only come from a limited range of their experience.

Over time the organisational pledge to woman-centred prisons has been eroded. While the discourse of gender and cultural sensitivity is deeply embedded in the rhetoric of Corrections Canada (one only has to visit the website to see this), the necessary structural reforms required to preserve the integrity of this initiative have not been implemented. As many have observed in other areas, the 'woman-centred' policies and practices that have emerged out of this effort are a consequence of organisational politics, legitimacy contests, and technical problems (Chan 1992).

The analogy of a round peg in a square hole captures the theme of encroachment (see Figure 11:1). When the circle is inserted into the square hole, the borders of the box are unchanged. If the box is a metaphor for the traditional structure of the corrections and correctional logic and if the circle symbolises the woman centred logic, then we can see how the woman centred logic is superimposed on the traditional structure without fundamentally altering it. The woman-centred logic appears isolated and contained within a pre-existent institutional framework. It seems as if a segment of the correctional population (women) can be compartmentalised and managed differently from the rest of the population. In this case the assumptions informing *Creating Choices* do just that, they propose to redefine the management of facilities for women according to feminist guiding principles and to build prisons in communities that can best service women and outsource programmes to the wider feminist and aboriginal service providers in the communities.

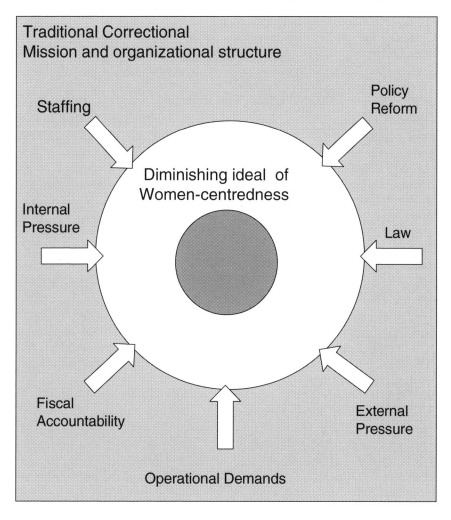

Figure 11.1 Encroachment of traditional corrections on the women's prisons

At the level of discourse, this reasoning offers a reasonable solution to many of the longstanding problems plaguing the management of women's prisons including geographical disparity, small numbers and fiscal problems contributing to the continued absence of gender and cultural sensitive programming. However, as expected, these ideas do not easily translate into practice precisely because of the limits imposed by the pre-existing bureaucratic and administrative processes. Many operational decisions are constrained by governmental processes, including formalised procedures for the acquisition of land upon which to build a new prison, legal and fiscal limitations, staff training, programme accreditation, contractual arrangements with service providers, public and political accountability.

There is no centralised control of the regional prisons. Instead, regional directors, who are also responsible for the management of considerably more and larger men's prisons independently, govern them through the regions. Given the vast size of Canada, Corrections is divided into five regional areas for administrative purposes. The Office of the Deputy Commissioner for Women that was envisioned in the recommendations of the Arbour Report (1996) to provide centralised control over the operations and policies informing these decisions was never fully implemented. Further, given the pre-existing institutional structure and division of corporate roles and responsibilities, it is questionable whether this proposal was even feasible. At present, this office has no direct line authority over the women's prisons and their staffing, budgets or daily operations.

The secondary nature of women's concerns, coupled with the complexities of jurisdictional authority, have decentralised the management of women's prisons across the country and severely limited the possibilities of uniformity, collegiality and accountability. Rather than have a coherent integrated system of corrections for women, there is considerable diversity in terms of how the woman-centred philosophy is operationalised. The regionalization of federally sentenced women, combined with the demands placed on each prison to comply with standardised policies and procedures[11] that do not take into account the gender based concerns raised in *Creating Choices,* has weakened the collective voice of women prisoners and eroded the organisational commitment to a 'new' gender based vision of women's corrections. To carry the analogy of Figure 11:1 further, what emerge are five small circles in a larger box (see Figure 11:2) constantly attempting to resist the internal and external pressure of the wider organisation while struggling to protect a founding vision that is quickly eroding.

In practice, this means that women's prisons, which are more expensive and perceived as new and well resourced, are always competing for resources with men's prisons. And secondly, that as new policies and correctional protocols are designed (as is constantly done in dynamic organisations), they are implemented throughout the system – including the women's prisons – with little concern or consideration given to the impact of these changes on women or in terms of their compatibility with that which the women's prisons are trying to achieve. This is extremely

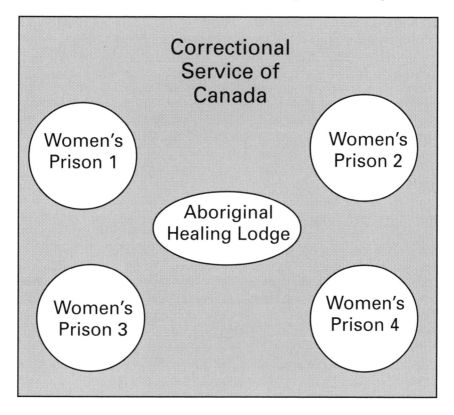

Figure 11.2 Decentralisation of Women's Corrections and Dilution of the Woman-Centred Model

frustrating for wardens, staff, and advocates in women's prisons that are committed to gender specificity, not to mention for prisoners.

While there are many examples that concretely illustrate this argument, for convenience I focus on the process of classification[12] because this is an institutional process that impacts many facets of the management of prisoners' sentences from programming, institutional placements and transfers to eventual release to the community.

Classification is a legal requirement in Canada. Under legislation, all federal prisoners are assigned a security classification and allocated to an appropriate institution (defined in terms of their potential for escape, their institutional conduct, and their risk to the public).[13] They will thereafter 'cascade' to lower security levels until eventual release. For women this has been an ambiguous requirement. Until the opening of new regional prisons, all federally sentenced women were housed in one maximum-security institution, the Prison for Women (P4W) or in provincial prisons.[14] While officially described as a 'multi-level' security institution, P4W was effectively maximum security, and from the 1980s classification within the institution utilised male-based instruments for security and release decisions as well as case-management.[15] *Creating Choices* advocated *assessment* of treatment needs, not classification, and argued that classification criteria discriminated against Aboriginal women in particular.[16] Women's treatment needs are interrelated, requiring a holistic rather than a hierarchical approach to programme provision.

In the implementation phase, attempts were made to develop a women-centred assessment system. An offender-management classification system based partly on that used in Shakopee women's prison in Minnesota was proposed (CSC 1995; Hannah-Moffat 1999). This incorporated gender-specific factors into security classification within the institution, and established performance expectations for reclassification. A woman-centred assessment tool (1994) was developed in one prison. Additionally, a guideline for using the new standardised, male-based Offender Intake Assessment tool (OIA) in women's prisons was prepared following its implementation across the federal prison system (CSC 1996). This took some account of the differences in the experiences of women compared with men, but essentially was an adaptation of a male model for use in the new women's prisons, including an Aboriginal healing lodge, while attempting to respond to gender and cultural differences and to create a distinct institutional culture.[17] Following the opening of the new facilities from 1995-97, however, neither the proposed security management model nor the 1996 women-centred guidelines appear to have been used. Instead women were, and still are, classified using the OIA, which was developed and validated on the male population.[18] Facilities, which were designed and developed on a feminist philosophy and model of corrections, now appear to have superimposed on them a quasi-actuarial model of assessment and review derived from the male population. It appears that the intent of this reform as well as the spirit of it have been compromised by wider organisational directive and by a failure to protect the idea of 'gender differences' which were fundamental to *Creating Choices*.

The management of women's prisons is not self-contained; it relies on facets of the wider correctional bureaucracy to carry out specialised tasks. This imposition of these wider processes, which are not vetted for their comparability with or potential impact on the new correctional ideal of woman-centeredness, has the effect of eroding the original ideal (which is increasingly seen as unworkable because it is being made to fit into the very structure it opposes). Indeed, individuals can influence this process by struggling to maintain the ideals by advocating for small procedural changes and exceptions, though such resistance is difficult to maintain and highly contingent on tireless charismatic leaders with a clear understanding and commitment to the original vision. Changes in personnel, the absence of an institutional memory, and small conciliations compromise the likely survival of the proposed reform and contribute to encroachment. When institutional bureaucracies are unleashed, the ideals of reformers are difficult to maintain and often lost in 'the process'.

What are the lessons to be learned?

Perhaps as Douglas (1986:92) suggests 'the necessary first step in resistance is to discover how the institutional grip is laid upon our mind'. I have outlined some of the organisational processes that contribute to the gap between the intentions of reformers and the outcome. Such processes should not contribute to a reform paralysis or deeply seated negativism that espouses, 'nothing works'. As Chan (1992: 2000) has argued, 'because the results of reforms are not always as envisioned by its advocates, there is always room for further repair work … to the extent that people become aware of, or discover, the shortcomings of previous reforms the repair process becomes increasingly necessary, yet difficult to achieve.' The question then is: how should that repair work be configured and what are some of the cautionary principles that can guide future reforms?

The first lesson is the importance of sustaining a 'truth in punishment' – in other words, of not losing sight of the experiential 'reality' of prison and of prisoners being involuntary subjects in regimes whose legal authority is derived from the power to punish. It is essential to maintain the 'visibility of imprisonment' for it is a valuable concept. Thinking about the 'unpleasantness of punishment' is not enjoyable; thinking of one's role in treatment, rehabilitation or public safety or in healing or empowering the disempowered is usually preferred. It is for this reason that the context of reform needs to be at the forefront of reformative projects. It reminds us of the limitation of reform and forces a discussion of what is possible 'within the context of imprisonment'. It dispels the illusionary and deceitful nature of holistic projects that profess to empower and heal and of institutions renamed from prisons to 'regional facilities' or 'healing lodges'. It points to the limits of punishment and underscores that some have the power to punish and others are relegated to the status of punished.

The second lesson is that change needs to be deeply embedded in the organisation structure – going beyond discourse and piecemeal practices. Linked to the concept I refer to as institutional integration is the fundamental issue of accountability and openness. This is a place where reformers and advocates have an important role. In order to have these initiatives work in practice, there needs to be centralised administrative control which is accountable[19], otherwise the situation we have in Canada will worsen and the integrity of the women-centred logic will be further eroded. The worst-case scenario is that in 15 years reformers will be facing five miniature P4Ws.

While most reformers and activists are well aware of the dangers of co-optation, (see, for example, Carlen and Tchaikovsky 1996) they remain committed to political action. Thus, it is better to do something than nothing. *Creating Choices* was a unique opportunity for many to articulate publicly concerns about the conditions of women's imprisonment in Canada. At a discursive level, the report reflected a unique, optimistic and well-intentioned programme of reform, which is now unfortunately seen to be a somewhat unachievable ideal. The danger that history reveals is that the good intentions of reformers and bureaucrats alike are absorbed by the prison and often result in little more than a re-formation or a reconfiguration of the prison, not a fundamental shift in how we punish or in how punishment is experienced.

A reflexive approach to strategic reforms and advocacy is based on recognition of the involuntary and repressive nature of and awareness and acknowledgement of the past. Fundamental shifts in how we punish are extremely difficult to achieve, as it is very difficult to fracture the prison/ punishment nexus. While we continue to live with the prison, we ought not accept its presence as inevitable. It is easy to dismiss those who advocate thinking outside of the penal box as impractical in an era where prisons more than ever before have a seeming permanency. However, the metaphorical box stifles thinking and creates the conditions for more of the same by structuring the possible changes along narrowly formulated and predetermined channels. Clearly, developments that appear more positive de-centre the prison and reduce the reliance on imprisonment while simultaneously acknowledging and addressing the plight of those who remain incarcerated. One can only hope that future reforms will be more successful than past efforts in de-centring the prison.

Concluding comment

While the seeds of change were planted with *Creating Choices,* wider organisational scheme stifled the growth of this vision and disillusioned reformers. The ongoing changes in women's prisons inspired by *Creating Choices* are part of a complex web of mixed intentions and purposeful actions, which help us understand the limits and possibilities of reform. The overall purpose of the chapter is to encourage systematic thinking about the limits of penal reform and about alternatives that destabilise the taken for granted or 'naturalised' assumptions of prisons and their transformation. Of central concern is the extent to which regimes of imprisonment can be modified for women. Canada's history of women's imprisonment reveals that building an institution based on the perceived needs and experiences of women prisoners, employing only female staff and administrators, and integrating feminist, maternal and therapeutic discourses with a penal regime is not original or radical (Freedman 1981; Rafter 1992; Strange 1983; Hannah-Moffat 2001). This is not to suggest that past and current regimes are the same or short-sighted; they are not. However, it does illustrate that certain institutional dynamics have continually undermined the successful implementation of reformers' ideals. The dominant feature of penal reform is its seeming inability to fracture the prison/punishment nexus.

Notes

1   A person serves a federal term of imprisonment when sentenced to imprisonment for a period of two years or greater; those sentenced to less than two years are imprisoned in a provincial institution.

2   The primary advocate for federally sentenced women in this context was the Canadian Association of Elizabeth Fry Societies. This national non-profit umbrella organisation operates for and on behalf of women in conflict with the law. Additional information on the mandate of this organisation and its member agencies can be located at www.elizabethfry.ca

3   The term classification refers to the designation of offenders and institutions as minimum, medium or maximum security.

4   Some women have requested a longer sentence to be housed in federal institutions. The reported reasons for these decisions include concerns about the conditions of confinement in provincial facilities, the location of the facility in relation to the woman's home community, the level and types of programmemes available, and a woman's belief that she may be released on community supervision sooner if in the federal system than the provincial

system because of the legislation governing release and the releasing patterns of various parole boards.

5 For a detailed critique of the concept of woman-centred prisons, see Hannah-Moffat 1995.

6 This term was originally associated with social movements in 1960s and 1970s that sought radical political changes in social relations. More recently, the concept of empowering individuals (whether they be the poor, workers, patients, immigrants, students, citizens or prisoners) has become a common tenet of several diverse political strategies and policy initiatives. The growing mass of policy and academic literature in education, health, legal, and labour reform and indeed penal reform confirms the widespread acceptance of empowerment strategies.

7 For a more detailed discussion of the contradictions of empowering incarcerated and involuntary populations see Hannah-Moffat 1985 and 2000.

8 Karla Homolka was convicted along with her husband Paul Bernardo of the murders of two teenage girls, who were held in captivity and repeatedly sexually assaulted prior to their deaths. This case outraged the public, as did the plea-bargained sentence of 12 years that Ms. Homolka received in exchange for testimony against her husband.

9 Following the April 1994 events, correctional officers and union representatives were picketing outside of the prison, demanding safer working conditions.

10 A detailed account of these events can be found in Hannah-Moffat 2001.

11 Some examples of such procedures include programme accreditation, the adoption of the Offender Intake Assessment – a new classification scheme for the assessment of criminogenic risk and needs.

12 This discussion is based on observations made by myself and Margaret Shaw while conducting a two year research project funded by the Status of Women of Canada on gender, diversity and classification in federally sentenced women's facilities. A detailed discussion of this project and its findings can be located on the website for Status of Women www.scw-cfc.gc.ca (also see Hannah-Moffat and Shaw 2001).

13 The Penitentiary and Parole Acts were replaced by the Corrections and Conditional Release Act in 1992.

14 From the 1970s some women stayed in their province under Exchange of Service agreements. Most provincial prisons are maximum security. A minimum-security federal prison for 11 women was opened in 1990 to meet criticism of the lack of alternatives.

15 I.e. the Wisconsin Case Management Strategy.

16 They are heavily over-represented. Up to 25% of federally sentenced women in prison are Aboriginal, compared with 2% in the country as a whole.

17 For example, full time work at home was to be assessed as full time employment. However, much of the women-specific information was to be recorded on the computer screen and made no difference to overall score calculation.

18 The exception is the SIR scale (Statistical Information on Recidivism), which is not valid or used for women.
19 See Carlen (2000a) for an insightful analysis of how similar ideas pertain to recent attempts to reform a Scottish women's prison.

Chapter 12

New discourses of justification and reform for women's imprisonment in England

Pat Carlen[1]

Introduction

This book is about penal reform and penal politics. But although several chapters uplift with tales of reformist endeavour, more tell a depressingly familiar story: of old and discredited penologies masquerading as new: and of the unexpected and retrogressively oppressive consequences of the best-intentioned reforms. Indeed, pessimists may have already concluded that in relation to penal reform 'nothing works', and, moreover, that this is inevitably so because of the seeming power of the state to incorporate all reformist discourse into the administrative machinery of the prison and the courts. One reading of what follows might suggest that that is my argument in this chapter. Such a reading would be unfortunate.

In what follows it will certainly be contended that there are necessarily limits to prison reform and that these limits – hereinafter termed 'carceral clawback' (Carlen 2002a) – logically inhere both in the involuntary nature of a subject's imprisonment and in the logical necessity of keeping a prisoner *in prison*. But the argument will distinguish between logical and political necessity and, in assuming that carceral clawback is a *logical* necessity, will not assume that, like the sentence of the court, it is a fairly direct outcome of the state's 'power to punish'. For the state's power to continue to punish by imprisonment, though formally vested in the criminal law, is, in the neo-liberal state, politically dependent upon the maintenance of the popular legitimacy of prison as an institution which *should* and *can* keep people in custody. The conditions under which that legitimacy can be maintained, however, vary between jurisdictions and according to specific mixes of cultural and political conditions. This chapter[2] will examine recent attempts to introduce innovative reforms in women's imprisonment in England with the aim of assessing both the extent to which carceral clawback is a necessary feature of imprisonment; and the different cultural and political conditions which facilitate carceral clawback taking the form it does.

In outline, the argument is as follows:

1. that, despite the appearance of reform in the regimes of the English women's prisons, a carceral clawback is already underway – made necessary by the prisons' continuing need for legitimacy and, in part, made possible by some of the constitutive common-sense elements of recent anti-prison discourses about women's imprisonment in England.

2. that most of the cosmetically-new policies currently reinvigorating the power of carceral clawback in the English women's prisons have been powered by the common-sense ideologies of optimistic campaigners (and prison-illiterate therapeutic experts) who have failed to remember (or who never have realised) that prison is for punishment by incarceration; and whose subsequent common-sense campaigning principles and strategies have been insufficiently theorised to protect them against incorporation into prison adminis-trative discourses wherein the necessity of carceral clawback (and its constant discursive renewal) is taken for granted; furthermore, that this ideological incorporation of reformist into administrative discourses is similar to that which occurred in Canada and which was first identified and analysed by Hannah-Moffatt (2001) and which is further discussed by the same author in chapter 11 of this book.

3. that in England carceral clawback is proceeding via financially co-erced, inclusionary controlling measures which are currently making imperialistic bids for greater control of ontological knowledge about the causes of crime and the causes of desistance from crime, together with epistemological claims about the only ways in which that knowledge can be obtained – and, for good measure, guaranteed via official accreditation.

4. that the need for accreditation of prison programmes in England converts the programme priorities of the supplying agencies from a professional concern about the therapeutic needs of the client into a functionalist concern about the survival of the organisational contract with the Prison Service; and that the new measures thereby being

brought into play are such that the language of auditable reform is able to paper over the cracks in the legitimacy of women's imprisonment without the threat to the *status quo* ever being realised, and, ironically, with its critics disarmed by the language of reform – unrealised.

The chapter is structured as follows: first, the formal logic of carceral clawback is explicated; secondly, the differences between common-sense and theoretical discourse are briefly described and their relationships in the construction of recent official discourse on women's imprisonment metaphorically analysed; thirdly, some of the substantive trans-formations of theoretical discourses into common-sense discourses which powered a new official discourse on women's prisons in England are described and located in their sustaining and converging ideologies in anti-prison, pro-prison and extra-prison discourses; and, lastly, the implications of the analyses and arguments are discussed.

The logic of carceral clawback

Prison is for punishment. It has other functions, but the only character-istic sentenced prisoners have in common is that they have been convicted of a crime for which the sentence of the court was punishment, either by a term of immediate imprisonment, or by one of those 'alternatives' to custody which are backed up by the explicit threat of incarceration for non-compliance with sentencing conditions. Like all other 'others', therefore, alternatives to imprisonment are predicated upon the continued existence of the binary partner; in this case, the prison itself.

Yet although prison is the most compelling symbol of the state's power to punish, it is also a politically dangerous symbol. The power to punish by imprisonment is not static and its legitimacy has to be constantly renewed in a political struggle wherein each side (for the purposes of this chapter, pro-and anti-prison ideologists) empowers the other at the moment of triumph of its own rhetoric. Indeed, it is partly because of the alternate triumphant insistence of both prison and prison-reformist claims that prison clawback takes the form it does.

Since the inception of penal incarceration, the punitive function of the prison has been occluded by governmental, professional or reformist claims that prisons – especially women's prisons – are, or could be, for something other than punishment: psychological readjustment, training in parenting, drugs rehabilitation, general education or … whatever else might provide a legitimating rationale for locking up not only women who commit very serious crimes but (when there is nowhere else to contain them – for example, family, the reformatory or the factory) also those who commit very minor ones, too.

Why do such myths about the possibilities of a benign prison persist and multiply? First, because imprisonment so nearly violates so many human rights and is so painful that democratic governments need continually to re-legitimate its systematic and almost exclusive use against certain classes and categories of lawbreakers for quite minor crimes (and especially nowadays when the promise of the state to reduce crime via its criminal justice apparatus has signally failed (Garland 1996, 2001); secondly, because the prison business is still (as it was during the early days of psychiatry) an opulent shareholder in the modernistic fashioning, retailing and consumption of new therapies and 'psy' sciences; and thirdly, because advocates of penal reform, becoming disillusioned by repeated failures of governments to reduce prison populations, have (though usually with ambivalence and in fear of co-optation) reluctantly (but repeatedly) accepted the invitation of prison administrations to help shape prison regimes designed to reduce both the pain and the damaging effects of imprisonment. The under-theorised nature of their reform attempts (in terms of the failure of the reformers to take seriously the nature of imprisonment and the way it might affect reform outcomes), together with the deliberate appeal to populist common-sense of their tactical rhetoric, have facilitated the incorporation of some key feminist concepts (for example, resistance to victim status, personal responsibility) into an official discourse on reform of the women's prisons and a currently vibrant carceral clawback (for example, in England the opening of two new private prisons for women, and the plans in late 2001 to convert two more male prisons for female use) which is far removed from the spirit of the reforming agendas of most anti-prison campaigners, many feminists, and many prison personnel too.

Common-sense, theory and official discourse

To make sense, all discourse has to exclude certain versions of reality and privilege others. The main difference between theoretical discourse and common sense discourse is that whilst the former has, by definition, to explicate and defend the ontological and epistemological assumptions and concepts of its knowledge claims, the meanings and referents of *common*-sense have, ironically, an infinite plasticity. As they are represented as being the consensual and natural constructions of reality held by all sane and respectable persons, they also appear at any one time to be both unchanging and at one with their conditions of existence. Consequently, the power of common-sense inheres in its ability constantly to adapt to oppositional discourses at the same time as calling into question the credibility and/or probity of the challengers. Common-sense discourses only have to be defended when challenged by a theoretical discourse which forces them to lay bare their ideological underpinnings, ambiguities and, in institutional and political terms, their choice of epistemological masters.

Some of the most sophisticated common-sense discourse is, as one might expect, official discourse i.e. the discourse which justifies the governmental pursuit of one course of action, programme or policy rather than another.

In the book *Official Discourse*, Burton and Carlen (1979) used the metaphor of the 'other' taken from psychoanalysis (Freud 1976; Lacan 1975) to describe how, when it is confronted by competing theories or pedagogies, official discourse has to erase the 'other' from the mirror of its own desire/imperative.

In the case of women's imprisonment in England at the dawn of the twenty-first century, the official imperative was to face a challenge to the legitimacy of disproportionately imprisoning poorer and ethnic minority women for relatively minor crimes. Through the closing-off of any alternative discourses about the extra-discursive conditions shaping women's imprisonment, an in-house prison service discourse had to be created, a 'prison-speak' which, by appearing to mirror many discursive elements of the critical discourse against women's imprisonment, could also absorb and neutralise the threat. Indeed, for the state or the prison (as for the oppressed) it is in the analytic resistance to the exercise of discursive power by theoretical or political opponents that the strongest ideological weapons for its own continuance are to be found (Foucault 1978).

Even at the end of twentieth century, neither of the main political parties in England was prepared to contest populist conceptions of the necessity and efficacy of imprisonment as the symbolic centrepiece of a punitive (if ineffective, in terms of crime reduction) criminal justice system. The only opposition to the increased use of imprisonment came from anti-prison theorists, the long-term campaigning organisations such as Women in Prison, Howard League, Prison Reform Trust and Nacro; together with the Prison Inspectorate, and some of the more enlightened amongst the judiciary and Prison Service personnel. By the mid-1990s, the strongest case for prison reductionism was being presented in relation to women's imprisonment. Women criminals were not seen as posing the same risks to the general public as men and, moreover, their claims to special treatment as mothers were receiving sympathetic publicity. To meet the threat of this ideologically obstructive Other, the Prison Service set up a Women's Policy Group to ensure that women prisoners' interests and different needs were in future taken seriously (in effect, authoritatively defined and circumscribed) by the Service itself. In other words, the Prison Service wanted to reassert ownership of a part of the prison population that it was constantly being accused of neglecting. (See chapter 9 for further discussion of the structural position and management of this Group.)

At the same time, many in the campaigning organisations were questioning the utility of their own 'outsider' and often abstract critiques of women's imprisonment and modifying them to appeal to the common-sense of a public which might be prepared to sympathise at least with women prisoners who had suffered abuse, or with children of prisoners damaged by their mothers' imprisonment. They were met halfway by the Prison Service's new Women's Policy Group which, in an attempt to diffuse the mounting criticism, went out of its way to consult with a range of campaigning, statutory and voluntary organisations.

The anti-prison campaigners were caught off-guard. Dispirited by their previous lack of success in reducing the female prison population (during the 1990s it had doubled in size), many abandoned the theoretical critique of the legitimacy (and social costs) of imprisoning non-violent women for minor crimes, and instead packaged their criticisms in the language of common sense with a populist (and official) appeal, content merely to argue, for instance, that it was important to treat women prisoners well because they were mothers and guardians of the next generation; that women in prison would be less likely to commit crime if they received some kind of therapy in prison; that women prisoners had been treated as victims by too many writers on women and crime when in fact there were many strong women in prison who would be even stronger if their custodial sentence could be made into a much more positive experience ... and so on. The dominant message was that women in prison should resist the 'deterministic' victimhood conferred upon them by critics of penal welfare; they should take responsibility for their lives by recognising their own needs; they should engage in activities that might enable them to be crime-free in the future; and they should have the opportunity to convert their period of imprisonment into a positive period wherein they might recuperate from the problems they had suffered outside prison. This insistence on responsibility and resistance to being a passive victim meshed very well with some elements in the rhetoric of welfare critics such as Charles Murray (1990) and even with some elements in the arguments of left-realist criminologists (e.g. Young 1986) who, like some anti-prison campaigners and feminists, were anxious to have their views on crime taken seriously by a New Labour government.

Meanwhile, in the reports on women's imprisonment, less and less mention was made of class or racism, until in 2000 the Wedderburn Report (Prison Reform Trust 2000) (based on the investigations of people chosen for their Establishment credentials and, in the main, their lack of 'contamination' through previous knowledge of women's prisons) marked the beginning of the new millennium by managing not to mention class and racism in the criminal justice system at all! Confusingly, the language of 'class' and 'racism' had been replaced by the New Labour 'speak' of 'social exclusion' – which, in terms of imprisonment must, literally, either be circular or oxymoronic.

Thus, by the beginning of the twenty-first century, and with the aid of its own new ideological machinery in the guise of the Women's Policy Group, the Prison Service had regrouped, and put its own gloss upon the common-sense (neutered-theoretical) arguments contained in reports such as those by Prison Reform Trust (2000) and Nacro (2001). In consultation meetings between the Prison Service and 'others', the challenge to the legitimacy of imprisoning disproportionate numbers of 'excluded' (working class and ethnic minority) women was common-sensically transformed (and theoretically neutralised) within the new orthodoxy about the efficacy of prison programmes in addressing social problems such as drug usage, sexual abuse and housing (to name but a few) from within the prison, and, overall, the whole process illustrated once more the point that Burton and Carlen made in 1979, that

> official discourse on law and order confronts legitimation deficits and seeks discursively to redeem them by denial of their material genesis. Such denial establishes an absence in the discourse. This absence, the Other, is the silence of a world constituted by social relations the reality of which cannot be appropriated by a mode of normative argument which speaks to and from its own self-image...
>
> (Burton and Carlen 1979:138)

At the time of writing (in December 2001) the newly-forged self-image of the women's prison system in the early twenty-first century in England is of a system legitimated by its provision of programmes, treatments and therapies, the underlying justifications for which mesh well with the common-sense rhetoric of some feminist criminologists and some anti-prison campaigners about the needs to de-victimise and 'empower' women in prison. (See chapter 10 for a critique of those programmes.) Moreover, many of the new programmes received the blessing (at a price) of the organisations which had previously put forward the radical critiques whose common-sense appeal had been partly responsible for the reforms taking the new forms they had. At the moment of official recognition of the utility of certain elements of those critiques to a new official discourse on women's crime and women's imprisonment, their theoretical sting had been drawn because:

> The ideological metonymies of official discourse are directed not only to the destruction of their real conditions of existence, but also, through denial of those conditions of existence, to their partial and surreptitious reproduction. To this extent, official discourse is always directed at discursive closure.
>
> (Burton and Carlen 1979:138)

In other words, because of the increase in populist punitiveness that had occurred as a result of the heightened awareness of criminal risk coinciding with a political, media and electoral demand for more and harsher custodial punishment, critical discourses presenting a threat to carceral increase had to be silenced or, at least, neutralised. The most threatening critical discourse at the end of the 1990s was in relation to the multiple jeopardy which women prisoners suffered as lawbreakers, women and members of ethnic minority groups. Via the newly-instituted Women's Policy Group alliances were forged with campaigning or non-statutory organisations and, in the Prison Service's revamping of its regimes for females, it began to appear as if much of the radical critique of women's imprisonment was being taken on board. Not so. When previous critics abandoned, modified or discursively adjusted their critiques of sentencing and prison policies, so that they might join as credible partners in common-sense policy-making with the Prison Service's Women's Policy Group, prison clawback was strengthened. Any further talk of the class- and ethnic minority-biased conditions of existence of the female prison population was now discursively erased as being 'unhelpful' and 'irrelevant'. Within the new official policy discourse of prison programming for self-governance, class and gender analyses were in future to be considered 'unspeakable': first, because theories which argued that class and gender discrimination played any part in explaining women's criminal careers were lacking in 'evidence'; and, more importantly, because, not being 'evidence-based' any 'programmes' based on such theories were definitely non-fundable!

I will now examine in more detail just how it was that a radical critique of prison legitimacy, based on structural analyses of class, racism and gender discrimination, produced the constitutive elements of a carceral clawback characterised by psy-technologies and programmes which, after abstracting women prisoners from their concomitantly recognised and denied structural conditions of existence outside prison, relocated and isolated them within psychological needs-based therapies for the governance of the self within prison.

How theoretical critique empowered contemporary official discourse on women's prisons in England

It has already been argued that by the mid 1990s, the British penal system was suffering a minor legitimacy crisis in relation to women's imprison-ment, a crisis made worse by a growing popular awareness that women prisoners were more likely to be suffering from multiple problems of material deprivation than male prisoners and less likely than males to be 'career' or 'dangerous' criminals; additionally, that as they were more likely than men to have dependent children for whom they were the main carers, their children at home could be expected to suffer all kinds of mental, emotional and psychological damage as a result of their mothers' imprisonment. Yet, at the same time there was a growth in punitiveness towards single mothers and an increasing number of sentencers who argued that if women wanted equality with men they should equally expect to receive equality of punishment with men when they broke the law. (See chapters 1, 2, 3 and 6 for discussion of different meanings of 'equality'.) There was no way that an official discourse (always dependent upon common-sense for its coherence in contradiction) could construct a populist argument around the complex notion of substantive rather than formal equality (see Heidensohn 1986). None the less, and as always, the constitutive threads of a new official discourse were there waiting to be metonymised from discourses contesting both the frequency and the nature of women's imprisonment. It did not take long to stitch them together in a new form – though still according to the old strategy of erasing from the new official discourse all reference to the material conditions of existence (characterised by poverty, racism and sexism) of a majority of female prisoners, and replacing it with an 'imaginary' realignment of signifiers (in this case the literal words and slogans of the prison critics) and signifieds – that is, differently contextualised meanings of those very same words. Displaced from their original theoretical or campaigning contexts, words such as 'responsibility', 'victim', 'need', 'citizenship', 'risk', 'accountability' 'rehabilitation', and 'choice' now took on very different meanings and referents. Moreover, they were destined to have entirely different effects from those envisaged by their radical authors. Other words such as class and racism were, as we have already seen, omitted altogether.[3]

In a new contextualisation of language taken from the discourses of the anti-prison campaigners and feminists, the criminological archives of a previous era were raided, and words like 'criminogenic' and 'criminal career' were dug out and put to new uses. While some critics were quick to point out that in many cases research commissioned by the Prison Service's Women's Policy Group was attempting to reinvent the wheel, other critics were more concerned that the new wheel was already careering in a penologically conservative direction. In other words, when the Women's Policy Group commissioned research into women's criminal careers, the purpose was more to investigate the psychological needs that prison therapists could claim to address within custodial programmes, than to investigate and address the tangle of social deprivations that so many female prisoners suffer outside prison. The main transformations in female prison reform discourse lay in the following areas:

1. *From 'Prison works' (Conservative Home Secretary Michael Howard) to 'Prison doesn't work, but we'll make it work' (Labour Home Secretary Jack Straw)*

The thrust of much anti-prison campaigning in the early 1990s was directed at refuting a Conservative Home Secretary's justification for increases in the prison population – the claim that 'prison works' in terms of reducing crime. In an address to the Howard League soon after the New Labour government came to power, the new Home Secretary amended that claim to: 'prison doesn't work, but we will make it work'. The repairing gel, we learned, was to be found in the magic of 'programming'. This move towards 'programming' could also claim to meet another objection to women's imprisonment: that the women most vulnerable to imprisonment were also those with multiple social problems and deprivations. 'Agreed', said Prison Speak. 'Therefore we must develop programmes to address those needs, and this can be done better in prison than in the community where the resources are just not available.' But the needs addressed turned out to be only those which could be represented as related to 'criminogenic' behaviour – that is, 'needs' rooted in the women, rather than in their social circumstances.

2. *From the demand for prison-accountability to the insistence on prisoner-accountability*

During the 1980s one recurring demand of reformers had been that prisons should be 'accountable', that structures should be put in place to safeguard prisoners' rights (Maguire *et al* 1985), and that a charter of minimum prison standards should be published and made enforceable by the courts. By the 1990s the concept of 'accountability' was well embedded in prison ideology, but the emphasis now was on the 'accountability' of the prisoner – not only for her own behaviour, but, via prisoner compacts and the Incentives and Earned Privileges Scheme, for the standard of her prison conditions and access to prison 'privileges' too.

The *coup* for official discourse inhered in the 'contractual' nature of the Incentives and Earned Privileges Scheme; it appealed to a liberal common-sense (about individual freedom and self-governance) and a feminist common-sense insistence that women take responsibility for their own lives and not be seen as victims. As David Garland (2001) points out, contractual modes of governance appeal strongly to the middle classes because, in mimicking traditional middle-class forms of self-governance they appear to be both 'obvious' and 'natural'. To give women in prison the opportunity to choose to govern their own lives may be an oxymoron, but if we add in the imaginary of the discursive desire of anti-prison campaigners that women prisoners should have equal opportunities with all other women, in other words, *as if they were not in prison*, it becomes unassailable 'common-sense'. Ironically, it also means that, in prison, women whose common-sense tells them that they can have very little real choice about how to govern their lives as prisoners can continue to be punished in the name of therapy and by professional women, for the very same characteristic that sent many of them there in the first place – not being middle class, and refusing to 'see things' as if they were middle class.

3. *From accountability to audit*

The shift in emphasis from prison accountability to prisoner account-ability has not lessened the degree of control experienced by prison managements. Indeed, in the wake of the escapes from Parkhurst and Whitemoor Prisons in the 1980s centralised control was increased, it became more managerialist and, concomitantly, the degree of discretion allowed to prison governors in the general governance of the prison was set at a minimum (Carlen 2002b).

The concept of prison 'accountability' as employed by prisoners' rights lobbyists in the 1980s posited an obligation for prison authorities to give accounts which would justify penal policies in terms of known rules and contestible principles of penal justice and prison governance.

> Garrett (1980) notes that many state departments are called upon to deliver services in which efficiency and economy cannot be measured directly in cost/output terms. They may provide services to which people are (to a more or less specified degree) entitled, or which must be distributed equitably within a fixed budget, or where provision to one group incurs disbenefits to others. In such cases accountability acquires social, political, legal and moral characteristics, raising difficult questions about the appropriate forms of audit and the yardsticks of assessment which should be employed.
>
> (Maguire *et al* 1985:2)

Auditability, however, unlike accountability, is not concerned with interpretation and debate. Instead, it demands that the workings of the system be made apparently transparent by being framed/measured within pregiven 'indicators' and 'standards'. Thus, while the concept of 'accountability' allows for openness and critique, audit via measurement closes off the possibility of critique by 'providing assurance that the system works well even when a substantive performance is poor' (Power 1997:60). In the move from prisons accountability to prisons audit, common-sense (this time in the template form of Key Performance Indicators and Standards) once more stifles critique.

4. From female prisoner resistance to class, gender, and penal victimisation and oppression – to responsibilisation

One of the transformations in discourse about women's imprisonment which has already been well-documented (see Hannah-Moffat and Shaw 2001; Hannah-Moffat 2001; Hannah-Moffat chapter 11 here) is that which, in my opinion, has its roots in feminist discourses which balked at representations of female lawbreakers in the criminal justice system as being solely victims of class or racist discrimination, and instead insisted that they should also be represented as survivors with an agency capable of resisting the various forms of oppression to which, it was usually admitted, they had indeed been subject. At its extreme, this argument was also put forward as an organising principle to explain the experiences of women in prison (see Bosworth 1999). But although none of the 'insistence on resistance' brigade actually denied that a majority of women prisoners had been subjected to various forms of oppression outside prison, many of them, especially if they held to a totally untheorised view of what prison actually entails – that is, punishment in the form of involuntary but secure custody – tended to underplay those aspects of custodial power which are necessarily activated and enhanced by prisoner resistance – in other words, the disciplinary and security mechanisms.

Within the women's prisons, a number of programmes were developed which, far from addressing the roots of women's oppression outside prison (and, incidentally, outside of their own or any one individual's sphere of direct influence), focused instead on the prisoners' attitudes to their criminal behaviour – on the rather simplistic grounds that changing how prisoners thought (within the prison) about their behaviour (outside the prison) would reduce their lawbreaking behaviour upon release. Thus it was that a progressive feminist exhortation – that oppressed women should take charge of their own lives and act to resist oppression – was transformed into a 'responsibilisation' of prisoners which (through silencing all reference to structural constraints) implied that not only were they solely responsible for their own behavioural choices, but also for the conditions in which those choices were made (see O'Malley 1992, 1996; Garland 1996, 2001, Hannah-Moffat 2001). Unlike the prison governor quoted below, many who helped to frame these programmes just did not take note of the prison's controlling imperative. Prison staff, on the other hand, take it for granted that the demands of prison security and the demands of therapeutic practice are inevitably antagonistic:

> We have the institutional dilemma of saying to women, 'Be assertive, be confident'. And as soon as they begin to exercise that assertiveness, staff say, 'Whoa. This is a prison. Get back there.'
>
> (Male Prison Governor in Carlen 1998:89; see also Hannah-Moffat 2001:18.)

5. The translation of 'risk as dangerousness' into 'risk as need'

In the 1980s and early 1990s, a number of campaigners against the imprisonment of minor female offenders had argued that women should only be imprisoned if they posed such a serious risk to public safety that a custodial sentence had to be imposed on the grounds of protection of the public. In the 1990s, however, 'risk' came to be translated into 'risk of committing another crime' and, especially in the case of women, 'risk to oneself'. Women with the greatest social needs were also seen as being those most 'at risk' of being in criminal trouble again in the future. As this new interpretation of risk took hold, prison could be justified on two related grounds: if a woman's needs were such that she was at increased risk of committing crime in the future she should go to prison because, being needy, she posed a risk; and by going to prison she could have her needs addressed and the risk diminished. Needless to say, the needs to be addressed in prison were psychological needs relating to the adjustment of how the woman viewed her criminal behaviour and social situation; rather than the material needs that, according to the anti-prison campaigners had, in part, created the conditions conducive to many women's lawbreaking behaviour in the first place.

6. *Holism and partnership operationalised as centralism*

One of the key features of late modern neo-liberal states according to Garland (1996) is the displacing of responsibility for crime control from the state to the citizen. Given that the criminal justice system can no longer make good its claim to deliver order and security via policing, the courts and the prisons, citizens have been subjected to a responsibilisation strategy whereby responsible citizens are expected to help themselves in these matters, for instance, via increased private security, insurance and a reliance upon other private organisations with whom the state may or may not claim to be 'in partnership'. In England, the Prison Service has certainly invited voluntary and other statutory organisations to join 'in partnership' in the design and running of many prison programmes and, because this has often been done under the ideological signs of 'interagency' or 'co-ordination', anti-prison campaigners at first applauded the approach as being 'holistic'. Once again, their approval was premature.

A recurring criticism directed at services for female offenders during the last decade related to the fragmented nature of service delivery. It was argued that too often provision by one agency undermined that of another; that although women in prison often required a great deal of specialist help, the expertise was not available within the prison and, furthermore, that although the relevant provision could be made by specialist agencies, the Prison Service did not make as much use of specialist agencies as it could. A third argument related to the need for 'one stop' provision – of information and all other types of service – so that ex-prisoners with children and/or a paucity of resources could easily identify and access their own specific mix of appropriate rehabilitative services. Proponents of these arguments (who included this author – see Carlen 1998) confidently believed that a holistic approach would lead to more and more 'community' organisations going into prisons with a greater variety of approaches to prisoners' 'needs' being practised. The reverse happened. Harnessing the perennial campaigning rhetoric about the desirability of higher standards in prison provision to a justification for a new accreditation process, one designed to authorise and recognise (for funding purposes) only those programmes deemed by the accreditors to address offending behaviour, the Prison Service fashioned a new machinery for the three-fold centralisation of penological knowledge: causes of criminal behaviour were located in individual offenders; the best way to remedy these criminogenic tendencies was by cognitive behavioural technique; and the best way to gain knowledge of anything penological whatsoever – success of therapeutic programmes, quality of prison and prison-officer performance – was to measure it.

7. From symbolic interactionism to construction of a new official criminology of women in prison

In the discourse of official knowledge there is a happy conjunction between necessity and desire. To be coherent, all discourse necessarily has to exclude certain statements and include others; to maintain its legitimacy, all official discourse desires to exclude oppositional knowledge of certain material conditions and replace it with an alternative world-view. Most of the academic books and campaigning and semi-official reports of the last decades of the twentieth century implicitly challenged the legitimacy of continuing to imprison so many women with such appalling histories of poverty and abuse as characterised a majority of women in prison. Having in part met the challenge to the legitimacy by claiming that the justification for imprisoning such women was that their needs would be met by the new prison regimes and programmes, official assurance had to be made doubly sure: first, by discrediting the knowledge claims of those who argued that in-prison programmes run by psychologists would hardly address the poverty-stricken circumstances to which so many prisoners would return upon release; and secondly, by making sure that all of those running the new programmes held to an ontology and epistemology of women's crime which would further bolster the legitimacy of imprisoning them.

The basic ontology of the New Official Criminology of Women in Prison is contained in a remarkably clever document entitled *The Government's Strategy for Female Offenders* (Home Office 2000a). In it, the arguments which had been put forward by some qualitative researchers that women committed crime because it appeared to them that they had few legitimate options (see Carlen 1988) were turned on their head. Implicitly allowing the symbolic-interactionist claim (and, incidentally, justification for qualitative, as opposed to quantitative, research) that their ways of seeing the world shape people's actions, the solution of the New Official Criminology for Women in Prison is simple. Change their *beliefs* about the world; the problem is in their heads, not their social circumstances:

> The characteristics of women prisoners suggest that experiences such as poverty, abuse and drug addiction lead some women to *believe* that their options are limited. Many offending behaviour programmes are designed to help offenders see there are always positive choices open to them that do not involve crime. At the same time, across Government, we are tackling the aspects of social exclusion that make some women *believe* their options are limited.
> (Home Office 2000a:7 emphases added)

This approach also justified the commissioning of new research into women's criminogenic needs, the only research to be welcomed in future being that which produces 'research evidence on effective ways to tackle women's re-offending' (Home Office 2000a:23). As the only programmes authorised for tackling women's offending behaviour are those which have been officially 'accredited', it seems that official discourse on women's imprisonment has indeed momentarily triumphed – by shoving the unofficial 'other' explanations of women's crime right out of the frame (especially the research funding frame!) – though not, of course, out of the archive.

Conclusion

I began this chapter by stating that I would not be arguing that prison reform is impossible because of some functionalist loop-back between the supposed 'needs' of the state and the forms that social change can take. Nor have I. In one sense, I have been more positivistic than that: I have argued that logically the prison necessarily has to engage in a carceral clawback whenever its being as a prison is threatened by prisoner emancipation – of mind or body. Yet that is a formal explanation. It does not begin to suggest why carceral clawback takes the form it does at a particular time and in a specific society. To help further understanding of that – of the substance of the politics of women's imprisonment in England at the end of the twentieth and beginning of the twenty-first century – it has been necessary to examine the changing ideologies of female poverty and oppression in the UK, and also the key political ideologies and organisational rhetorics of legitimate penal governance.

During the last two decades, UK jurisdictions have (like many others) had an increasingly troublesome problem of legitimacy in relation to women's imprisonment. The main discursive configuration within which that particular legitimation deficit has now been framed (and is currently being addressed) has involved a separation of reformist discourses from their extra-discursive referents. In England the process has been facilitated by the abandonment by campaigning anti-prison critics of a coherent (and watchful) theoretical approach to female prison reform so that they might more easily enjoy a 'common-sense' 'partnership' with the Prison Service in order to 'get something done'. Something is being done; and oppositional discourses supposed to be championing a reduction in the women's prison population are unwittingly helping to fashion a new policy discourse on women and crime, an official discourse which will justify more and more women being locked up in the future – so that their 'criminogenic needs' can be met – not somehow, but legitimately![4]

Notes

1 The author thanks Kelly Hannah-Moffat for very helpful comments on an earlier draft of this chapter.
2 Part of this chapter was originally published as Carlen 2002c.
3 In a Home Office (2001b) consultation paper published just as this chapter was being completed, the link between women's 'life experiences' was acknowledged, but then dismissed by the old device of pointing out that 'not all women who suffer social exclusion turn to crime'. The paper recorded a range of criticisms of the previous paper (Home Office 2000a), one of the most telling being that from Dorothy Wedderburn: 'There is the danger that concentration upon individual characteristics of offenders, which may not be very amenable to change in the short run, will be at the expense of attention to social circumstances which can be influenced by government policy' (p. 17).
4 Between 1993 and 2001 the female prison population for England and Wales increased by over 145%.

References

Alamagno, S. A. (2001) 'Women in Jail: Is Substance Abuse Treatment Enough?' *American Journal of Public Health*, 91(5): 798–800

Allen, H. (1987a) *Justice Unbalanced*, Buckingham: Open University Press

Allen, H. (1987b) 'Rendering Them Harmless: Professional Portrayals of Women Charged with Serious Violent Crimes' in P. Carlen and A. Worrall (eds), *Gender, Crime and Justice*, Milton Keynes: Open University Press

Andrews, D. (1989) 'Recidivism is Predictable and Can Be Influenced: Using Risk Assessments to Reduce Recidivism', *Forum on Corrections Research*, 1 (2): 11–18

Andrews, D. and Bonta, J. (1998) *The Psychology of Criminal Conduct*, rev. edn. Cincinnatti OH: Anderson Publishing

Andrews, D., Bonta, J. and Hoge, R. (1990) 'Classification for Effective Rehabilitation', *Criminal Justice and Behaviour*, 17 (1):19–52

Andrews, D., Zinger, I., Hope, R., Bonta, J., Gendreau, P. and Cullen, F. (1990) 'Does Correctional Treatment Work? A Clinically Relevant and Psychologically Informed Meta-analysis', *Criminology*, 28(3): 369–494

Arbour, the Honourable Justice Louise, Commissioner (1996) *Report of the Commission of Inquiry into Certain Events in the Prison for Women in April of 1994*, Ottawa, Solicitor General of Canada

Ashworth, A. and Wasik, M. (eds) (1998) *Fundamentals of Sentencing Theory*, Oxford: Clarendon Place

Bailey, S. (2000) 'Violent Adolescent Female Offenders' in G. Boswell (ed.) *Violent Children and Adolescents: Asking the Question Why*, London: Whurr Publishers

Baker-Miller, J. (1976) *Towards a New Psychology of Women*, Boston: Beacon Press

Ballinger, A. (2000) Dead Women Walking: Executed Women in England and Wales, 1900–1955, Aldershot: Ashgate

Barker, E. T. and Buck, M. F. (1977) 'LSD in a Coercive Milieu Therapy Program', *Canadian Psychiatric Association Journal*, 22: 311–314

Barker, E. T. and Mason, M. H. (1968a) 'The Insane Criminal as Therapist', *Canadian Journal of Corrections*, 10:553–561

Barker, E. T. and Mason, M. H. (1968b) 'Buber behind Bars', *Canadian Psychiatric Association Journal*, 13: 61–72

Barker, E. T., Mason, M. H. and Wilson, J. (1969) 'Defence-Disrupting Therapy', *Canadian Psychiatric Association Journal*, 14: 355–358

Barnett, S., Corder, F. and Jehu, D. (1989) 'Group Treatment For Women Sex Offenders Against Children', *Practice*, 2: 148–159

Barnardos (1998) *Whose Daughter Next? Children Abused Through Prostitution*, Barnardos, Ilford

Batacharya, S. (2000) *Racism, girl violence and the murder of Reena Virk*, unpublished MA thesis, University of Toronto

Bazelon, D. L. (1976) 'The Morality of Criminal Law', *Southern California Law Review*, 49: 385–403

Beck, U. (1992) *Risk Society: Towards A New Modernity*, London: Sage

Bill, L. (1998) 'The Victimization and Revictimization of Female Offenders', *Corrections Today* 60(7): 106–114

Birch, H. (1995) 'A Special Kind of Evil', *The Independent*, 23 November

Blanchfield, M. and Bronskill, J. (2001) 'Psychologist, Ottawa Admit Giving LSD to Teen Inmate', *National Post*, June 23

Blanchfield, M. and Bronskill, J. (1998) 'An Extreme Case of Questionable Ethics', *Ottawa Citizen*, September 28

Blume, E. S. (1990) *Secret Survivors: Uncovering Incest and Its Effects in Women*, New York: Wiley and Sons

Bosworth, M. (1999) *Engendering Resistance: Agency and Power in a Women's Prison*, Aldershot: Dartmouth

Bottoms, A. E. (1983) 'Neglected Features of Contemporary Penal Systems' in D. Garland and P. Young (eds) *The Power to Punish: Contemporary Penality and Social Analysis*, London: Heinemann

Bottoms, A. (1995) 'The Philosophy of Punishment and Sentencing' in C. M. V. Clarkson and R. Morgan (eds), *The Politics of Sentencing Reform*, Oxford: Clarendon Press

Bowker, L. H. (1993) 'A Battered Woman's Problems Are Social Not Psychological' in R. J. Gelles (ed.) *Current Controversies on Family Violence*, London: Sage

Braithwaite, J. and Pettit, P. (1990), *Not Just Deserts: A Republican Theory of Criminal Justice*, Oxford: Clarendon Press

Brinkworth, L. (1994) 'Sugar and Spice and Not at All Nice', *Sunday Times*, 27 November 1994

Brinkworth, L. (1996) 'Angry Young Women', *Cosmopolitan*, February

Briscoe, S. and Coumarelos, C. (2000) 'New South Wales Drug Court Monitoring Report', *Crime and Justice Bulletin* No. 52, December, NSW: Bureau of Crime Statistics and Research

Brody, S. R. (1976) *The Effectiveness of Sentencing*, Home Office Research Study No 35. London: HMSO

Brogden, M. and Harkin, S. (2000) *Male Victims of Domestic Violence: Report to the Northern Ireland Domestic Violence Forum*, The Queens University of Belfast, unpublished

Bronskill, J. and Blanchfield, M. (2001) 'Psychologist, Ottawa, Admit Giving LSD to Teen Inmate', *National Post*, June 23.

Browne, A., Miller, B. and Maguin, E. (1998) 'Prevalence and Severity of Lifetime Physical and Sexual Victimization Among Incarcerated Women', unpublished, Buffalo, N.Y: Research Institute on Addictions

Bullock, R., Little, M. and Millham, S. (1998) *Secure Treatment Outcomes: The Care Careers of Very Difficult Adolescents*, Aldershot: Ashgate

Bureau of Justice Statistics (1998) *Prison and Jail Inmates at Midyear 1998*, Washington D.C: US Department of Justice

Burton, F. and Carlen, P. (1979) *Official Discourse*, London: Routledge and Kegan Paul

Carlen, P. (1983) *Women's Imprisonment*, London: Routledge

Carlen, P. (1985) 'Law, Psychiatry and Women's Imprisonment: A Sociological View' *British Journal of Psychiatry*, 146 (June): 618-621

Carlen, P. (1986) 'Psychiatry in Prisons: Promises, Premises, Practices and Politics' in P. Miller and N. Rose (eds), *The Power of Psychiatry*, Cambridge: Cambridge University Press

Carlen, P. (1988) *Women, Crime and Poverty*, Milton Keynes: Open University Press

Carlen, P. (1989) ' Crime, Inequality and Sentencing' in P. Carlen and D. Cook, *Paying For Crime*, Milton Keynes: Open University Press

Carlen, P. (1990) *Alternatives to Women's Imprisonment*, Milton Keynes: Oxford University Press

Carlen, P. (1994) 'Why Study Women's Imprisonment? Or Anyone Else's?' in R. King and M. Maguire (eds) *Prisons In Context*, Oxford: Clarendon Press

Carlen, P. (1995) 'Virginia, Criminology and the Anti-Social Control of Women' in T. Blumberg and S. Cohen (eds) *Punishment and Social Control*, New York: Aldine de Gruyter

Carlen, P. (1996) *Jigsaw: A Political Criminology of Youth Homelessness*, Buckingham: Open University Press

Carlen, P. (1998) *Sledgehammer: Women's Imprisonment at the Millennium*, London: Macmillan

Carlen, P. (2000a) 'Against the Politics of Sex Discrimination' in D. Nicolson and D. Bibbings (eds), *Feminist Perspectives on Criminal Law*, Oxford: Clarendon

Carlen, P. (2000b) 'Youth Justice? Arguments for Holism and Democracy in Responses to Crime' in P. Green and A. Rutherford (eds), *Criminal Policy in Transition*, Oxford: Hart Publishing

Carlen, P. (2001a) 'Death and The Triumph of Governance? Lessons from the Scottish Women's Prison', *Punishment and Society*, 3 (4): 459–471

Carlen, P. (2001b) 'Questions of Survival for Gender-Specific projects for Women in the Criminal Justice System', *Women, Girls and Criminal Justice*, 2 (4): 51–52&64

Carlen, P. (2002a) 'Carceral Clawback: The Case of Women's Imprisonment in Canada', In *Punishment and Society* 4 (1)

Carlen, P. (20002b) 'Governing the Governors' in *Criminal Justice*, 2 (1)

Carlen, P, (2002c) 'Controlling Measures: The Repackaging of Common Sense Opposition to Women's Imprisonment in England and Canada' in *Criminal Justice*, 2 (2)

Carlen, P., Hicks, J., O'Dwyer, J. Christina, D. and Tchaikovsky, C. (1985) *Criminal Women*, Cambridge: Polity Press

Carlen, P. and Tchaikovsky, C. (1996) 'Women's Imprisonment in England at the End of the Twentieth Century: Legitimacy, Realities and Utopias' in R. Matthews and P. Francis (eds) *Prisons 2000: An International Perspective on the Current State and Future of Imprisonment*, New York: St Martin's Press

Carrabine, E., Lee, M. and South, N. (2000) 'Social Wrongs and Human Rights in Late Modern Britain: Social Exclusion, Crime Control and Prospects for a Public Criminology', *Social Justice* 27 (2): 193–251

Carter, H., Klein, R. and Day, P. (1992) *How Organisations Measure Success: The Use of Performance Indicators*, London: Routledge

Castel, R. (1991) 'From Dangerousness to Risk' in G. Burchell, C. Gordon and P. Miller (eds), *The Foucault Effect: Studies in Governmentality*, Chicago: University of Chicago Press

Chan, J. (1992) *Doing Less Time: Penal Reform in Crisis*, Sydney: Institute of Criminology Monograph Series No.2

Chaudhuri, A. (2000) 'Twisted Sisters', *The Guardian*, 15 August

Chesney-Lind, M. (2000) *Program Assessment of 'Women at Risk Program of Western Carolinians for Criminal Justice, Ashville, North Carolina: Report Prepared for the National Institute of Corrections*. Ashville: Women at Risk

Chiquada, R. (1997) *Black Women's Experience of Criminal Justice: A Discourse on Disadvantage*, Sussex: Waterside Press

Christie, N. (1986a) 'Suitable Enemies' in H. Bianchi, and R. van Swaaningen, (eds) *Abolitionism – Towards a Non-Repressive Approach to Crime*, Amsterdam: Free Academic Press

Christie, N. (1986b) 'The Ideal Victim' in E. Fatah (ed.) *From Crime Policy to Victim Policy*, London: Macmillan

Christie, N. (2001) 'International Crime Trends', Plenary Speech at *Crime and Punishment Conference*, London: 19 September

Clark, D, and Howden-Windell, J. (2000) *A Retrospective Study of Criminogenic Factors in the Female Prison Population*, London: HM Prison Service

Cohen, S. and Scull, A. (1983) *Social Control and the State*, Oxford: Basil Blackwell

Cohen, S. (1985) *Visions of Social Control*, Oxford: Polity

Coles, B. (1995) *Youth and Social Policy: Youth Citizenship and Young Careers*, London: UCL Press

Cook, D. (1997) *Poverty, Crime and Punishment*, London: Child Poverty Action Group

Cook, P. W. (1997) *Abused Men: The Hidden Side Of Domestic Violence*, London: Praeger

Cook, S. and Davies, S. (1999) *Harsh Punishment: International Experiences of Women's Imprisonment*, Boston: Northeastern University Press

Cooke, R. (2001) 'Snap Decisions', *The Guardian*, 30 October: G2: 8

Cooper, S. (1987) 'The Evolution of the Federal Women's Prison' in E. Adelberg and C. Currie (eds) *Too Few To Count*, Vancouver: Press Gang

Cornell, D. (1995) *The Imaginary Domain*, London: Routledge

Correctional Service Of Canada (CSC) (1994) *Correctional Program Strategy for Women*, Ottawa: Correctional Service of Canada

Correctional Service Of Canada (CSC) (1995) *Security Management System*, Ottawa: Correctional Service of Canada, Federally Sentenced Women's Program

Correctional Service of Canada (CSC) (1996) *FSW Facilities Offender Intake Assessment Guidelines*, Ottawa: Correctional Service of Canada

Correctional Service of Canada (1998) *Board of Investigation into the Allegations of Mistreatment by Former Inmate at the Prison for Women Between March 22 1960 and August 1 1963* Ottawa: Correctional Service of Canada

Covington, S. (1999) *Helping Women Recover: A Program for Treating Addiction*, San Francisco: Jossey-Bass Publishers

Covington, S. and Beckett, L. (1988) *Leaving the Enchanted Forest: The Path from Relationship Addiction to Intimacy*, New York: HarperCollins Publishers

Covington, S. and Bloom, B. (1999) 'Gender-Responsive Programming and Evaluation for Women in the Criminal Justice System: A Shift from What Works? To What Is The Work?' Paper Presented at the 51st Annual Meeting of the American Society of Criminology, Toronto:17–20 Nov

Crow, I. (2001) *The Treatment and Rehabilitation of Offenders*, London: Sage

Curran, S., DeCou, K., Dusek-Gomez, N., Haven, T. and Rodriguez, M. (2000) *Fundamental Fairness: Providing Intermediate Sanctions for Women*, Ludlow, Massachusetts: Hampden County Correctional Centre

Daly, K. (1994) *Gender, Crime and Punishment*, New Haven: Yale University Press

Daly, K. (1997) 'Different Ways of Conceptualising Sex/Gender in Feminist Theory and their Implications for Criminology', *Theoretical Criminology*, 1(1): 25–51

De Cou, K. and Van Wright, S. (2001) 'A gender-specific intervention model for incarcerated women: *women's V.O.I.C.E.S.*, in G. Landsberg, M. Rock and L. K. W. Berg (eds) *Serving Mentally Ill Offenders And Their Victims: Challenges and Opportunities and Other Mental Health Professionals*, New York, N.Y.: Springer Publishing Co.

Denton, B. (2001) *Dealing: Women in the Drug Economy*, Sydney: University of New South Wales Press

Department of Health (1999) *Working Together to Safeguard Children*, London: HMSO

Department of Health and Home Office (2000) *Safeguarding Young Children Involved in Prostitution*, London: HMSO

Devlin, A. (1998) *Invisible Women. What's Wrong with Women's Prisons?* Winchester: Waterside Press

Donzelot, J. (1979) *The Policing of Families*, London: Hutchinson

Douglas, M. (1986) *How Institutions Think*, New York: Syracuse University Press

Dowden, C. and Andrews, D. (1999) 'What Works For Female Offenders? A Meta-analytical Analytic Review', *Crime and Delinquency*, 45 (4): 438–452

Doyal, L. and Gough, I. (1991) *A Theory of Human Need*, London: Macmillan

Duff, R. A. (1996) 'Penal Communications: Recent Work in the Philosophy of Punishment' in M. Tonry (ed.) *Crime and Justice: A Review of Recent Research*, 20: 1–97 Chicago, University of Chicago Press

Duff, R. A. (1998) 'Law, Language and Community: Some Preconditions of Criminal Liability', *Oxford Journal of Legal Studies:* 189–206

Duff, R. A. (1999) 'Punishment, Communication and Community' in M. Matravers (ed.) *Punishment and Political Theory*, Oxford: Hart Publishing

Eaton, M. (1986) *Justice for Women? Family, Court and Social Control*, Milton Keynes: Open University Press

Eaton, M. (1993) *Women After Prison*, Buckingham: Open University Press

Eaton, M. and Humphries, J. (1996) *Listening to Women in Special Hospitals*, Twickenham: St Mary's University College, Strawberry Hill

Edwards, S. (1984) *Women On Trial*, Manchester: Manchester University Press

Ehrenreich, B. and English, D. (1979) *For Her Own Good*, London: Pluto Press

Ericson, R. and Haggerty, K. (1997) *Policing The Risk Society*, Toronto: University of Toronto Press

Evans, D. (1993) *Sexual Citizenship: The Material Construction of Sexualities*, London: Routledge

Eveson, M. (1964) ' Research With Female Drug Addicts at the Prison for Women', *Canadian Journal of Corrections*, 6: 21–27

Fabiano, E. and Ross, R. (1983) *The Cognitive Model of Crime and Delinquency: Prevention and Rehabilitation*, Toronto: Planning and Research Branch of the Ontario Ministry of Correctional Services

Fabiano, E., Porporino, P. and Robinson, D. (1990) *Rehabilitation Through Clearer Thinking: A Cognitive Model of Correctional Intervention*, Research Brief No B-04. Ottawa

Farrington, D. and Morris, A. (1983) 'Sex, Sentencing and Reconviction', *British Journal of Criminology*, 30 (4): 449–75

Feeley, M. and Little, D. (1991) 'The Vanishing Female: The Decline of Women in the Criminal Process, 1687–1912', *Law and Society Review* 25 (4)

Feeley, M. and Simon, J. (1992) 'The New Penology: Notes on the Emerging Strategy of Corrections and its Implications', *Criminology* (30) 4: 449–75

Finkelstein, N. and Piedade, E. M. (1993) 'The Relational Model and the Treatment of Addicted Women', *The Counselor*, 8–10

Fletcher, B. R., Shaver, L. D. and Moon, D. G. (1993) *Women Prisoners: A Forgotten Population*, Lanham, Md: American Correctional Association Press

Folkard, M. S., Smith, D. E. and Smith, D. D. (1976) *IMPACT. Intensive Matched Probation and After-Care Treatment, Vol.11.* Home Office Research Study No 36. London: HMSO

Forbes, J. (1992) 'Female Sexual Abusers: The Contemporary Search for Equivalence', *Practice*, 6 (2): 102–111

Ford, F. (2001) 'Rise in Women Inmates Swamps Prisons', *The Times*, 26 November

Foucault, M. (1977) *Discipline and Punish*, Harmondsworth: Penguin

Foucault, M. (1978) 'Politics and the Study of Discourse', *Ideology and Consciousness*, Spring 1978

Foucault, M. (1981) *The History of Sexuality*, Vol. 1, London: Penguin

Fowler, R. (1999) 'When Girl Power Packs a Punch', *The Guardian, 12 July*

Fox, K. (2001) 'Self-Change and Resistance in Prison', in Gubrium, J. and Holstein, J. (eds) *Institutional Selves: Troubled Identities in a Post-Modern World*, Oxford: Oxford University Press

Freedman, E. (1981) *Their Sisters' Keepers: Women's Prison Reform in America, 1830–1930*, Ann Arbor: The University of Michigan Press

Freud, S. (1976) *The Interpretation of Dreams*, Harmondsworth: Penguin

Garland, D. (1990) *Punishment and Modern Society*, Chicago: University of Chicago Press

Garland, D. (1996) 'The Limits of the Sovereign State', *British Journal of Criminology*, 36 (4): 445–71

Garland, D. (1997) 'Governmentality and the Problem of Crime', *Theoretical Criminology*, 1 (2): 196–97

Garland, D. (2000) 'The Culture of High Crime Societies: Some Preconditions of recent "Law and Order" Policies', *British Journal of Criminology*, 40 (3): 347–75

Garland, D. (2001) *The Culture of Control: Crime and Social Order in Contemporary Society*, Oxford: Oxford University Press

Garland, D. and Sparks, R. (2000) 'Criminology, Social Theory and The Challenge of Our Times', *British Journal of Criminology*, 40 (2): 189–204

Garrett, J. (1980) *Managing The Civil Service*, London: Heinemann

Gelsthorpe, L. (2001) 'Accountability, Difference and Diversity in the Delivery of Community Penalties' in A. Bottoms, L. Gelsthorpe and S. Rex (eds) *Community Penalties: Change and Challenges*, Cullompton, Willan

Gendreau, P., Little, T. and Goggin, C. (1996) 'A Meta-analysis of the Predictors of Adult Offender Recidivism: What Works!', *Criminology*, 34: 575–607

Gendreau, P. and Ross, R. (1979) 'Effective Correctional Treatment: Bibliography for Cynics', *Crime and Delinquency*, 25: 463–489

Gendreau, P. and Ross, R. (1987) 'Revivication of Rehabilitation: Evidence from the 1980s', *Justice Quarterly*, 4: 349–408

George, M.J. (1994) 'Riding the Donkey Backwards: Men as the Unacceptable Victims of Marital Violence', *The Journal of Men's Studies*, 3 (2): 137–159

Giddens, A. (1990) *The Consequences of Modernity*, Cambridge, Polity Press

Gilligan, C. (1982) *In a Different Voice*, Cambridge, Mass: Harvard University Press

Gilmore, N. and Somerville, M. A. (1998) *A Review of The Use of LSD and ECT at the Prison for Women in the Early 1960s*, Ottawa: Correctional Service of Canada

Girshick, L. (1999) *No Safe Haven: Stories of Women in Prison*, Boston: Northeastern University Press

Globe and Mail (1999) 'Ontario Apologises for Grandview Abuse', 17 November: 3

Glover, J. (1999) *Humanity: A Moral History of the Twentieth Century*, London: Jonathan Cape

Gorman, K. (2001) 'Cognitive Behaviourism and The Holy Grail: The Quest for a Universal Means of Managing Offender Risk', *Probation Journal*, 48 (1): 3–39

Grandview Agreement Between Grandview Survivors Support Group and Government of Ontario, 30 June, 1994

Gray, T., Mays, G. and Stohr, M. K. (1995) 'Inmate Needs and Programming in Exclusively Women's Jails', *The Prison Journal*, 75 (2): 186–202

Green, P. (ed.) (1991) *Drug Couriers*, London, Howard League for Penal Reform

Green, P. (1996) 'Drug Couriers: The Construction of a Public Enemy' in P. Green (ed.) *Drug Couriers: A New Perspective*, London, Quartet Books

Greenberg, D. (1975) 'Problems in Community Corrections', *Issues in Criminology*, 19: 1–34

Groves, W. B. and Frank, N. (2001) 'Punishment, Privilege and Structured Choice' in J. Halliday, C. French and C. Goodwin *Making Punishment Work: Review of the Sentencing Framework for England and Wales*, London: Home Office

Hagan, J., Simpson, J. and Gillis, A. (1979) 'The Sexual Stratification of Social Control', *British Journal of Sociology*, 30: 25–38

Halliday, J., French, C. and Goodwin, C. (2001) *Making Punishments Work: Review of the Sentencing Framework for England and Wales*, London, Home Office

Hannah-Moffat, K. (1999) 'Moral Agent or Actuarial Subject: Risk and Canadian Women's Imprisonment', *Theoretical Criminology*, 3 (1): 71–94

Hannah-Moffat, K. (2000) 'Prisons That Empower: Neoliberal Governance in Canadian Women's Prisons', *British Journal of Criminology*, 40 (3): 510–531

Hannah-Moffat, K. (2001) *Punishment in Disguise: Penal Governance and Federal Imprisonment of Women in Canada*, Toronto: University of Toronto Press

Hannah-Moffat, K. and Shaw, M. (2000a) 'Thinking About Cognitive Skills? Think Again!' in *Criminal Justice Matters*, 39: 8–9

Hannah-Moffat, K. and Shaw, M. (eds.) (2000b) *An Ideal Prison? Critical Essays on Women's Imprisonment in Canada*, Halifax: Nova Scotia, Fernwood Publishing Press

Hannah-Moffat, K and Shaw, M. (2001) *Taking Risks: Incorporating Gender and Culture into the Classification and Assessment of Federally Sentenced Women in Canada*, Ottawa: Status of Women. www.swc-cfc.gc.ca

Hannah-Moffat, K. and Singh, A. M. (1996) 'Corrective Vision: Rights, Accountability and the Prison for Women', Imbizo 2

Harkness, J.M. (1996) *Research Behind Bars: A History of Non-Therapeutic Research on American Prisoners*, unpublished doctoral dissertation, University of Wisconsin-Madison: Department of History

Harris, R. and Timms. N. (1993) *Secure Accommodation in Child Care: Between Hospital and Prison or Thereabouts?* London: Routledge

Hayman, S. (2000) 'Prison Reform and Incorporation: Lessons from Britain and Canada' in K. Hannah-Moffat and M. Shaw, (eds) *An Ideal Prison? Critical Essays on Women's Imprisonment in Canada*, Halifax: Fernwood Publishing

Hedderman. C. and Gelsthorpe, L. (1997) *Understanding the Sentencing of Women*, Home Office Research Study 170, London: HMSO

Hedderman, C. and Hough, M. (1994) 'Does the Criminal Justice System treat Men and Women Differently?' in *Research Findings 10*, London: Home Office, Research and Statistics Department

Heidensohn, F. (1986) 'Models of Justice? Portia or Persephone? Some Thoughts on Equality, Fairness and Gender in the Field of Criminal Justice', *International Journal of the Sociology of Law* 14, 3–4: 287–298

Herman, J. L. (1992) *Trauma and Recovery*, New York: Basic Books

Hetherton, J. (1999) 'The Idealisation of Women: Its Role in the Minimization of Child Sexual Abuse by Females', *Child Abuse and Neglect*, 23 (2): 161–164

HM Inspectorate of Prisons (1997) *Women in Prison: A Thematic Review*, London: Home Office

HM Inspectorate of Prisons (2001) *Follow Up to Women in Prison, A Thematic Review*, London: Home Office

HM Inspectorates of Prisons and Probation (2001) *Through the Prison Gate*, London: Home Office

HM Inspectorate of Probation (1991) *Women Offenders and Probation Service Provision*, London: HMSO

Home Office (1957) *The Wolfenden Committee's Report on Homosexual Offences and Prostitution*, London: HMSO

Home Office (1992a) *The National Prison Survey: Main Findings*: Home Office Research Study 128, London: HMSO

Home Office (1992b) *Gender and the Criminal Justice System*, London: Home Office

Home Office (1992c) *Race and The Criminal Justice System*, London: Home Office

Home Office (1996) *Protecting the Public: The Government's Strategy on Crime in England and Wales*, London: HMSO

Home Office (2000a) *The Government's Strategy for Women Offenders*: London, Home Office

Home Office (2000b) *Criminal Statistics England and Wales Supplementary Tables 1999*, Vols. 1&2, London: HMSO

Home Office (2001a) *Criminal Justice: The Way Ahead*, London: Home Office

Home Office (2001b) *The Government's Strategy for Women Offenders: Consultation Report*: London: Home Office

Home Office (2001c) *Statistics on Women and the Criminal Justice System*, London: HMSO

Hornblum, A.M. (1998) *Acres of Human Experimentation at Holmsburg Prison*, London: Routledge

Howard League (2000) *A Chance to Break the Cycle: Women and the Drug Treatment and Testing Order*, London: Howard League for Penal Reform

Howden-Windell, J. and Clark, D. (1999) *Criminogenic Needs of Female Offenders. A Literature Review*, London: HM Prison Service

Hudson, B. (1987) *Justice Through Punishment: A Critique of the 'Justice' Model of Corrections*, Basingstoke: Macmillan

Hudson, B. (1988) *Content Analysis of Social Enquiry Reports Written in the Borough of Haringey*, unpublished report, Middlesex Area Probation

Hudson, B. (1993) *Penal Policy and Social Justice*, Basingstoke: Macmillan

Hudson, B. (1995) 'Beyond Proportionate Punishment: Difficult Cases and the 1991 Criminal Justice Act', *Crime, Law and Social Change*, 22: 59–78

Hudson, B. (1996) *Understanding Justice: An Introduction to Ideas, Perspectives and Controversies in Modern Penal Theory*, Buckingham: Open University Press

Hudson, B. (1998) 'Doing Justice to Difference' in A. Ashworth and M. Wasik, (eds) *Fundamentals of Sentencing Theory*, Oxford: Clarendon Press

Hudson, B. (1999) 'Punishment, Poverty and Responsibility: The Case for a Hardship Defence', *Social and Legal Studies*, 8 (4): 583–593

Hudson, B. (2000) 'Punishing the Poor: Dilemmas of Justice and Difference', in W. C. Heffernan and J. Kleinig (eds) *From Social Justice to Criminal Justice: Poverty and the Administration of Criminal Law*, New York: Oxford University Press

Hudson, B. (2001) 'Punishment, Rights and Difference' in K. Stenson and R. Sullivan (eds) *Crime, Risk and Justice: The Politics of Crime Control in Liberal Democracies*, Cullompton: Willan Publishing

Immarigeon, R. and Chesney-Lind, M. (1992) 'Women's Prisons: Overcrowded and Over-Used', Madison Wi: National Council on Crime and Delinquency

Irigaray, L. (1994) *Thinking the Difference*, trans. K. Montin, London: Athlone

Jackson, P. and Stearns, C. A. (1995a) 'Gender and Jails: the Myth of the Universal Inmate', *American Jails*, 33–39

Jackson, P. and Stearns, C. A. (1995b) 'Gender Issues in a New Generation Jail' *The Prison Journal*, 75, 2: 203–221

James, O. (1995) *Juvenile Violence in a Winner-Loser Culture*, London: Free Association Books Ltd

Johnstone, G. (1996) *Medical Concepts of Penal Policy*, London: Cavendish

Keller, J., Bertoldo, E. and Dudley, W. (1999) 'Females in Court Ordered Domestic Violence Interventions: A Closer Look at Victim or Perpetrator' *Humanity and Society*, 23 (4): 539–365

Kelly, B. (1992) *Children Inside: Rhetoric and Practice in a Locked Institution for Children*, London: Routledge

Kemshall, H. (1995) *Good Practice in Risk Management*, London: Jessica Kingsley

Kemshall, H. (1998) *Risk in Probation Practice*, Aldershot: Ashgate

Kendall, K. (1998) 'Evaluation of Programmes for Female Offenders', in R. Zaplin (ed.) *Critical Perspectives and Effective Intervention*, Gaithersburg, Maryland: Aspen

Kendall, K. (2000) 'Anger Management with Women in Coercive Environments' in R. Horn and S. Warner (eds) *Positive Directions for Women in Secure Environments*, Leicester: British Psychological Society

Kendall, K. and Pollack, S. (forthcoming) 'Cognitive Behaviouralism in Women's Prisons: A Critical Analysis of Therapeutic Assumptions and Practices' in B. Bloom (ed.) *Gendered Justice: Programming for Women in Correctional Settings*, Chapel Hill: University of North Carolina Press

Kendall, K. and Proctor, D. (2001) 'Human Experimentation in Canadian Federal Penitentiaries'. Paper presented at the British Sociological Association, Medical Sociology Group Conference, University of York, 21–23 September

Kerruish, V. (1991) *Jurisprudence as Ideology*, London: Routledge

Kirsta, A. (1994) *Deadlier than the Male: Violence and Aggression in Women*, London: Harper Collins

Kittrie, N. (1971) *The Right To Be Different: Deviance and Enforced Therapy*, Baltimore: Johns Hopkins Press

Knelman, J. (1998) *Twisting in The Wind: The Murderess and The English Press*, Toronto: Toronto University Press

Knowsley, J. (1996) 'Girls Gangs Rival Boys to Rule The Streets', *The Sunday Telegraph*, 6 May

Kurz, D. (1993) 'Physical Assaults by Husbands: a Major Social Problem' in R. J. Gelles and D. R. L. Loseke (eds) *Current Controversies on Family Violence*, London: Sage

Lab, S. P. and Whitehead, J. T. (1990) 'From "Nothing Works" to "the Appropriate Works": The Latest Stop in the Search for the Secular Grail', *Criminology*, 28: 405–417

Lacan, J. (1975) *The Language of the Self*, New York: Delta

Lacey, N. (1996) ' Normative Reconstruction in Socio-Legal Theory', *Social and Legal Studies* 5 (2): 131–157

Laffargue, B. and Godefroy, T. (1989) 'Economic Cycles and Punishment: Unemployment and Imprisonment: A Time Series Study: France 1920–1985.' *Contemporary Crises*, 13: 371–404

Laframboise, D. (1997) 'Who's the Victim Now?' *Globe and Mail*, 8 November: D3

Laidler, K.J. and Hunt, G. (2001) ' Accomplishing Femininity Among Girls in the Gang', *British Journal of Criminology*, 41 (4): 656–678

Lee, M. and O'Brien, R. (1995) *The Game's Up: Redefining Child Prostitution*, London: The Children Society

Lipton, D., Martinson, R. and Wilks, J. (1975) *The Effectiveness of Correctional Treatment: A Survey of Treatment Evaluation Studies*, New York: Praeger

Lloyd, A. (1995) *Doubly Deviant, Doubly Damned: Society's Treatment of Violent Women*, Harmondsworth: Penguin

Lloyd, G. (1984) *The Man of Reason: 'Male and Female' in Western Philosophy*, London: Methuen

Loader, I. (1996) *Youth, Policing and Democracy*, Basingstoke: Macmillan

Logan, C. H. (1972) 'Evaluation Research in Crime and Delinquency: A Reappraisal', *Journal of Criminal Law, Criminology and Police Science*, 63: 378–387

Loucks, N. (1997) *HMPI Cornton Vale: Research into Drugs and Alcohol, Violence and Bullying, Suicide and Self-Injury Backgrounds of Abuse.* Edinburgh: Scottish Prison Service Occasional Papers, Report 1/98

MacDonald, R. (ed.) (1997) *Youth, The Underclass and Social Exclusion*, London: Routledge

MacKinnon, C. A. (1987) *Feminism Unmodified: Discourse on Life and Law*, Cambridge Mass: Harvard University Press

MacKinnon, C. A. (1989) *Toward a Feminist Theory of the State*, Cambridge Mass: Harvard University Press

Maguire, M., Vagg, J. and Morgan, R. (1985) *Accountability and Prisons*, London: Tavistock

Maher, L. (1997) *Sexed Work: Gender, Race and Resistance in a Brooklyn Drug Market*, Oxford: Oxford University Press

Mair, G. (1997) 'Community Penalties and Probation' in M. Maguire, R. Morgan and R. Reiner (eds) *The Oxford Handbook of Criminology*, 2nd edn. Oxford: Oxford University Press

Mair, G. (2000) 'Credible Accreditation?' *Probation Journal*, 47 (4): 268–271

Malloch, M. S. (2000) *Women, Drugs and Custody*, Winchester: Waterside Press

Martin, D., MacCrimmon, M., Grant, I. and Boyle, C. (1991) 'A Forum on Lavallee v. R: Women and Self-Defence', 25 *University of British Columbia Law Review*, 23

Martinson, R. (1974) 'What Works? Questions and Answer About Penal Reform', *Public Interest*, 35: 22–45

Mathiesen, T. (1974) *The Politics of Abolition*, Oxford, Martin Robertson

Matravers, A. (1997) 'Women and The Sexual Abuse of Children', *Forensic Update*, 5 (1): 9–13

Matravers, A. (2001) 'Breaking the Silence', *Guardian*, 15 February

Matravers, M. (2000) *Justice and Punishment: The Rationale of Coercion*, Oxford: Oxford University Press

Matthews, R. (1986) 'Beyond Wolfenden' in R. Matthews and J. Young (eds) *Confronting Crime*, London: Sage

Mauer, M. (1999) *Race to Incarcerate*, New York: New Press

Maybrick, F. E. (1905) *Mrs Maybrick's Own Story – My Fifteen Lost Years*, New York and London: Funk and Wagnell

McColgan, A. (1993) 'In Defence of Battered Women Who Kill', *Oxford Journal of Legal Studies*, 13.(4): 508–529

McMahon, M. (1998) 'Assisting Female Offenders: Art or Science?' Chairperson's commentary on the 1998 Annual Conference of the International Community Corrections Association, Arlington, Virginia, 27–30 Sept

Melossi, D. (1998) 'Introduction' in D. Melossi (ed.) *The Sociology of Punishment*, Aldershot: Ashgate

Melrose, M., Barrett, D. and Brodie, I. (1999) *One Way Street? Retrospectives on Childhood Prostitution*, London: The Children Society

Messerschmidt, J. (1986) *Capitalism, Patriarchy and Crime*, Totowa, NJ: Rowan and Littlefield

Minow, M. (1990) *Making All the Difference*, Ithaca, N.Y: Cornell University Press

Miller, D. (1994) *Women Who Hurt Themselves*, New York: Basic Books

Miller, J. (2001) *One of the Guys: Girls, Gangs and Gender*, Oxford: Oxford University Press

Mirrlees-Black, C. (1999) *Domestic Violence: Findings From A New British Crime Survey Self Completion Questionnaire*, Home Office Research Study 191, London: Home Office

Mitford, J. (1974) *The American Prison Business*, London: Allen & Unwin

Monture, P. (2001) 'Aboriginal Women and Correctional Practice: Reflections on The Task Force on Federally Sentenced Women' in K. Hannah-Moffat and M. Shaw *An Ideal Prison: Critical Essays on Women's Imprisonment Canada*, Halifax: Fernwood

Moran, R. (1992) 'The Search for the Born Criminal and the Medical Control of Criminality' in P. Conrad and J. Schneider (eds) *Deviance and Medicalization: From Badness to Sickness*, exp.edn. Philadelphia: Temple University Press

Morash, M., Bynum, T. and Koons, B. (1998) *Women Offenders: Programming Needs and Promising Approaches*, National Institute of Justice Research in Brief

Morgan, R. and Carlen, P. (1999) 'Regulating Crime Control' in P. Carlen and R. Morgan (eds) *Crime Unlimited?* London, Macmillan

Morris, A., Wilkinson, C., Tisi, A., Woodrow, J. and Rockley, A. (1995) *Managing the Needs of Female Prisoners*, London: Home Office

Morse, S. (2000) 'Deprivation and Desert', in W. C. Heffernan and J. Kleinig, (eds) *From Social Justice to Criminal Justice: Poverty and the Administration of Criminal Law*, New York: Oxford University Press

Motz, A. (2001) *The Psychology of Female Violence: Crimes Against the Body*, Hove: Brunner-Routledge

Moxon, D. (1988) *Sentencing Practice in the Crown Courts*, Research Study No. 103, London: Home Office

Muncer, S., Campbell, A., Jeris, V. and Lewis, R. (2001) ' "Ladettes", Social Representations and Aggression', *Sex Roles*, 44 (1/2): 33–44

Muncie, J. (1998) *Youth and Crime*, London: Sage

Muncie, J. (2000) 'Pragmatic Realism? Searching for Criminology in the New Youth Justice' in B. Goldson (ed.) *The New Youth Justice*, Lyme Regis: Russell House Publishing

Murray, C. (1990) *The Emerging British Underclass*, London: Institute of Economic Affairs

Nacro (1991) *A Fresh Start for Women Prisoners*, London: Nacro

Nacro (1993) *Women Leaving Prison*, London: Nacro

Nacro (1996) *Women Prisoners: Towards A New Millennium*, London: Nacro

Nacro (2001) *Women Beyond Bars*, London: Nacro

Naffine, N. (1990) *Law and the Sexes*, London: Allen and Unwin

Naffine, N. (1997) *Feminism and Criminology*, Cambridge: Polity Press

Nelken, D. (1989) 'Discipline and Punish: Some Notes on the Margin' *Howard Journal* 28, (4): 345–354

New South Wales Department of Corrective Services, (2001) *Evaluation of the Parramatta Transitional Centre*, Sydney: Corporate Planning and Development Unit

O'Donovan, K. (1993) 'Law's Knowledge: The Judge, The Expert, The Battered Woman, and Her Syndrome', *Journal of Law and Society* (20)4: 427–437

O'Dwyer, J. and Carlen, P. (1985) 'Josie: Surviving Holloway and Other Women's Prisons' in P. Carlen, J. Hicks, J. O'Dwyer, D. Christina and C. Tchaikovsky (1985) *Criminal Women*, Cambridge: Polity Press

O'Malley (1992) 'Risk, Power and Crime Prevention', *Economy and Society*, 21 (3): 252–75

O'Malley, P. (1996) 'Post Keynsian Policing', *Economy and Society*, 25 (2): 137–55

O'Malley, P. (2000) 'Risk Societies and the Government of Crime', in M. Brown and J. Pratt (eds) *Dangerousness, Risk and Modern Society*, London: Routledge

Owen, B. (1998) *In The Mix: Struggle and Survival in a Women's Prison*, Albany: State University of New York Press

Parton, N. (1991) *Governing the Family: Childcare, Child Protection and the State*, London: Macmillan

Pearson, P. (1998) *When She Was Bad: How Women Get Away With Murder*, London: Virago Press

Phoenix, J. (1999) *Making Sense of Prostitution*, London: Methuen

Pitts, J. (1997) 'Causes of Youth Prostitution, New Forms of Practice and Political Responses' in D. Barrett (ed.) *Child Prostitution in Britain: Dilemmas and Practical Responses*, London: The Children Society

Pollak, O. (1950) *The Criminality of Women*, Philadelphia: University of Pennsylvania Press

Power, M. (1997) *Audit Society*, Oxford: Oxford University Press

Prison Reform Trust (1991) *The Identikit Prisoner*, London: Prison Reform Trust

Prison Reform Trust (2000) *Justice for Women: The Need for Reform* (The Wedderburn Report), London: Prison Reform Trust

Probation Studies Unit (2000) *Draft Report on the Retrospective Study of the Hereford and Worcester Probation Service Women's Programme* (unpublished) University of Oxford Centre for Criminological Research

Probation Studies Unit (2001) *ACE Profiles for Female, Ethnic Minority and Young Offenders* (unpublished. Quoted with permission) University of Oxford Centre for Criminological Research

Pryor, S. (2001) *The Responsible Prisoner*, London: Home Office

Rafter, N. (1992) *Partial Justice: Women, Prison and Social Control*, New Brunswick, NJ: Transaction Publishers

Rafter, N. and Stanley, D. (1999) *Prisons in America: A Reference Handbook*, Santa Barbara: ABC Clio

Rex, S. (2000) 'Beyond Cognitive Behaviouralism? Reflections on the Effectiveness Literature'. Paper Presented at the 24th Cropwood Conference: Future Directions for Community Penalties: University of Cambridge

Roberts, C. (1987) *First Evaluation Report, Young Offender Project*, Department of Social and Administrative Studies, University of Oxford

Roberts, J. and Domurad, F. (1995) 'Re-engineering Probation: Lessons from New York City', *Vista*, 1 (1): 59–68, Worcester: Association of Chief Officers of Probation

Robinson, J. and Smith, G. (1971) 'The Effectiveness of Correctional Programs', *Crime and Delinquency*, 17: 67–80

Rock, P. (1996) *Reconstructing a Woman's Prison: The Holloway Redevelopment Project: 1968–88*, Oxford: Clarendon Press

Rose, N. (1996) *Inventing Our Selves: Psychology, Power and Personhood*, Cambridge: Cambridge University Press

Rose, N. (1999) *Governing the Soul*, 2nd edn. London: Free Association Books

Rose, N. (2000) 'Government and Control', *British Journal of Criminology*, 40 (2): 321–339

Rose, N. and Miller, P. (1992) 'Political Power Beyond The State: Problematic of Government', *British Journal of Sociology*, 43: 173–205

Rose, R. (1993) *Lesson-Drawing in Public Policy*, New Jersey: Chatham House

Ross, R. and Fabiano, E. (1985) *Time To Think: A Cognitive Model of Delinquency Prevention and Offender Rehabilitation*, Johnson City, Tennessee: Institute of Social Sciences and Arts

Ross, R. and Fabiano, E. (1986) *Female Offenders: Correctional Afterthoughts*, Jefferson, North Carolina: McFarland

Ross, R., Fabiano, E. and Ross. R. (1988) 'Rehabilitation Through Education: A Cognitive Model for Corrections', *Journal of Correctional Education*, 39(2): 45

Ross, R. and McKay, H. B. (1976) 'Adolescent Therapists', *Canada's Mental Health*, 24 (2) June:15–17

Ross, R. and McKay, H. B. (1979) *Self-Mutilation*, Toronto: Lexington Books

Ross, R. and Ross, R. (1995) *Thinking Straight: The Reasoning and Rehabilitation Program for Delinquency Prevention and Offender Rehabilitation*, Ottawa: Air Training and Publications

Rothman, D. (1980) *Conscience and Convenience: The Asylum and its Alternatives in Progressive America*, Boston: Little Brown

Rumgay, J. (1996) 'Women Offenders: Towards Needs-Based Policy', *Vista* 2:(2)

Sandel, M. (1982) *Liberalism and the Limits of Justice*, Cambridge: Cambridge University Press

Scull, A. (1984) *Decarceration: Community Treatment and the Deviant*, Cambridge: Polity Press

Seear, N. and Player, E. (1986) *Women in the Penal System*, London: Howard League

Select Committee on the Increase in The Prisoner Population (2000) *Interim Report: Issues Relating to Women*, Sydney: New South Wales, Government

Shaw, M. (1993) 'Reforming Federal Women's Imprisonment' in E. Adelberg and C. Curtis (eds) *In Conflict With The Law: Women and The Canadian Justice System*, Vancouver: Press Gang Publishers

Shaw, M. (1997) *Conflicting Agendas: Evaluating Feminist Programmes for Women Offenders*, unpublished doctoral dissertation: University of Nottingham

Shaw, M. (2001) 'Women, Violence and Disorder in Prisons', in K. Hannah-Moffat and M. Shaw, *An Ideal Prison? Critical Essays on Women's Imprisonment in Canada*, Halifax: Fenwood

Shaw, M. and Hannah-Moffat, K. (2000) 'Gender, Diversity and Risk Assessment in Canadian Corrections', *Probation Journal*, 47(3): 163–172

Sim, J. (1990) *Medical Power in Prisons*, Open University Press

Simon, J. (1988) 'The Ideological Effects of Actuarial Practices', *Law and Society Review*, 22 (4): 772–800

Singer, M. I., Bussey, J., Song, L. and Lunghofer, L. (1995) 'The Psychosocial Issues of Women Serving Time in Jail', *Social Work*, 40 (1): 103–113

Slack, P. (1990) *The English Poor Law, 1531–1782*, London: Macmillan

Smart, C. (1989) *Feminism and the Power of Law*, London: Routledge

Smart, C. (1992) *Regulating Womanhood*, London: Routledge

Smart, C. (1995) *Law, Crime and Sexuality: Essays in Feminism*, London: Sage

Social Work Services and Prisons Inspectorates for Scotland (1998) *Women Offenders: A Safer Way*, Edinburgh: HMSO

Somerville, M. A. and Gilmore, N. (2000) *A Report on Research on Inmates in Federal Penitentiaries*, prepared for the Correctional Service of Canada, 14 Feb

Stanko, E. A. (2001) 'The Day to Count: Reflections on a Methodology to Raise Awareness about the Impact of Domestic Violence in the UK', *Criminal Justice*, 1 (2): 215–226

Stanko, E. A. and Scully, A. (1996) 'Retelling the Tale: the Emma Humphreys Case' in A. Myers and S. Wight (eds) *No Angels: Women Who Commit Violence*, London: Pandora

Stenson, K. and Sullivan, R. (2001) (eds) *Crime, Risk and Justice: The Politics of Crime Control in Liberal Democracies*, Cullompton: Willan Publishing

Stewart, B. (2001) 'Not a Country Club', *Macleans*, April 9: 34–38

Stewart, C. (2000) 'Responding to the Needs of Women in Prison', *Prison Service Journal*, 132: 41–43

Stitt, S. and Macklin, A. (1995) *Battered Husbands: the Hidden Victims of Domestic Violence*, Liverpool: John Moores University Centre for Consumer Education and Research

Strange, C. (1983) 'The Velvet Glove: Maternalistic Reform at the Andrew Mercer Ontario Reformatory for Females, 1874–1901', M.A. Dissertation, University of Ottawa, Department of History

Straus, M. A. (1993) 'Physical Assaults by Wives: A Major Social Problem' in R. J. Gelles and D. R. Loseke (eds) *Current Controversies on Family Violence*, London: Sage

Stubbs, J. and Tolmie, J. (1994) 'Battered Women Syndrome in Australia: a Challenge to Gender Bias in the Law' in J. Stubbs (ed.) *Women, Male Violence and the Law*, Sydney: Institute of Criminology

Tadros, V. (1998) 'Between Governance and Discipline: The Law and Michel Foucault', *Oxford Journal of Legal Studies*, 4 (Spring): 75–103

Task Force on Federally Sentenced Women (TFFSW) (1990) *Creating Choices – The Report Of The Task Force On Federally Sentenced Women*, Ottawa: Solicitor General of Canada

Teplin, L. A., Abram, K. M. and McClelland, G. M. (1996) 'Prevalence of Psychiatric Disorders Among Incarcerated Women', *Archives of General Psychiatry*, 53: 505–512

Terr, L. C. (1990) *Too Scared to Cry: How Trauma Affects Children and Ultimately Us All*, New York: Basic Books

Valverde, M. (1996) 'Social Facticity and the Law: A Social Expert's Eyewitness Account of Law', *Social and Legal Studies*, 5 (2): 201–218

Vanstone, M. (2000) 'Cognitive-Behavioural Work With Offenders in the UK: A History of Influential Endeavour', *The Howard Journal*, 39 (2): 171–183

Van Wormer, K. S. and Bartollas, C. (2000) *Women and the Criminal Justice System*, Boston: Allyn and Bacon

Venhard, J., Sugg, D. and Hedderman, C. (1997) 'Part I: the Use of Cognitive-Behavioural Approaches with Offenders: Messages from the Research', in *Changing Offenders' Attitudes and Behaviour: What Works?* Home Office Research Study 171. London: Home Office Research and Statistics Directorate

Veysey, B., DeCou, K. and Prescott, L. (1998) 'Effective Management of Jail Detainees with Histories of Physical and Sexual Abuse', *American Jails*, 7 (2): 50–56

von Hirsch, A. (1986) *Past or Future Crimes: Deservedness and Dangerousness in the Sentencing of Criminals*, Manchester: Manchester University Press

von Hirsch, A. (1992) 'Proportionality in the Philosophy of Punishment', in M. Tonry (ed.) *Crime and Justice: An Annual Review of Research*, vol. 16, Chicago: University of Chicago Press

von Hirsch, A. (1993) *Censure and Sanctions*, Oxford: Clarendon Press

Walker, L. (1984) *The Battered Woman Syndrome*, New York: Sage

Walker, L. (2000) *The Battered Woman Syndrome* (2nd ed.), New York: Springer Publishing Co

Walkowitz, J. (1992) *City of Dreadful Delights*, London: Routledge

Wasik, M. and von Hirsch, A. (1994) 'Section 29 Revised: Previous Convictions in Sentencing', *Criminal Law Review*, June: 409–418

Weeks, J. (1981) *Sex, Politics and Society: The Regulation of Sexuality Since 1800*, Longman: London

Welldon, E.V. (1988) *Mother, Madonna, Whore: The Idealisation and Denigration of Motherhood*, London: Free Association Books Ltd

Wilczynski, A. (1997) 'Mad or Bad? Child Killers, Gender and the Courts', *British Journal of Criminology*, 37 (3): 419–436

Women's Policy Group (2001) 'Cognitive Skills Programmes', correspondence between the author and the Women's Policy Group, HM Prison Service

Worrall, A. (1990) *Offending Women: Female Lawbreakers and the Criminal Justice System*, London: Routledge

Worrall, A. (1997) *Punishment in the Community*, Harlow: Longman

Worrall, A. (2000a) 'Governing Bad Girls: Changing Constructions of Female Juvenile Delinquency' in J. Bridgeman and D. Monk (eds) *Feminist Perspectives on Child Delinquency Law*, London: Cavendish Publishing

Worrall, A. (2000b) 'Failure Is The New Success', *Prison Service Journal*, 132: 52–54

Worrall, A. (2000c) 'What Works at One Arm Point? A Study in the Transportation of a Penal Concept', *Probation Journal*, 47 (4): 243–249

Worrall, A. (2001) 'Nasty Little Madams: Changing Perceptions of Girls' Violence', unpublished paper given to 'Still Standing Strong Conference' University of Melbourne: February

Yeoman, B. (1999) 'Bad Girls', *Psychology Today*, 2 (6): 54–57&71

Young, I. (1994) 'Punishment, Treatment, Empowerment: Three Approaches to Policy For Pregnant Addicts', *Feminist Studies*, 20 (1): 33–57

Young, J. (1975) ' A Working Class Criminology' in I. Taylor, P. Walton and J. Young (eds) *Critical Criminology*, London: Routledge and Kegan Paul

Young, J. (1986) ' The Failure of Radical Criminology: The Need for a Radical Realism', in R. Matthews and J.Young (eds) *Confronting Crime*, London: Sage

Zedner, L. (1991) *Women, Crime and Custody in Victorian England*, Oxford: Clarendon Press

Index